Harry Rand

HUNDERTWASSER

Benedikt Taschen

Front cover:
Detail from 625 *Wintergeist – Tableau d'hiver – Winterbild – Polyp –
Winter Painting,* Giudecca, April 1966
(see ill. p. 131)

Back cover:
The Hundertwasser House, Vienna
Photo: Karl Heinz Koller

Frontispiece:
Hundertwasser at work on the paper model of the "Slit Eye" House,
1972

© 1991 Benedikt Taschen Verlag GmbH
Hohenzollernring 53, D-5000 Köln 1
© 1991 for the illustrations: Gruener Janura AG, Glarus, Switzerland
Editor: Sally Bald, Cologne
Graphic design and cover: Peter Feierabend, Berlin
Production: Gudrun Bailly, Assunta Ahrens, Cologne
Printed in Germany
ISBN 3-8228-0555-6
GB

Contents

INTRODUCTION

The aesthetic field worked with such fertile results by the artists of turn-of-the-century Vienna subsequently lay fallow for three generations. Until Friedensreich Hundertwasser reaped the harvest.

Hundertwasser's is a fine accomplishment. He has earned personal recognition, and international respect for Austrian art. He is now an international celebrity, and Vienna, a moribund city at mid-century, has returned to its sparkling prominence of old. Hundertwasser's voice is heard worldwide; and, while his art and philosophy have been condemned, his instincts about the future have proven correct. Time already looks set to vindicate his beliefs, and his art can be regarded as a genuine alternative to the vacuities of so much modern art. His work constitutes a rebuttal of legions of aestheticians, especially those descended from Duchamp.

There is little in the way of rigorous logic in Hundertwasser's art. Despite his manifestoes, he is a sensualist – giving all, nakedly, luxuriously, without a trace of the minimalist reductionism that has been in vogue elsewhere. In his work it is the object itself that is pre-eminent, not its implications. He avoids theory, preferring the realm of the senses. There is little in his introspective art of a purely speculative nature.

Predictably enough, this has irritated and confused many of his more literal-minded critics, who suppose that an art as rational as Hundertwasser's must also be ploddingly logical. Others, though, delight

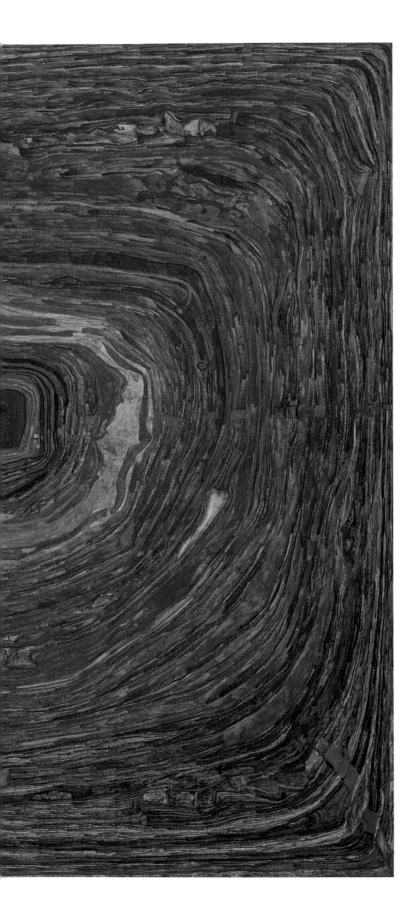

in the flamboyance with which the artist sends his objects into the world. It is a relief, a sensuous oasis in a desert of arid theory. Of course the aesthetic conjectures of conceptual artists are by no means without value; but the beauty of the object tends to be ignored. Hundertwasser, far from being a logician, might be described as a pastoral philosopher.

Hundertwasser has been a dedicated artist and craftsman for forty years, and has earned a place in the front rank of those who craft their artwork well and do not merely offer it up as an illustration of an idea. Control and skill are virtues which are again being recognised and rewarded as the twentieth century draws to a close. Representational art was out of fashion for decades, but, with its return, the attractions of a personal mythology are growing. Furthermore, after a generation of minimalist colorists, the lush opulence of Hundertwasser's colours is winning admirers by sheer force of contrast. And finally, while he has been associated with many extra-artistic causes, Hundertwasser is undogmatic about the relations of society to art. He is not an artist to throw humanity overboard for the sake of aesthetics; and his moderation ensures that his doctrines are never tainted with fanaticism.

224 *Le grand chemin – Der große Weg – The Great Way,*
St. Mandé/Seine, June 1955
Mixed media: polyvinyl acetate on two joined strips of canvas primed with chalk and zinc white, 162 x 160 cm

YOUTH

Stowasser	STOWASSER
Fritz	FRITZ
Friedrich	FRIEDRICH
Friederich	FRIEDERICH
Friedereich	FRIEDEREICH
Friedenreich	FRIEDENREICH
Hundertwasser	HUNDERTWASSER
Friedensreich	FRIEDENSREICH
Regentag	REGENTA G
Dunkelbunt	DUNKELBUNT

JW 198/KK 47 *Selbstportrait mit blauem Sweater – Self-Portrait with Blue Sweater,* March 1948, oil on wrapping paper, ca. 40 x 30 cm

On 15 December 1928 Friedrich Stowasser (Friedensreich Hundertwasser) was born in Vienna, Austria. In that same city, within a few months, Arik Brauer and Ernst Fuchs also came into the world. All three were half-Jewish. Miraculously, and improbably, all three survived the Second World War. They became friends and the pre-eminent artists of the Austrian post-War period. Hundertwasser achieved a worldwide recognition unlike that of any other artist of our time.

Friedrich's was not an illustrious or even an old Viennese family, and the family's history is unclear. His mother's was a very poor Jewish family without trade or profession; they subsisted almost as beggars, living on the fringes of society. He was an only child, and just days after his first birthday, his father, who was not Jewish, a jobless technical engineer who had served with distinction in the Austrian army, died while undergoing an appendectomy.

Since the boy had never felt his father's personality as a formative influence, there was nothing callous in his discounting that loss. Compensations for this loss included being made to feel special among his peers. The boy also enjoyed his remaining parent's undivided attention and affection. Thus, in diminished circumstances, the youngster's character was formed in an emotional and intellectual climate determined solely by his mother Elsa.

His mother's world was a restricted one: poverty, her Jewish identity, widowhood, and Slavic origins, all imposed limits. Friedrich's world was only slightly less circumscribed. His mother worked in a bank, and her time away from the household gave the boy long periods by himself. By the time he was five, he was beginning to express himself in art. In 1936 he was enrolled in Vienna's Montessori School. It was an unusual choice. Elsa was not a political woman, and she was not "making a statement" of liberalism. Unable to distinguish finer grades of literacy herself, she wanted the best possible education for her son, one that would enable him to enter into the ranks of the great conformist majority and earn a living.

After just a year, Friedrich was withdrawn from the Montessori School; it was expensive, and did not seem to be preparing the boy to earn a living. School reports did have good words for his "unusual sense of colour and form", though. "My mother was very upset by this. She wanted me to have a good sense of mathematics and German. For her, that was the school's way of saying: 'Your child is stupid. He excels at basketweaving.'"

Hundertwasser recalls that at the Montessori School "We were treated individually. They watched each of us to see whether we played with puppets or engines or whatever. Me, I painted." Individual instruction distinguished the Montessori

JW 33/KK XX *Kleiner Blumenstrauß aus Frühlingsblumen – Small Bouquet of Spring Flowers,* Obere Donaustraße, Vienna, April 1944
Pencil and watercolour on drawing paper, 14 x 14 cm

JW 26 *Portulaca,* September 1943
Pencil and watercolour on paper, 11 x 11 cm

Right: Hundertwasser in Dalmatia with his mother, ca. 1932

schooling from rigorous Catholic education, trade schools, or military schools – which were still the predominant types of Austrian educational institution at that time.

In 1937 Friedrich Stowasser was baptized. That spring, sinister events were moving rapidly. On 12 March 1938 the German army entered Austria, which was incorporated into the Third Reich. The next day, the *Anschluss* was proclaimed – formal union of Germany and Austria.

On 14 March Adolf Hitler arrived in Vienna and, amidst hysterically happy Austrian crowds, took formal possession of the country. On 10 April an Austrian plebiscite produced a 99.75 % vote in favour of the *Anschluss,* thus making Austria a new state in the German Reich, with seven districts. Subsequently, the Nazis' opponents committed suicide, fled, were murdered or were forced into concentration camps.

The eleven-year-old Hundertwasser discovered how the infamous Nuremberg Race Laws categorized him. Perversely, converts were the target of more rapid liquidation. To try to preserve her Jewish family, Stowasser's mother enrolled him in the Hitler Youth.

Every day young Friedrich returned from school – to the apartment, which by law had to carry a yellow star – and slept until midnight when the SS made their usual inspections. The boy had to fend off the SS officers. Knocks on the door alerted him to don his Hitler Youth swastika pin and an armband with a swastika to meet the SS men at the door; he also wore the medals his father had earned as a German officer in World War I. His medal-bedecked uniform was meant to demonstrate his pure Aryan blood. Twice the boy's bold confrontation parried the Nazis' midnight raids, but the ruse had only to fail once for disaster to strike. In 1943 those who knew the bitter secrets of evasion – equally threatened, equally doomed Jewish commandos with red armbands – knocked on the door with the yellow star and abducted his aunt and grandmother; they were never to be seen again.

At the same time, 1943, Hundert-

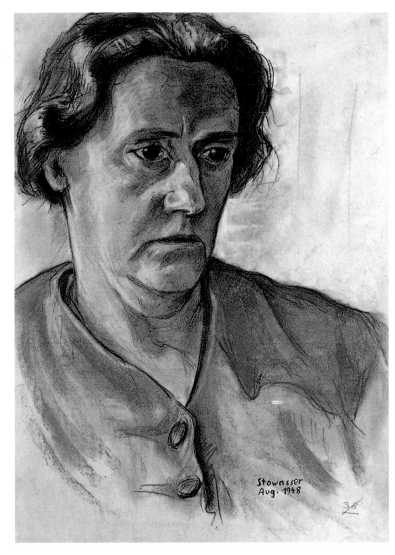

JW 136/KK 29 *Portrait meiner Mutter – Portrait of My Mother*, Obere Donaustraße, Vienna, August 1948
Crayon on drawing paper, 62 x 43 cm

During the Anglo-American bombing and the fighting for Vienna in 1944, Hundertwasser and his mother lived in the cellar of their house near the Danube canal (where the family had been obliged to live since forced resettlement in 1938). A watercolour from this period, *Ferry over the Danube Canal* (p. 15) does not record the terror; the teenager's technique developed amid a menacing situation. As the war neared its end in 1945, Hundertwasser and his mother hid before the Russians conquered Vienna; his mother was terrified they would be denounced to the SS as Jews and be killed.

Other juvenilia also ignore the terrible circumstances in which they were composed. Numerous pieces depict a beautiful springtime of youth, a fairy-tale setting (though one which, as we know, was a breeding-ground of inhumanity).

Near-famine came with the surrender, and to ease rationing, families sent their children to the countryside. The farmer in Schwanenstadt who lodged Hundertwasser gave him food during the couple of months in 1946 that the youth worked as a farmer. He was profoundly moved by the green plants and the brown earth, whose vivid-

wasser first consciously drew in pencil from nature, though he soon graduated to crayon, and began to collect pressed flowers. Untutored, these works display a distinct personality. His journal for Monday, 23 August 1943, contains a landscape tersely recorded in crayon. The washed-out browns and greens suggest something forlorn and abandoned, a timeless backwater described in the shimmering blaze of midsummer. His watercolours show the picturesque woods and the palaces of old Vienna.

About 1936–37, in church, Friedrich, along with the other children, was given little votive pictures, and one showed a naïve painting of a black madonna with a child – this is the earliest work he recalls affecting him. He began to collect postage stamps in 1940, a hobby he continued until 1947.

Mother – Elsa Stowasser – in the Obere Donaustraße, Vienna, ca. 1954

JW 25/KK XIV *Heiligenkreuzerhof-Tor – Heiligenkreuzerhof Gate,*
Schönlaterngasse, Vienna, September 1943
Pencil and watercolour on paper, 20 x 15 cm (16 x 14)

and I left. I did not protest. Christian Andersen did not leave any mark." Hundertwasser's disillusionment was prompted by figure studies expounded in theory and by models. Once he had learned the rudimentary principles of organizing observation into design, school held little for him. He left once he had acquired the basic skills of abstracting the body, drawing from the nude, and copying from nature.

Formal training did next to nothing to shape Hundertwasser's evolution. The example of Egon Schiele, on the other hand, made a considerable impact. In 1948 the Vienna Albertina held an exhibition commemorating Schiele's death in 1918, and Hundertwasser first encountered the earlier artist's work (from the Nierenstein Collection) in that show, in a small gallery. Schiele's influence was decisive, and far more powerful than the role subsequently played in Hundertwasser's development by Klimt. For the rising young artist, Schiele's

ness convinced him to become a painter. This experience, not the product of an art school's drudgery, or even the blaze of youthful talent discovering its unfettered freedom, is almost unique in the annals of art – we are perhaps reminded of van Gogh's Christian religion and his need to preach through paint, or of Mahler's youthful infatuation with nature. The boy decided that only art could be the adequate expression of this feeling of nature, thereafter his life's principal concern.

After this epiphany of nature the artist's first significant works appeared, indicators of his growing talent and feeling, as *Selbstbildnis* (Self-Portrait, p. 13 below).

In 1948 – after his school-leaving exams, which had been interrupted by the Nazi regime – Hundertwasser entered the Vienna Academy of Fine Arts in Robin Christian Andersen's class. Hundertwasser declares he was uninfluenced. "I felt bored

JW 98/KK 22 *Selbstbildnis – Self-Portrait,* December 1947
Pencil on drawing paper, 30 x 22 cm

JW 74/KK 13 *Blick auf Stiefern – View of Stiefern,* Kamptal, September 1945
Watercolour on drawing paper with wrapping paper border, 31 x 23 cm

plastic expression of peaceful beauty, a glimpse of another world. In that realm Hundertwasser found the equivalent of a symphony in which the listener wanders oblivious to others.

Twenty years old when he saw Egon Schiele's works, Hundertwasser was impressed by Schiele's colours and especially the cities he conjured. In these spaces, as in Cezanne's, there was compression and a taut energy. Schiele's buildings seemed vitally, soulfully human – nothing like real architecture, or the houses conceived by other painters.

H. R.: How important for you were particular works of Schiele?
F. H.: Very important. It is the walls. The walls of the towns and the houses. I was very impressed by this. They were all glowing in the dark. For me the houses of Schiele were living beings. For the first time I felt that the outside walls were skins. He painted them as if there were no difference between the skin of a naked girl and the skin of a house. It is the third skin which really demonstrated something that cries, that lives, it is amazing. When you look at these houses you feel that they are humans.

Young Hundertwasser recognized the same inner luminosity in the work of Walter Kampmann (who died in 1945 in Berlin). An exhibition of Kampmann's work at the Albertina stirred Hundertwasser, for Kampmann depicted a different dream world. Daintier than Schiele's private realm, Kampmann's radiantly transparent trees seemed each an immobile saint. Kampmann's insight into nature's vitality heightened Hundertwasser's innate love of plants. He was fascinated "to see trees portrayed as living beings on a personal,

work evoked a special kind of beauty, as Hundertwasser (with apparent difficulty) explains: "It was *awe-ful,* and impressed me with a kind of *tristesse* that still gives me happiness very deep inside – happiness without a smile."

Schiele's work offers many rewards, but his expressive draughtsmanship, a marvel of intense eloquence, was not the main allure for Hundertwasser; such drawing was not the means to Hundertwasser's goal. Nor did Hundertwasser adopt Schiele's frankly sensual subjects – massively offensive in their time, today they confront (rather than affront) us with their utmost honesty of vision. What Hundertwasser derived from Schiele's art was the

human level". These two resurrected personalities competed with the great reputations of Paul Klee and Gustav Klimt.

In January 1949, at Schloss Leopoldskron, Salzburg, Hundertwasser delivered a speech in English: "Art is always changing, we must be creative." In October of that year Hundertwasser first exhibited one picture in an Academy student exhibition at the Secession. (His first exhibited picture was *A Birch Grove.*) A *Self-portrait* of that year (p. 8) indicates his development.

Hundertwasser travelled to Italy, and in a little Roman café the melting colours of ceramic tiles covering the walls deeply impressed him.

F. H.: They were a liquescent colour, with action-style drippings. I kept going back and seeing all kinds of things in them. That is how I discovered Jackson Pollock. I was onto action painting from the start . . but I didn't do it myself. Oh, I tried! But instead of dripping and letting things happen, I kept dominating them. My paintings look like action paintings that were actually painted. I painted every line. Maybe it was the formal structured Austrian in me. (In Alan Levy, "Art News", October 1976)

During July 1949 he painted *Via Porta Sporano con Grattacielo* (p. 16), the view of a

long, perspectivally receding street, dark in the shadows. Here we begin to glimpse the complex strands embedding Hundertwasser's work within the fabric of modern art history, for this painting has diverse and unexpected formal and emotional precedents. (Seventy-five years before, in Algeria, Albert Lebourg's sense of wonder – in light and dark and the looming of a building above a narrow street – anticipated Hundertwasser's.) On each side of *Via Porta Sporano con Grattacielo* the sheer sides of buildings form two containing walls; at the end of this street rises, gleaming from the shadows, a fantastic pile, Hundertwasser's nemesis – the skyscraper (behind an arched gateway). Hundertwasser sought the sub-

ject of urbanism from an impulse stronger than any artistic heritage, although his treatment derived its authority from a range of artistic possibilities. (For example, in the extreme foreground, a white-shirted figure adds a splash of light that compresses distance and proximity between two high-valued passages, a device typical of Jacob van Ruisdael and his uncle Salomon van Ruisdael.)

Composition with Sunflowers (p. 18) is a harsher watercolour, its fierce colours recalling Emil Nolde's bluntness. In Tuscany Hundertwasser joined three French painters hitchhiking: René Brô, Bernard, and Micheline. Together they journeyed to Sicily, then Hundertwasser went with them north to Paris where he remained through 1950. Brô became the young artist's close friend. That October, Hundertwasser first exhibited pictures in Paris in the Galerie Librarie Palmes.

In the winter of 1949–50, the artist chose the name by which he would be known thereafter, and which Viennese critics for some time refused to accept. In the Slavic languages "sto" (or "sta") means one hundred, thus out of Stowasser emerged Hundertwasser – hundred waters. (A few early works are signed simply "HUWA", an abbreviation Hundertwasser quickly dropped. Ten years later he discovered that his name meant "dammed-up water" in the Tyrolean dialect – thus he had made a mistake in translating his name into German.) The attraction of water, in whatever language, is real to him. "I think water is an uncanny element, and that there are any number of possibilities in it. It is a fact that water fascinates me a great deal. I see water as a sort of refuge, an escape to which I can always resort." (Soundtrack of work 707)

He transformed his first name in 1961 – when he lived in Japan for a year – from Friedrich to Friederich, then to Friedereich,

JW 224/KK 56 *Via Porta Sporano con Grattacielo*, Genoa, July 1949
Charcoal and watercolour on brown wrapping paper, 31 x 22 cm

and finally to Friedensreich. ("Regentag" is the name Hundertwasser gave his ship, and he frequently calls himself "Mr. Regentag" or "Captain Regentag". As a name, Regentag, rainy day, occurred to him when he noticed how colours shine in the rain. For him, rainy days are the most beautiful, "the days on which I can work, on which I am most happy". Paul Klee painted a picture titled "Regentag" in 1931; 1950 marks the most decisive period of Paul Klee's influence on Hundertwasser.) Thus, his full name became Friedensreich (rich in peace) Hundertwasser (hundred waters) Regentag (rainy day). All of these three names, or any combination of them, may appear on his work, as he answers to all of them and signs his work with whichever name he feels appropriate. Recently he added another name: Dunkelbunt, dark-colourful. In Hundertwasser's life his name has changed several times. There are numerous precedents for the ritualistic changing of names dependent on circumstance.

In the Bible, Abram became Abraham and Jacob's name was changed to Israel; Joseph took an Egyptian name. The Japanese have sometimes used different names for each stage of their lives, dependent on professional status, general condition, and even mood. And politicans have taken memorable names: Lenin, Trotsky. There are stage names, pen names ("noms de plume"), and "noms de guerre" ("El Cid", "Tito").

H. R.: Why do people change names?
F. H.: There are many reasons. Sometimes a man wants to change his name. Out of courtesy, others call him whatever he wants. When he says, "My name is Joseph", people call him Joseph. That's why he gets called that name: because he wants it. And he gets nicknames. Hokusai had a hundred names. Whenever he changed residences, he changed his name – that's quite wise. One man has one name; when he has many names he is many persons. That is very good. I have many names and am many persons. I am a painter, an architect, an ecolo-

gist. One name does not correspond exactly to one of these professions. I always have the problem of being only one. There are so many things to do and I always say: I'd like to be ten Hundertwassers to do ten times more things. Although I cannot do that, at least I can have many names.

H. R.: Should everybody use many names for each of their activities?

F. H.: Yes, if they are strong enough. Why not? Generally they don't and have a hard time filling one name with meaning. That is another problem: when you have filled one name with meaning, then you need another name – because I don't want to put too many things into one name. It is like a rebirth. You start anew with a new name.

H. R.: Is there any meaning in the name you are given at birth?

F. H.: No. If you keep the name you are given, then you are a coward, you are not able to be yourself. Then you always do what society or your family has prepared for you. You will never step out of line, you will never be an independent personality. The family name is more an accidental name be-

JW 227/KK 59 *Sonnenblumen-Komposition – Composition with Sunflowers,* San Gimignano, August 1949

Watercolour on yellow Italian market wrapping paper, 32 x 26 cm

Photo: Hundertwasser, 1952

Photo: Hundertwasser, taken with delay timer, Vienna, 1952

cause it's over generations, but the first name is your label. It is very obvious that when somebody wants to be himself he finds a new name that corresponds to him. Everybody should name himself – like a king who crowns himself.

89 *Frau mit Luftballons – Woman with Balloons,* St. Mandé/Seine, April 1950
Watercolour and charcoal on wrapping paper, ca. 40 x 30 cm

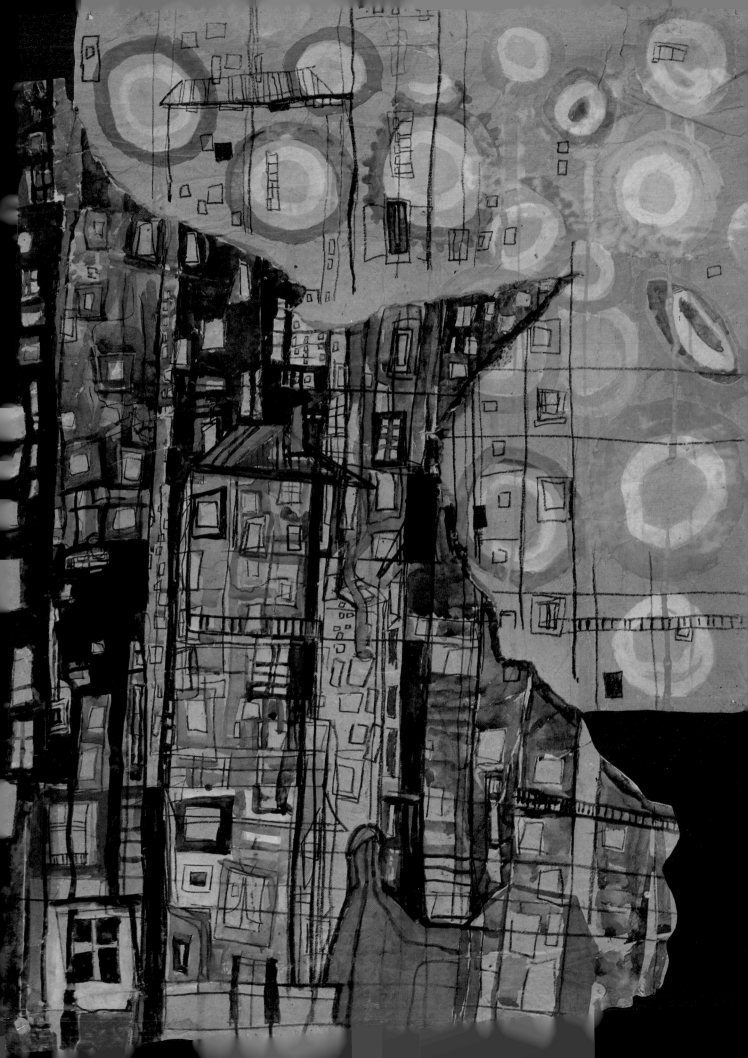

PARIS

Stowasser

Fritz

Friedrich

Friederich

Friedereich

Friedenreich

Hundertwasser

Friedensreich

Regentag

Dunkelbunt

STOWASSER

FRITZ

FRIEDRICH

FRIEDERICH

FRIEDEREICH

FRIEDENREICH

HUNDERTWASSER

FRIEDENSREICH

REGENTAG

DUNKELBUNT

JW 274/KK 77 *Les tournesols et la cité – Die Sonnenblumen und die Stadt – The Sunflowers and the Town,*
St. Mandé/Seine, December 1949
Watercolour and charcoal on two pieces of irregularly torn, overlapping wrapping paper, 70 x 50 cm

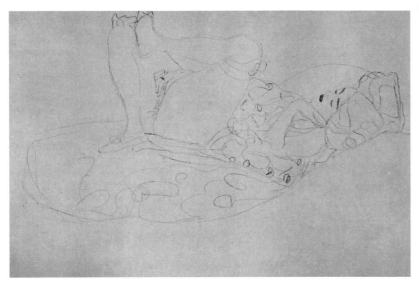

Gustav Klimt
Recumbent Semi-Nude from the Right, 1914/15
Blue crayon, 37 x 56 cm

Brô told me that wheat is the cheapest food if you get it from the farmer, not the shop. It is just amazing how little you can live on and be independent, because if you want to be independent you must be independent of money. My mother said you must have a profession to earn money, otherwise you cannot survive. I told her: "Money is of no importance and I can live without money, or with so little money that it does not count." I went to Paris and I actually lived on $ 50 a year, and after a year I still had that money in my pocket, because you can easily get a dollar from a friend. "Give me a dollar," and they give it to you and you live for a week on it. It is not a struggle. It was just to prove things, and it made me extremely happy. In that way I lived for several years, I painted happily, I lived with friends, they invited me. I had a bicycle somebody lent me, so I did not have to spend any money.

F. H.: When I was in Paris I rode a bicycle to a neighbouring farmer to get wheat. For one day's work I would get 10 kilos of wheat, on which I could live for three months. I divided the wheat into portions and had a fantastic meal every day.
H. R.: What would you do with the wheat?
F. H.: I could have it ground; eat it as a soup; make bread; bake little cakes; make a salad.

In January 1950 Hundertwasser left Brianchon's class at the Ecole des Beaux-Arts after only a few hours, as Brianchon realized that Hundertwasser didn't need academic training. His one class drawing, *Nude*, was a laconic, thoroughly modern rendition of the figure – a finely modelled and thoroughly convincing attempt.

Since 1949 Hundertwasser had been living in quarters provided by a family that saw promise in the young artist. For seven years he was a guest of the Dumage family; he lived and painted in their pavilion near the Bois de Vincennes on the Avenue Daumesnil in St. Mandé/Seine. On a brick wall on the second floor of this remarkable structure, Hundertwasser and Brô painted their mural. Hundertwasser and Brô decided not to paint their second mural directly onto the walls. Instead, they opted to paint *The Miraculous Catch* (above) on pa-

nels. They reasoned that, when the time came for the old hunting pavilion to be demolished one day, they would be able to save their work. And so they carried the pressed fibreboard through the streets of Paris on a handcart. Then they divided up the creative task: Brô did most of the sketching, establishing the forms with quick, sure lines, while Hundertwasser slowly coloured the design. The colouring was tedious work, and Brô sometimes joined in, while Hundertwasser for his part occasionally added to the drawing.

The middle tone of *Gepflügter Acker am Rundhang im Regen, Ploughed Field on a Slope in the Rain (p. 38)*, painted during this period, was established by the dark yellow paper on which it was painted. Lighter values and darker shades were added with paint. The perspective is more complex than first appears. A kind of anti-perspec-

Left: 81 *Aktzeichnung – Nude,* Paris, January 1950
Charcoal drawing on paper, 65 x 50 cm

Top: 97 *La pêche miraculeuse – Der wunderbare Fischfang – The Miraculous Catch,* St. Mandé/Seine, June 1950
Mixed media: chalk, casein on four pressed wood fibre boards, each 2.75 x 1.25 m, together 2.75 x 5 m

23

tive combines a central vanishing point and another converging perspective – slightly displaced to the lower left. Catching the spectator's eye, two figures look directly out of the picture towards us. A third, something of a surrogate for the viewer, gazes away into the composition's distant centre.

For several years Hundertwasser subsisted happily in Paris – which was so different from the grim post-War drabness of Vienna. He painted incessantly and absorbed the life of the city around him. He visited galleries to see what was current in the art world. In coffeeshops, like all young artists, he took part in earnest discussions which shaped his values and outlook. He went to exhibitions, and he found a gallery, Facchetti, which exhibited mostly French, and some American artists. This is of some significance, because it meant that from an early moment Hundertwasser was exposed to the most advanced European and American thinking on art.

It is youthfully immature not to accept limits, but art attempts the impossible. If

96 *Pays des hommes, oiseaux et navires – Land der Menschen, Vögel und Schiffe – Land of Men, Birds and Ships*, St. Mandé/Seine, May 1950
Mural in distemper, carried out in collaboration with René Brô (drawing by Brô, colours by Hundertwasser) in the Countess Castiglione's former hunting lodge, demolished in 1964, 2.75 x 5 m

24

one loves architecture, what is true for people is true for buildings. Hundertwasser combined favourite features of disparate places in *City View Half Siena, Half Paris* (below), a panoramic vista that combines glimpses of one city with parts of another. It is a witty work, free of the astringency of modernism. A structural grid recalls Klee's fluttering background. A city composed of elements from two others conveys the impression of a place that never was, yet a place that combines sensations of each of its sources. Human nature – affection and infatuation – is paramount here, as space and time are transcended for the sake of emotion.

Le Ligne de Sceaux, Die Bahn Nach Sceaux, Railway to Sceaux (p. 30) is composed of ascending horizontal registers, a treatment which became increasingly important to Hundertwasser; in his later works extreme backgrounds were characterized by these registers (sky, sea, land, or indeterminate space). The sky above *Rail-*

way to Sceaux fades in successive registers, reaching, finally, deepest blue, which recalls Klee's use of banded colours, but also invokes the ultimate source in modern art

Top: Working on the mural on p. 24, 1950

84 *City View (Half Siena, Half Paris),*
St. Mandé/Seine, probably March 1950
Oil and charcoal on white primed wood fibreboard, 58 x 55 cm

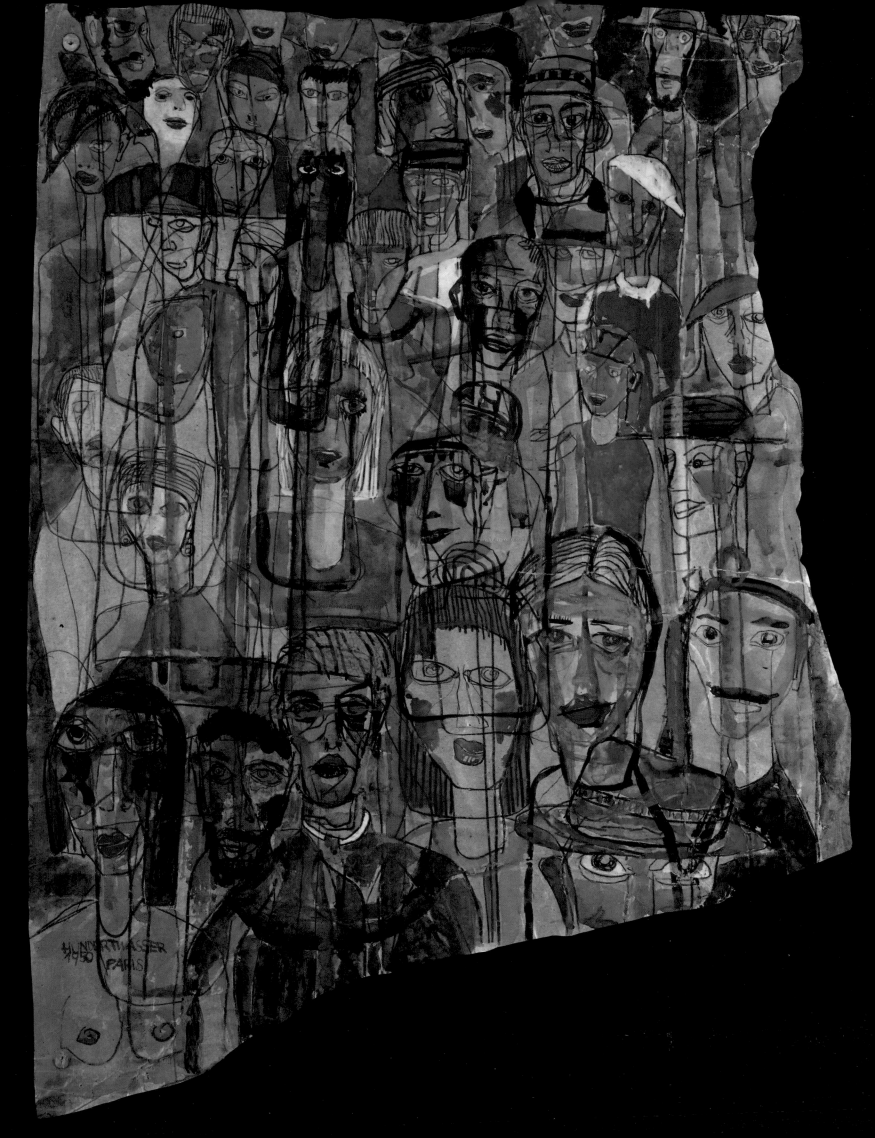

"The wind carried off the sister picture 'Trees (Complement to People)' during the brief time I was in the château fetching a camera."

78 *People (Complement to "Trees")*, St. Mandé/Seine, January 1950
Watercolour and charcoal on yellow irregular wrapping paper, 59 x 44 cm

for such images: Japanese wood-block prints. The sky is further subdivided by telephone lines. And beneath this striped sky, a brown train moves jerkily through blue-green fields in which there is also a green path. Reality is untethered from the here-and-now, and things seem too beautiful for the world we know, but that is precisely Hundertwasser's message: that the world as it is, unornamented, is gorgeous. The *Railway to Sceaux* cites inspiration in the past, captures something of the vitality and energy of the young artist's intense vision, and suggests that the work contains the seeds from which a great career will grow. Hundertwasser flourished in Paris and his art began attracting attention. He conceived of more ambitious, if not larger, works.

In *People* (p. 26) he broke away from naturalistic description, albeit relying on imaginative recombinations. As parts of a city had represented the best of urbanism, humanity too is depicted with only a hint of perspective. The faces near the top are smaller than those near the bottom, which are closer to the viewer. Some (indeterminate) distance is implied. A cross-section of humanity is presented – some with fair hair, negroes, etc. The irregular shape of the paper is both "primitive", in that it looks technologically undeveloped, and a clever way of stressing the painting's medium, a modernist ideal.

Superimposed hulls in *Les Transatlantiques, Singende Dampfer I, Singing Steamers I* (above) create a sense of depth. The overlapping shapes exemplify "descriptive perspective". As in *People* the ships get smaller as they move upward. We must be on some elevated point as we can look down upon the deck of the steamer nearest to the viewer. This work seems a dream of ships, as once Hundertwasser painted a dream of streetcars. The ships have gathered in sleep before the morning sends them to unknown ports. The image is majestic in a way that is rare in post-War pictorial art.

Despite the overall calm and dignity of

86 *Les Transatlantiques – Singende Dampfer – Singing Steamers (I),*
St. Mandé/Seine, probably May 1950

Watercolour and charcoal on primed, crumpled wrapping paper, varnished later, 52 x 74 cm

the scene, the **picture's** surface is a dazzling, flickering **pattern**. The dots of portholes form a series of bands – the hulls. Columns of steam become vertical bars interrupted by glimpses of the sea in rectangular patches. And above all, the night sky seals the painting with a bar of dark blue. The colour and subject have the effect of taming the animated composition. The scene exudes contentment; as is so often the case in good art, polar opposites are reconciled. Here Hundertwasser proved to be an agile student of Klimt – the master of the seething arrangement which yet remains lyrical and calm.

Hundertwasser spent the first half of 1951 in Morocco and Tunisia. In spite of the move from Europe to North Africa, he felt surprisingly at home in his new architectural environment. He was attracted to Arab music and impressed by the expressive freedom of Arabic painting. The unself-conscious drawings done by African children resembled Klee's archaic, witty forms. "Every Arab boy makes Klee paintings without thinking - and look at how they paint the outsides of their cafes! They know nothing about modern art. If they saw their coffee shops in a book or a museum, they would laugh." Outside his native culture, Hundertwasser recognised the universality of humankind's finest achievements.

29

H. R.: Who were the first artists you really admired?

F. H.: The artists who worked before the rational age, before the nonsense about perspective started. The mediaeval painters - and, of course, the Indian, East Asian, African and Red Indian prehistoric cave paintings, and Maori painters. They were all true works of art that do not lie, works of art that present facts.

Some distorted minds consider ugliness beautiful and beauty ugly. In today's museums, beauty is now considered bad, a negative idea, and ugliness is considered good, seen as positive. First this was an unspoken law. Now it is voiced aloud, and people consider themselves brave if they take this position. They say beauty is dangerous. They say beauty is negative.

North Africa did not feel like an alien environment to Hundertwasser. Quite the contrary: he felt at home there. So much so that in May the French authorities asked him to leave Morocco, where he had been living among North Africans in the manner

85 La ligne de Sceaux – Die Bahn nach Sceaux – Railway to Sceaux,
St. Mandé/Seine, probably March 1950
Watercolour and charcoal on primed wrapping paper, 50 x 65 cm

Right: *87 Part of a Steamer – Teil eines Dampfers,*
St. Mandé/Seine, March 1950
Watercolour, charcoal and oil on primed wrapping paper, 52 x 74 cm

Self-Portrait, ca. 1952

of the local people. Hundertwasser travelled to Austria via Tunisia and Sicily, and on his return exhibited the work he had done in North Africa. That September he became a member of the Vienna Art Club, where his work was shown and promoted for the next three years.

The connection with the Art Club's Di-

rector, Alfred Schmeller, fortuitously brought Hundertwasser to the attention of a printing firm that used the Rotaprint process (a kind of lithography on zinc rolls). The firm's facilities had just been released from requisition by the occupying powers; and its commercial lithographic capacity was offerd as a cheap, simple means for artists to begin graphic production. Hundertwasser availed himself of the opportunity and produced a portfolio consisting of a cover and nine lithographs. The cover shows an inverted house; as well as attesting Hundertwasser's debt to Schiele's architectural views, it also suggests that architecture in general will be a major theme thereafter, and that human welfare and the dignity of life are central to his artistic agenda. Astonishingly, given the humble beginnings of these ideas, years later he had a chance to demonstrate his

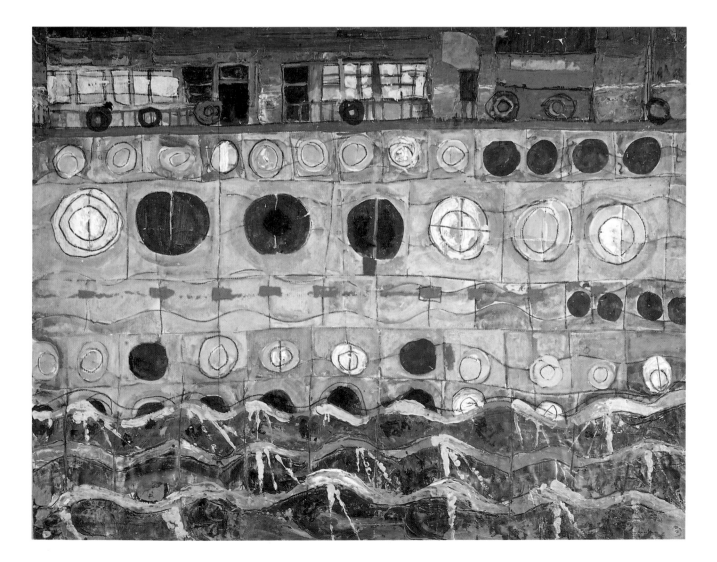

I *City suburb from above* (black and vermilion)

III *Girl with Glasses* (green, blue and red)

II *Skyscraper with Trees* (black, green and red)

IV *Boy with House and Girl with Bird* (black, blue and green)

132 Art Club Rotaprint Portfolio, Vienna 1951
29.5 x 21 cm
Edition of 100 numbered and signed on the introductory page.
9 Rotaprint lithographs in 1 to 3 colours. Published by Art Club, Alfred
Schmeller, Vienna 1951

V *Face* (carmine and vermilion)

VII *Faces Looking Out of Windows* (black)

VIII *Singing Steamer* (red, blue and green)

VI *House with Flowers* (black and blue-green)

IX *Cyclist in the Rain* (dark blue, light blue and green)

124 *Singender Vogel auf einem Baum in der Stadt – Singing Bird in a Tree in the City,* Aflenz, Steiermark, August 1951
Watercolour on wrapping paper primed with chalk zinc white, 65 x 45 cm

most fastidious of graphic artists, never misrepresenting anything about a print's production. Whatever the graphic process, Hundertwasser takes the greatest care to present the exact situation with regard to edition sizes, the technique employed and the degree of the artist's manual involvement, designated publisher, printer, paper and all particulars.

Hundertwasser has now produced nearly one hundred different prints in lithography, silkscreen, woodblock, etching, linocut, multimedia prints – and this first edition in Rotaprint. He spent long periods experimenting with print techniques and distinguished himself with uncommon creativity and formal invention. As his interest in prints increased, Hundertwasser's paintings became rare and precious. In December 1951, in a sale show for Christmas (in "Das gute Bild für Jeden", Künstlerhaus, Vienna – his first public work in Vienna), one painting, "European Holding His Moustache", created a widespread impression. A harrowing reaction from the press prompted public scorn, which was followed by scandal. The frame had been made by hand from parts of a bed and wooden shutters, the wood still showing signs of woodworm, and the painting itself

sense of the integration of architectural function, human betterment, and regard for nature when he was given the chance to build an AGIP service station in Vienna (p. 29).

The 1951 portfolio forcefully indicated his differences from the then-prevalent "tachisme" and from advocates of the unfettered and amoral unconscious. This first graphic edition of one hundred, each signed and numbered, was also pulled in an unspecifiable number of proofs and imperfect trail proofs. This imprecision of numbering soon vanished from Hundertwasser's graphics. Now he is among the

105 *Gelbe Schiffe – Gelbe Küsse/Yellow Ships – Yellow Kisses,*
Marrakesh, February 1951
Watercolour on paper bag primed with chalk zinc white, 39 x 51 cm

was naive in style, done entirely without perspective.

Full of direct observation (recalling the so-called Siennese "primitives") - *Cathedral I*'s (p. 37) pre-renaissance flatness differs from modernism, where every item generates its own native space. *Cathedral's* many cheerful details unite in the most delightful and magical harmony and ignite memory.

Yellow Ships – Yellow Kisses (p. 34) was painted in the same year. Once invented, the shape of the "kiss boat" reappeared in Hundertwasser's work over the years. Conflated lips and a boat play wittily with space; near and far space elide. The lips focus the field of view tightly; the boat becomes a small object in the distance - outlined, recognizable, but without details. The combined distances place the lips into space, floating without a face (echoes of

Man Ray) and locate boats close-up, without supporting water or any spatial matrix.

During this period, Hundertwasser also painted *Singing Bird in a Tree in the City* (p. 34). From the base of a tree, a woman stares at the viewer. Her clothes are permeated by liquid colours. Above all, bands of Klee-like greens tinge the painting. Through the centre of the painting passes the dark column of the tree's trunk. This division only highlights the blue windows that are the city. Enlivened by the birdsong, buildings shine on the right side of the picture. The stellate shapes of the tree's leaves (superimposed like a green sun on the entire design) spread a patterned order from the centre. The living tree invigorates the city's regularity. And, fairy-tale-like, a bird with unknown powers sings a majestic song. So the city and its life are brought together in a way that is rare in reality but

127 *Almhütten auf grünem Platz – Mountain Cabins on Green*,
Aflenz, Steiermark, August 1951
Watercolour on wrapping paper primed with chalk, zinc white and fish glue, 35 x 67 cm

is, nonetheless, the essence of the experience. If this balance is rarely encountered, painting can encourage proper action; it can envision the impossible.

F. H.: For me pictures are gateways through which – when I succeed – I can burst into a world which is at once very close to us and very distant; a world to which we have no access, where we find ourselves, but which we cannot perceive; a world which is opposed to the real world. Our parallel world, from which, in a sense, we alienate ourselves. And this is paradise. We are inside it, we are imprisoned in it, and yet some inexplicable power denies it to us.

I have managed to open some windows onto this world. How I have managed it is difficult to explain. It certainly wasn't by force, not by selection, not by intelligence, not even exactly by intuition, but almost by a kind of sleepwalking. The work of an artist is very difficult, precisely because it cannot be done with force, with diligence, or with intelligence. I mean, you can do everything else in life using strength and application and intellect, but in art these things produce absolutely no result.

Drawn from nature in the Schiele style, the mountain pastureland of *Mountain Cabins on Green* (p. 35) presents translucent, graded values of green by letting different quantities of colour float in different areas. These greens are an image of a thriving farm economy. As in other compositions, Hundertwasser used one element – a reddish-brown barn that touches the paper's right edge – as a detail to anchor the design to the surface. A whitewashed house's windows glow a deep yellow, suggesting a surrounding darkness and indicating warmth and life within; the windows recall Schiele's influence. Though depicting a specific locale that he witnessed, *Mountain Cabins on Green* has universal qualities basic to any farming community.

The Schiele-like observations of detail are combined with other, intuited or learned, inventions of modern art. Not all of them were part of the mainstream. Hundertwasser's colour sense seems to owe

something to Fauvism, which aroused vigorous objections and was as disturbing in its day as Schiele or any other controversial Central European artist. This Western European colourist tradition – canonized for its classicism and yet revolutionary – also fostered Hundertwasser's art. As part of the

general climate of modern art, Fauvism prepared the way for this quintessential colourist.

Part of the essential history of recent art pivots on the figure of van Gogh. *Bürgeralm Landscape* (p. 39) recalls van Gogh's reed-pen drawings of southern France and

Ill. p. 37: 104 *Kathedrale (I) – Cathedral (I),* Marrakesh, February 1951
Watercolour on brown cement bag, primed with chalk, zinc white and fish glue, later mounted on canvas, 67 x 29 cm

JW 273/KK 75 *Gepflügter Acker am Rundhang im Regen – Ploughed Field on a Slope in the Rain,* Charenton/Seine, October-November 1949
Watercolour and charcoal on yellowish-brown paper, ca. 60 x 40 cm
In memory of Hochegg

128 *Bürgeralmlandschaft – Bürgeralm Landscape*, Aflenz, Steiermark, August 1951
Watercolour on wood fibreboard, primed with chalk, zinc white, 38 x 48.5 cm

his late landscapes. A split-rail fence cuts diagonally across the foreground and, in the opposite direction (and swinging the gaze in a gentle rhythm), a hedge moves into the middleground. A cottage occupies the work's centre. We begin to discover Hundertwasser's compositional proclivities. A pine forest blankets the mountain, and above it, like a celestial object, the artist's name appears in syllables of bright yellow. Carefully retracing the history of recent art (as did Gorky, De Staël and Morandi, each in his own way), Hundertwasser was testing the resources of modern art for incompletely exploited possibilities.

Hundertwasser's fluent forms and natural transcription of the scene of *Bügeralm Landscape* suggest his untroubled mind at the time. In the future, his condition – his human worries and everyday troubles – would be reflected in an agitated working method. But at the moment his life was steady and happy; he wanted for nothing. At an early age, Hundertwasser decided that money was not important.

F. H.: How little you need to live. At that time I already had my philosophy. I said: how silly to always ask for more. The Communists, the Socialists, the unions – everybody is concentrating on trying to get more, to get more money and more of what money can buy. What would happen if people instead of asking for more and more would ask for less and less? They would be happier, would be healthier, wouldn't eat rich food, they'd give up their cars for bicycles, grow vegetables in the garden; everyone would need less money – I think that would be an interesting experiment.

Eventually Hundertwasser's art attracted buyers, but he resisted the idea of selling because he didn't need the money and wanted to keep his paintings. Purchasers negotiated, raised their initial offers, and were refused. Offers doubled and redoubled and when Hundertwasser at last sold a work, he discovered he had inadvertently acquired the reputation of a shrewd businessman.

F. H.: Strangely, when you don't need money, money runs after you. I try to explain this to people, that when you try to make money you will never get any.

As guest of the Bargellini family in Tuscany, 1952

H. R.: It seems true . . . on a small scale.

F. H.: There is something to it. Of course, you could say or act as if you do not need money, but this does not work. You must really believe in it.

When he came back to Vienna in 1952 he stayed with his mother in the Russian-occupied zone. Fears were abroad. Hitchhiking back to Paris he was picked up by a civilian car chauffeured by a Russian soldier. The civilian in the back seat asked him his destination, his exact street address in Vienna and if he collected postcards or was interested in photography. Hundertwasser informed him that he collected stamps, which was not good enough. The Russian, who claimed to be a "collector", said that Hundertwasser would be paid to send him postcards and maps of cities in West Germany. When Hundertwasser next returned to Vienna he found that the Russian had visited his mother at midnight and two in the morning asking for Hundertwasser; soon after, the Russian was waiting for him and drove him to the Prater, where he was paid 150 Schillings to send postcards whenever he passed through Germany, and Hundertwasser complied, after a fashion, by mailing postcards of churches. Thus ended his espionage activities.

Hundertwasser mounted his first one-man show in February 1952, at the Art Club in Vienna. At the opening he gave a lecture, "My Aspiration: To Free Myself from the Universal Bluff of Our Civilization". In response to the scathing reaction his work elicited, Hundertwasser replied to his critics with a series of "open letters" directed at galleries, public officials, and critics. The exhibition and the show produced a divided public: one critical camp was offended by his work, others supported

it. As a result of the show Hundertwasser was invited to produce a linocut, a work which became *Three Houses.* (Also in February, Hundertwasser had his first one-man show at the Galeria Sandi in Venice.)

Hundertwasser painted the watercolour to transform into the linocut. The work proved crucial, and stated a major theme that was to reappear in his art. The image depicts the sheer expanse of a city, with only the slightest suggestion of distance contributed by the diminution of the rectangular elements as they recede toward the work's top. He was exposing the inhuman regularity of the modern city, a "machine for living" in which life conforms to the tempo of the machine. This image later figured in one of Hundertwasser's most famous prints, *Good Morning City* (p. 125), itself based on an early work, *Bleeding Houses* (p. 42).

STRAIGHT LINES

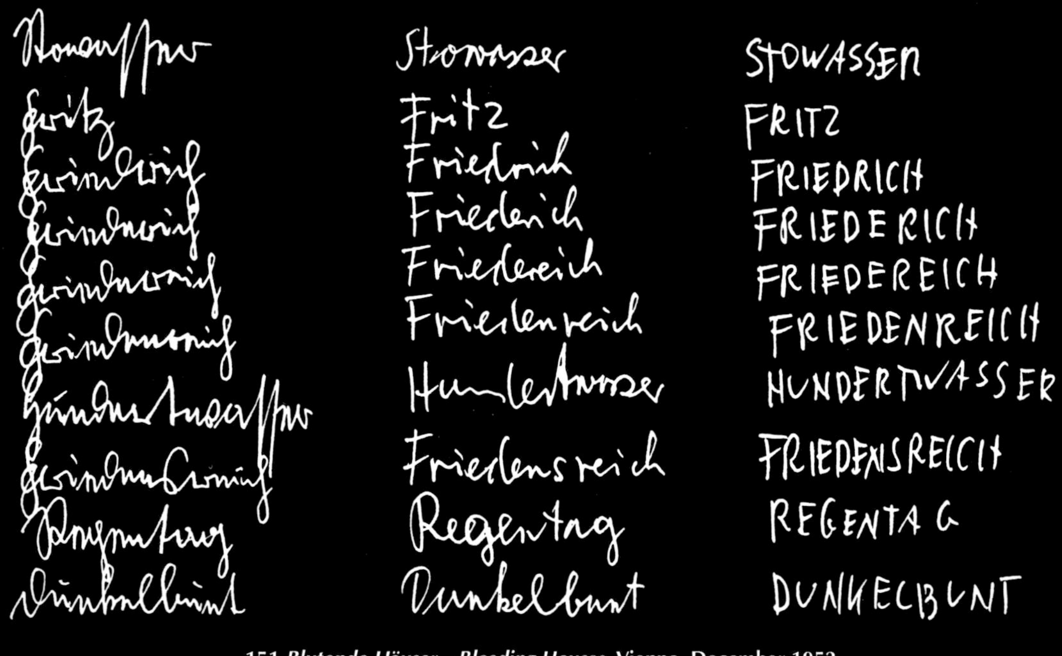
Stowasser
Fritz
Friedrich
Friederich
Friedereich
Friedenreich
Hundertwasser
Friedensreich
Regentag
Dunkelbunt
STOWASSER
FRITZ
FRIEDRICH
FRIEDERICH
FRIEDEREICH
FRIEDENREICH
HUNDERTWASSER
FRIEDENSREICH
REGENTAG
DUNKELBUNT

151 *Blutende Häuser – Bleeding Houses,* Vienna, December 1952
Mixed media: egg tempera on hard fibreboard, primed with chalk, zinc white and fish glue, 104 x 60 cm

Hundertwasser's revulsion for the rectangular rationality of the mechanisms into which life is forced derives from impressions made by the Austrian Baroque's voluptuousness and by the curvaceous richness of Jugendstil ornamentation. Hundertwasser – captivated by Klimt and Schiele in the early 1950s – found fresh stimulus in Persian miniatures, the paintings of Giotto and Uccello, the woodcuts of Hokusai, Paul Klee, and the Douanier Rousseau. These artists were governed by an under-

lying faith in the animated line, not the product of a draughtsman's ruler. Hundertwasser believes that ruled straight lines are unhealthy in the most fundamental and organic sense.

It would be easy to assume that his affection for the vital line and distrust of straight lines arose only from the lingering strains of earlier Viennese art that still informed the environment of his youth. The culture of his youth confirmed the experiences of his travel. Hundertwasser con-

167 *La cité – Die Stadt – The City*, St. Maurice/Seine, August 1953
Mixed media: oil and casein on wood fibreboard, primed with chalk zinc white and fish glue, surrounded by a "baguette électrique", 74 x 176 cm

tends that ruler-drawn straight lines make people sick because, not occurring in nature, they incessantly subject people to an irritation for which the organism is unprepared. In the modern city the insult of the straight line is relentless, and comparable to the assault of chemical carcinogens, of pollutants that cause fearful diseases. At a basic level, Hundertwasser is well aware that "We are made up of cells, organically built up into humans [. . .] So when these seeing cells perceive something that is alien to them, alien to organic forms, they transmit an alarm signal to the brain."

F. H.: If a lion is stalking you, or a shark is out to kill you, you are of course in mortal danger. We have lived with these dangers for millions of years. The straight line is a man-made danger. There are so many lines, millions of lines, but only one of them is deadly and that is the straight line drawn with a ruler. The danger of the straight line cannot be compared with the danger of or-

CHILDREN'S DAY CENTRE
HUNDERTWASSER ARCHITECTURAL PROJECT FOR
FRANKFURT-HEDDERNHEIM

1. INCREASE IN NATURE IN ANSWER TO THE INDISCRIMINATE
   SETTLEMENT OF THE LANDSCAPE
2. A LIFE IN HARMONY WITH NATURE
3. COUNTRY AIR INSTEAD OF CITY AIR
4. YEARNINGS FOR ROMANTICISM AND CREATIVITY MADE REALITY
5. FULLY GRASS-COVERED ROOFTOPS FOR WALKING AND WANDERING ABOUT
   ON
6. ENERGY-SAVING HOUSES WHICH ARE COOL IN SUMMER AND WARM IN WINTER
7. BETTER QUALITY OF LIVING FOR NEIGHBOURS AND NON-RESIDENTS
8. A CREATIVE WAY OUT OF THE DEAD-END OF URBAN PLANNING WHICH WILL SET
   A WORLDWIDE PRECEDENT

WHEREBY SUCH INNOVATIONS ARE NOTHING NEW! THE AIM IS RATHER TO RE-GAIN HUMAN DIGNITY IN ARCHITECTURE. OR SIMPLY TO REGAIN HUMAN DIG-NITY. WHY THE RELENTLESS USE OF THE RULER WHEN EVERYONE KNOWS THAT THE STRAIGHT LINE IS A DANGEROUS, COMFORTABLE ILLUSION WHICH LEADS TO RUIN? IT IS INCREDIBLE THAT BUILDING CONTINUES TO BE UNHUMAN AND UN-NATURAL DESPITE THE BAUHAUS MENTALITY HAVING PROVED ITSELF A DEAD END DECADES AGO.

THE BAUHAUS MENTALITY BEHIND RESIDENTIAL ARCHITECTURE CAN BE DE-SCRIBED AS UNFEELING, EMOTIONLESS, DICTATORIAL, HEARTLESS, AGGRESSIVE, SMOOTH, STERILE, UNADORNED, COLD, UNPOETIC, UNROMANTIC, ANONYMOUS AND YAWNINGLY VOID. AN ILLUSION OF FUNCTIONALITY.

HOUSES WITH PEOPLE INSIDE THEM MUST NOT BE ABANDONED TO AN INTERNA-TIONAL ARCHITECTURE MAFIA WHICH IS MOTIVATED BY CULTURAL POLITICS AND WHICH PLAYS NIHILISTIC-AESTHETIC GAMES WITH PEOPLE.

IT IS NOT QUITE SO BAD WHEN AN ART MAFIA SEEKS TO FORCE UPON THE GENERAL PUBLIC - VIA MUSEUMS AND ART MAGAZINES - A NEGATIVELY UGLY STYLE OF PAINTING CURRENTLY IN FASHION. MODERN ART TRENDS CHANGE FROM YEAR TO YEAR, AND YOU NEED NEITHER BUY NOR EVEN LOOK AT THEM.

BUT WHEN THIS INTELLECTUAL MAFIA, ENEMY OF MAN AND NATURE, FORCES PEOPLE TO LIVE FOR GENERATIONS IN HOUSES OF PERVERSELY FASHIONABLE DE-SIGN AND SOULLESS CONSTRUCTION, IT COMMITS A PERMANENT CRIME.

IT IS PRECISELY THIS ENFORCED ENDURANCE OF DICTATORIAL HOUSES BY THEIR INHABITANTS THAT FORMS THE BASIS OF THE GENERAL SPIRITUAL AND PHYSICAL PRIVATION SUFFERED BY OUR WESTERN CIVILIZATION, THE STATE, NATURE AND BY US OURSELVES.

THE ARCHITECT AND TOWN PLANNER IS TODAY, MORE THAN EVER BEFORE, THE SPINELESS PUPPET OF UNSCRUPULOUS CLIENTS.

HE IS A SUBORDINATE EXECUTOR OF THE MASS-PRODUCTION LOBBY, THE MONEY MAFIA AND POWER POLITICS. LIKE A WAR CRIMINAL, AND USUALLY AGAINST HIS CONSCIENCE (SHOULD HE HAVE ONE), HE OBEDIENTLY FOLLOWS ORDERS AND BUILDS CONCENTRATION CAMPS IN WHICH NATURE, LIFE AND THE HUMAN SOUL ARE SYSTEMATICALLY DESTROYED.

THE BLIND, COWARDLY AND STUPID APPLICATION OF THE GEOMETRIC STRAIGHT LINE HAS MADE DESOLATE WASTES OF OUR CITIES, FROM THE AESTHETIC, SPIRI-TUAL AND ECOLOGICAL POINTS OF VIEW.

THE STRAIGHT LINE AND ITS PRODUCTS ARE CANCEROUS ULCERS POISONING URBAN PLANNING AND PHYSICAL HEALTH EQUALLY.

OUR CITIES ARE THE CONCRETIZED CRACKPOT WHIMS OF CRIMINAL ARCHITECTS WHO NEVER TOOK THE HIPPOCRATIC OATH OF ARCHITECTURE: I REFUSE TO BUILD HOUSES WHICH MIGHT DAMAGE NATURE AND PEOPLE.

TWO GENERATIONS OF ARCHITECTS WITH A BAUHAUS MENTALITY HAVE DE-STROYED OUR LIVING ENVIRONMENT.

THE ARRIVAL OF THE URBAN PLANNER HAS MADE OUR CITIES UGLY.

MAN HAS LOST CONTACT WITH THE EARTH.

MAN LIVES IN ISOLATION FROM THE EARTH AND FROM HIS NATURAL ENVIRON-MENT.

WE INSULATE OURSELVES WITH CONCRETE AND PLASTIC.

EVEN RAIN WATER IS NO LONGER PERMITTED TO SEEP INTO URBAN SOIL, BUT IS PIPED AWAY ELSEWHERE.

EVEN OUR DEAD, BURIED 12 FEET DEEP BELOW THE HUMUS LAYER IN AIRTIGHT AND WATERTIGHT COFFINS, ARE NOT ALLOWED TO COME INTO CONTACT WITH PLANTS NOR BECOME HUMUS.

THE ALTERNATE PROFITABILITY OF THE HEDDERNHEIM COMPLEX AS A WHOLE IS HUGE, AND THE FOLLOWING SHOULD BE NOTED REGARDING COST-EFFICIENCY CALCULATIONS FOR THE COMPLEX: DATA ON ECOLOGICAL AND CREATIVE NEEDS AND ON PEOPLE'S YEARNINGS AND SPIRITUAL REQUIREMENTS MUST BE STORED IN OUR COMPUTERS AND GIVEN CONSIDERATION BEFORE ALL ELSE. THE MODERN MEANS OF COMPUTERS MAY THUS BE APPLIED TO ARCHITECTURE, URBAN PLAN-NING, ECONOMY, TRANSPORT, ENERGY AND AGRICULTURE IN ORDER TO CALCU-LATE WHAT IS CHEAP AND WHAT IS EXPENSIVE, WHAT IS MEANINGFUL AND WHAT IS HARMFUL, WITHIN ITS OVERALL CONTEXT.

A CONSIDERATION OF ALL OF THE AVAILABLE DATA, INCLUDING ECOLOGICAL AND OTHER DATA, MUST BECOME AN ABSOLUTE PRECONDITION OF ALL CALCU-LATIONS.

WHAT IS THE POINT OF, E.G., A HOUSE WHICH IS CHEAP BECAUSE THE PLANNERS AND ARCHITECTS TOTALLED UP ONLY THE COSTS OF MATERIALS, LAND AND LA-BOUR, BUT FOR WHICH WE WILL ULTIMATELY PAY DEARLY?

THEIR BILL DID NOT INCLUDE THE OTHER COSTS WHICH WILL BE INCURRED, DE-SPITE THEIR BEING EQUALLY EASY TO PROJECT: INCREASED EXPENDITURE ON HEAT-ING AND COOLING, DUST AND NOISE-PROOFING AND AIR POLLUTION SIMPLY BECAUSE, E.G., NO GRASS ROOF WAS PLANNED FROM THE START.

COSTS WILL ESCALATE AS A RESULT OF VANDALISM, CRIMINALITY, DISCONTENT, NEUROSES, UNEMPLOYMENT, HOSPITAL EXPENSES, EXODUS FROM THE CITIES, IN-JURED SELF-ESTEEM AND DIGNITY AND THE MUZZLING OF INDIVIDUAL CREATIV-ITY, ALL PROVOKED BY MISTAKEN PLANNING AND THE FAILURE TO CONSIDER ECO-LOGICAL AND CREATIVE COMPONENTS IN THEIR RICH INTERPLAY AND COMPLEX WHOLE.

THIS BILL WILL UNDOUBTEDLY BE PRESENTED, BUT AT A LATER DATE, MAKING IT EASY FOR PLANNERS UP TILL NOW TO SHRUG OFF CONNECTIONS, CAUSES AND EFFECTS - IN SHORT, RESPONSIBILITY.

MY CREATIVE CONTRIBUTION TO THE BUILDING OF THIS COMPLEX SHOULD THEREFORE BE SEEN SIMPLY AS AN ADVANCE TOWARDS THE CREATIVITY OF EACH INDIVIDUAL.

NATURE, ART AND CREATION ARE A SINGLE UNITY. WE HAVE SIMPLY SEPARATED THEM.

IF WE RAPE THE CREATION OF NATURE, IF WE ANNIHILATE CREATION IN US, THEN WE DESTROY OURSELVES. ONLY NATURE CAN TEACH US CREATION, CREATIVITY. OUR TRUE ILLITERACY IS OUR INABILITY TO BE CREATIVELY ACTIVE.

WE MUST SEEK A PEACE TREATY WITH NATURE, THE SOLE CREATIVELY SUPERIOR POWER, UPON WHICH MANKIND IS DEPENDENT.

SUCH A PEACE TREATY WITH NATURE SHOULD INCLUDE THE FOLLOWING POINTS:
1. WE MUST LEARN THE LANGUAGE OF NATURE, IN ORDER TO COMMUNICATE WITH HER.
2. WE MUST RETURN TO NATURE TERRITORIES WHICH WE HAVE ILLEGALLY APPRO-PRIATED AND RAVAGED, E.G. ON THE PRINCIPLE THAT EVERYTHING HORIZON-TAL UNDER THE OPEN SKY BELONGS TO NATURE, INCLUDING E.G. ROOFS AND ROADS.
3. TOLERATION OF SPONTANEOUS VEGETATION.
4. THE CREATION OF HUMANKIND AND THE CREATION OF NATURE MUST BE RE-UNIFIED. THE DIVISION OF THESE CREATIONS HAS HAD CATASTROPHIC CONSE-QUENCES FOR NATURE AND MAN.
5. LIFE IN HARMONY WITH THE LAWS OF NATURE.
6. WE ARE MERELY GUESTS OF NATURE AND SHOULD BEHAVE ACCORDINGLY. MAN IS THE MOST DANGEROUS PARASITE EVER TO HAVE RAVAGED THE EARTH. MAN MUST PUT HIMSELF BACK IN HIS ECOLOGICAL PLACE TO ALLOW THE EARTH TO REGENERATE.
7. HUMAN SOCIETY MUST ONCE AGAIN BECOME A WASTELESS SOCIETY. FOR ONLY THOSE WHO RESPECT AND RECYCLE THEIR WASTE IN A WASTELESS SOCIETY TRANSFORM DEATH INTO LIFE AND ARE ENTITLED, SINCE THEY RESPECT THE CYCLE AND ALLOW LIFE TO BE REBORN, TO CONTINUE ON THIS EARTH.

MAN'S YEARNING FOR A HOME IN HARMONY WITH NATURE AND HUMAN CREA-TIVITY IS IMMENSE. BUT IT IS PRECISELY THIS MOST UNDERSTANDABLE OF DESIRES WHICH IS DENIED TO RESIDENTS, AND IN PARTICULAR TO CHILDREN AND PUPILS.

PEOPLE ARE STILL REQUIRED TO LIVE AND LEARN IN CONCENTRATION-CAMP PRE-FABRICATIONS AND SOULLESS, COLD AND EMOTIONLESS BUILDINGS.

WHAT IS THE POINT OF ALL OUR NEW MATERIALS IF WE DO NOT USE THEM TO BRING NATURE BACK INTO THE CITY?

WE HAVE CEMENT, REINFORCED CONCRETE, PLASTIC, BITUMEN, SYNTHETIC RUB-BER, STAINLESS STEEL, EXPANDED CLAY AND MIXTURES OF ALL THESE MATERIALS, AS WELL AS THE TRADITIONAL MATERIALS OF TAR, BRICK, WOOD, RUBBER AND SO ON.

IT SHOULD BE A CHALLENGE TO EVERY ARCHITECT TO BUILD A HOME NOT ONLY FOR PEOPLE BUT, IN PARTICULAR, FOR WILD-GROWING SPONTANEOUS VEGETA-TION IN THE CITY.

A GOOD BUILDING SHOULD ACHIEVE AND UNITE TWO THINGS:

HARMONY WITH NATURE AND HARMONY WITH INDIVIDUAL HUMAN CREATION.

TOO LONG HAVE WE MADE THE EARTH OUR SLAVE, WITH THE CATASTROPHIC RESULTS WITH WHICH WE ARE ALL TOO FAMILIAR.

IT IS NOW HIGH TIME TO REVERSE THE ROLES, TO PLACE OURSELVES BELOW THE EARTH, TO HAVE THE EARTH OVER US. THIS BY NO MEANS INVOLVES DWELLING IN DARK CAVES AND DAMP CELLARS - QUITE THE OPPOSITE.

WE CAN HAVE EARTH AND TREES OVER OUR HEADS, AND STILL HAVE LIGHT AT THE SAME TIME. PLACING OURSELVES BENEATH NATURE MEANS, SYMBOLICALLY AND LITERALLY, LIVING IN HOUSES WHERE NATURE IS OVER US; IT IS OUR DUTY TO REPLACE ON OUR ROOFTOPS THE NATURE WE KILL WHEN WE BUILD A HOUSE. THUS THE NATURE WHICH WE HAVE ON OUR ROOFS IS THE PIECE OF EARTH WHICH WE HAVE KILLED BY PLACING A HOUSE ON IT.

WE NEED BEAUTY BARRIERS TO MAKE THE WORLD BIGGER AGAIN. INSTEAD, WE DO AWAY WITH EVERYTHING WHERE WE ARE AND EVERYTHING WHERE NATURE IS STILL UNSPOILT. AND IN ORDER TO GET THERE, WE BUILD UGLY ROADS WHICH DO AWAY WITH EVERYTHING IN BETWEEN.

THUS THE WORLD EVERYWHERE IS BECOMING SMALL AND UGLY. WHAT WE URGENTLY NEED ARE BEAUTY BARRIERS. THESE BEAUTY BARRIERS CONSIST OF NON-REGULARIZED IRREGULARITIES, AND THESE NON-REGULARIZED IRREGULARITIES CONSIST OF EITHER SPONTANEOUS VEGETATION OR THE CREATIVITY OF THE INDIVIDUAL.

BOTH ARE CREATIONS WHICH MUTUALLY COMPLEMENT ONE ANOTHER.

IF INDIVIDUALS IN THEIR OWN SPACE ASSERT THEIR "WINDOW RIGHT" AND DESIGN THEIR ENVIRONMENT, IF EACH PERSON IN THEIR OWN SPACE GIVES SPONTANEOUS VEGETATION A CHANCE, THE NEXT KINGDOM WILL SOON BE REACHED. FOR PARADISE IS AT YOUR NEIGHBOUR'S JUST AROUND THE CORNER, OR WHERE YOU ARE YOURSELF. PARADISES CANNOT BE SOUGHT AND FOUND, PARADISES CANNOT BE REQUISITIONED OR MANUFACTURED BY THE AUTHORITIES. THE HEDDERNHEIM COMPLEX WILL SET AN EXAMPLE TO THE WORLD. LIVING AND WORKING IN DECENT CONDITIONS AND CLOSE TO NATURE IS NOT ONLY ATTAINABLE AND FEASIBLE FOR ALL, BUT IS MORE ECONOMICAL, TOO: AS STATED ABOVE, THE ALTERNATE PROFITABILITY OF THE OVERALL COMPLEX IS HUGE. IT IS THE NORMAL METHODS OF INHUMAN, UNNATURAL BUILDING FOR WHICH WE ALL HAVE TO PAY SO DEARLY.

1. SEEN FROM ABOVE, THE HEDDERNHEIM COMPLEX IS ENTIRELY GREEN, LIKE NATURAL WOODED FIELDS AND PARKS. THE UNCOMPROMISING COVERING OF THE HOUSE WITH GRASS AND TREES PROVIDES OPTIMUM HEAT INSULATION: COOL IN SUMMER, WARM IN WINTER. IN MY HOUSE IN LÖWENGASSE, VIENNA, JUST 1 OF THE 3 RADIATORS AVAILABLE IS NEEDED TO HEAT THE ENTIRE APARTMENT (HEATING AND COOLING SAVINGS = SAVINGS IN ENERGY COSTS).

2. INSTEAD OF GOING AWAY ON HOLIDAY, PEOPLE WILL PREFER TO STAY AT HOME, IN A HOUSE IN WHICH THEY ARE AT LAST HAPPY AND UTTERLY AT EASE.

3. THE AIR IS BETTER, RICHER IN OXYGEN, OF STABLE HUMIDITY AND ALMOST DUST-FREE. THE ENTIRE CLIMATE IS BETTER, AND NOISE POLLUTION IS DRASTICALLY REDUCED.

4. GENERAL WELL-BEING IS INCOMPARABLY IMPROVED: PEOPLE FEEL HEALTHIER, HAVE FEWER HEADACHES, FEWER DEPRESSIONS, FEWER ILLNESSES (THE SAVINGS THIS BRINGS IN TERMS OF MEDICINES, DOCTORS, HOSPITAL AND SANATORIUM STAYS, PYSCHIATRIST'S FEES ETC. ARE IMMENSE. IN THE LONG TERM THESE WILL FAR OUTWEIGH INITIAL CONSTRUCTION COSTS).

5. THE TERRIBLE CONSEQUENCES OF LIVING AND WORKING IN INHUMAN, UNNATURAL BUILDINGS - VANDALISM, TERRORISM, MENTAL SUFFERING AND SUICIDE - WILL ALSO BE LARGELY AVOIDED.

I SEE THE ONLY DISADVANTAGE IN THE FRANKFURT-HEDDERNHEIM COMPLEX, AS IN THE HUNDERTWASSER HOUSE, IN ITS DAILY STREAM OF VISITORS, WHO COME FROM ALL OVER THE WORLD TO LOOK AT THE COMPLEX BECAUSE THEY TOO WANT TO LIVE IN A HARMONIOUS ENVIRONMENT SUCH AS THIS.

THE SOLUTION IS FIRST TO ESTABLISH BOUNDARIES TO PROTECT THE USERS OF THE COMPLEX, AND THEN TO BUILD MORE SUCH HOUSES; THE DEMAND IS ENDLESS.

THE ROOFS FOR "WALKING AND WANDERING ABOUT ON" ARE FULLY GRASSED AND ACCESSIBLE TO USERS. THERE IS NO PART OF THE HOUSE WHICH CANNOT BE EASILY REACHED. YOU CAN RELAX ON THE ROOF ON GRASS AND UNDER TREES.

A UTOPIAN, FAIRY-TALE VISION OF THE FUTURE, SUCH AS ONLY CHIDREN DARE DREAM OF, WILL HERE BECOME A TANGIBLE REALITY IN THE TRUEST POSSIBLE SENSE.

ROOFING THE HOUSES WITH TREES AND NATURE WILL ALMOST DOUBLE THE SPACE AVAILABLE FOR LEISURE ACTIVITIES, SINCE IT TURNS THE OTHERWISE STERILE, DEAD ROOF INTO A GRASSY MEADOW, A WOOD, A HILL, A VIEWING TOWER, A PARK AND A GARDEN.

THE USERS WILL BE PROUD OF THEIR GOOD CONSCIENCE VIS-A-VIS NATURE.

EVERYTHING HORIZONTAL UNDER THE OPEN SKY BELONGS TO NATURE. THIS IS HERE MADE REALITY.

MAN IS THE GUEST OF NATURE AND SHOULD BEHAVE ACCORDINGLY. THIS IS HERE MADE REALITY.

MAN, ON HIS ROOFTOPS, MUST RETURN TO NATURE THAT WHICH HE HAS ILLEGALLY TAKEN FROM HER IN BUILDING HIS HOUSE. THIS IS HERE MADE REALITY.

THIS IS AN ACTIVE CONTRIBUTION TOWARDS PEACE WITH NATURE - NOT JUST TALKING, BUT ACTING AND SETTING A LIVING EXAMPLE.

THIS GRASS-ROOFED COMPLEX IS A FORWARD-LOOKING SOLUTION TO THE INDISCRIMATE SPRAWL OF OUR CITIES.

THE ANONYMITY OF HUMAN MASSES STACKED IN HOUSING SILOS ONE ABOVE THE OTHER IS WRONG.

EQUALLY WRONG IS THE SETTLEMENT AND DESTRUCTION OF HUGE AREAS OF NATURE WITH ENDLESS, MONOTONOUS SUBURBAN ESTATES; LOS ANGELES IS A PARTICULARLY HORRIFIC EXAMPLE. VERTICAL HIGH-RISE HUMAN STACKING IS JUST AS WRONG AS HORIZONTAL SPRAWLING ACROSS NATURE. IN GRASS AND TREE-ROOFED ESTATES, ON THE OTHER HAND, NATURE IS INCREASED.

FOR DESPITE CREATING LIVING SPACE FOR PEOPLE, GREATER LIVING SPACE IS ALSO CREATED FOR NATURE. A NEW LANDSCAPE IS CREATED.

THE HUNDERTWASSER HEDDERNHEIM COMPLEX REALIZES THE YEARNINGS CHERISHED BY PRESENT-DAY MAN FOR SECURITY, ROMANTICISM AND COMMUNITY IN HARMONY WITH NATURE. FOR THE ADULT SUFFERING FROM THE CREATIVE IMPOTENCE INSTILLED INTO HIM FROM YOUTH, THE SOLE REMAINING POSSIBILITY IS TO THINK BACK TO HIS OWN CHILDHOOD AND TO START AGAIN FROM THE

POINT WHERE HE WAS TORN FROM HIS DREAMS, WHICH WERE NOT DREAMS AT ALL, BUT HIS REAL BASIS, THE ROOTS OF HIS EXISTENCE, WITHOUT WHICH HE CAN NEVER TRULY BE A PERSON.

TERRIBLE SINS HAVE BEEN COMMITTED IN THE PAST IN THE FIELD OF ARCHITECTURE FOR YOUNG PEOPLE IN PARTICULAR, I.E. SCHOOLS, CHILDREN'S HOMES ETC.

COLD-HEARTED RECTILINEAR REPRESSION OF THE CHILDISH SOUL AND SUPPRESSION OF ITS GERMINATING CREATIVITY HAVE BEEN PRACTICED FOR DECADES, SIMPLY BY MEANS OF THE AGGRESSIVE, LEVELLING ARCHITECTURE IN WHICH OUR YOUNG PEOPLE HAVE TO SPEND THE MOST IMPORTANT YEARS OF THEIR LIVES.

THE MENTAL ABUSE COMMITTED BY SCHOOLS BUILT IN SUCH CONCENTRATION-CAMP STYLE EXCEEDS EVEN THE PHYSICAL PUNISHMENT THEY REPRESENT.

FOR THE YOUNG GENERATIONS WHO HAVE HAD TO SPEND THE LAST DECADES GROWING UP IN EDUCATIONAL INSTITUTIONS AND NURSERY SCHOOLS HOSTILE TO NATURE AND CREATIVITY, THE LASTING PSYCHOLOGICAL DAMAGES ARE IMMENSE.

CHILDREN ARE EVEN LESS ABLE THAN ADULTS TO DEFEND THEMSELVES AGAINST A PREPLANNED, SOUL-DESTROYING, LIFE-DESTROYING ENVIRONMENT.

IN HEDDERNHEIM, YOUNG PEOPLE WILL BE IN UNINTERRUPTED, LIVELY, POSITIVE CONTACT WITH NATURE, BEAUTY AND CREATIVITY.

IT WILL STAMP THEIR LIVES, AND THE CHILDHOOD YEARS SPENT IN THIS HOUSE WILL REMAIN FOR EVER IN THEIR MEMORIES AS SOMETHING BEAUTIFUL, AND WILL POSITIVELY INFLUENCE THEIR LIVES.

THEY WILL ALSO SHARE WITH OTHER PEOPLE WHAT THEY HAVE PERSONALLY EXPERIENCED AS POSITIVE AND BEAUTIFUL, AND THUS CARRY IT OUT INTO THE WORLD.

HEDDERNHEIM HUMAN BEINGS WILL BE TRULY FREE - AND NOT CAST DOWN BY INTELLECTUAL, THEORETICAL BUILDINGS.

PARADISES CAN ONLY BE MADE BY WE OURSELVES, WITH OUR OWN CREATIVITY, IN HARMONY WITH THE FREE CREATIVITY OF NATURE.

HUNDERTWASSER   VIENNA, 14 MAY 1987

ganic lines described by snakes, for instance. The straight line is completely alien to mankind, to life, to all creation.

Measured against the history of life on earth, the straight line seems an ideal fiction with a purely conceptual existence. In the view of Hundertwasser, it is a fiction that "exists everywhere you live. Our whole civilization is founded on the straight line." The straight line came to humanity with the brick, with modular construction.

Bleeding Houses reappeared as a central image in Hundertwasser's later work. In this first appearance of the theme we see the clear presentation of seven large, pris-

matic, vertical structures. The buildings which dominate the piece represent the unrelievedly massive constructions that are the target of Hundertwasser's anger. Looming up into the painting's centre, two buildings touch the top edge and two the bottom, fixing the composition in space. One abuts the middle left margin, locking the picture into the surface of the painting, and another building touches the lower left corner. One more brushes the centre right edge and this same building on the right just grazes the picture's upper border. These contact points secure the buildings' considerable masses upon the painting's face. Moving in from the painting's outer fringes, small "unpainted" areas circulate

Top left and p. 49: Model of the Children's Day Centre, Heddernheim

Exterior views of construction work shortly before completion of the Children's Day Centre

between these towering skyscrapers. Mindlessly repeated architecture, such as is parodied in this work, permits no vistas – and prohibits the open pedestrian traffic of older cities. Though some architecture critics resisted the endless repetition of modernist building, Hundertwasser was the only painter to take this oppressiveness as his theme. The painting's title indicts the buildings' anti-humane fortress-like impregnability.

His rebuke became a practical solution. When the time came for Hundertwasser to respond with an idea for an urban complex, he proposed the *Frankfurt-Heddernheim,* which shows an alternative to the world of *Bleeding Houses.*

The City (pp. 44–45) represented a continuation of Hundertwasser's dialogue with architecture. (Architecture is the most conservative of the arts. The architect builds for others. He must explain his ideas, plan clearly, and marshal large labour gangs. A patron or the state delegates resources greater than an artist's. To place this capital in the service of the architect, his ideas must be conventional; the building's function must have a name and a type: bank, school, hospital, church, house, factory, etc. With the rarest exception, there can be no solitary architectural van Gogh.) Hundertwasser believes modern architecture failed when an initially benign rationality became inhuman.

The model of the Children's Day Centre was built by Alfred Schmid, 1987–88

EARLY STYLE

	Stowasser	STOWASSEN
Stowasser	Fritz	FRITZ
Fritz	Friedrich	FRIEDRICH
Friedrich	Friederich	FRIEDERICH
Friedrich	Friedenreich	FRIEDENREICH
Friederich	Hundertwasser	HUNDERTWASSER
Friedenreich	Friedensreich	FRIEDENSREICH
Hundertwasser	Regentag	REGENTA G
Friedensreich	Dunkelbunt	DUNKELBUNT
Regentag		
Dunkelbunt		

In his picture *Trams from Vienna, Munich and Stuttgart* (above), Hundertwasser's powerful imagination has included trams from three different cities. A convention of red, blue, and yellow trams course the imaginary avenues of a make-believe city. The trams are surrogates for geometric abstraction's nameless vertical and horizontal colour-blocks (on the left, a white rectangle surrounds one tram). But the trams frolic like puppies or children. Hundertwasser enlivened the small geometric units Klimt had enlisted to brighten a background or amplify a portrait's cadence. The experiment proved successful.

Outlines describe the *Car with Red Raindrops* (p. 58), painted about the same time. A red network indicates rainwater streaming off the car's body. Each red line ends with a bulbous raindrop. All is seen from above, from a window looking into the street. By means of colour, viewpoint, and stylization of the car's details an otherwise commonplace scene was transformed. The automobile's shape is rotund and compact, and the rain, blood-scarlet, balances what would otherwise have been perhaps too charming.

On the Sunny Side of the Street (p. 55) takes its title from a popular American song. Thin, slightly wavering, vertical bands progress over the surface in parallel. The painting (in primary colours with green accents throughout) has secondary accents

162 *Strassenbahnen von Wien, München und Stuttgart – Trams from Vienna, Munich and Stuttgart,* painted on the roof of a boarding house in Stuttgart, June 1953
Watercolour on white paper, 48 x 63 cm

in brown. Against the stripes are set oblongs in primary colours, the most prominent of which, a red square in the lower left, anchors the composition to the surface's edge – as had the houses in *Bleeding Houses* (p. 42). It makes an abstractly energetic impression.

In 1953 Hundertwasser visited Paris for the second time. During this sojourn the Galerie Paul Facchetti began to represent him. Facchetti, who had been a photographer, had introduced Pollock and Dubuffet in Europe. Hundertwasser's first exhibition at the gallery was mounted in January 1954. Remarkably, for a first show by an unknown artist, notices appeared far and near. (Besides French periodicals, the influential Japanese art journal "Bijutso Techo" carried a review by the art critic Shinichi Segui, who was fluent in French.) Many years later Jeanne Facchetti recalled that Hundertwasser had first come to the gallery's attention in 1950; she remem-

bered him as "a handsome young man, somewhat timid, quiet, but very strong-willed . . . I can still see him before me . . . on his bicycle, carrying his paintings on his back. He wore a pullover of his own design, grey with bright red, blue, green, and orange stripes. His long slender hands disappeared under the dangling sleeves which were much too long for him . . . (he) wore a collarless shirt and self-made sandals."

On the gallery's floor, Hundertwasser spread out his work before the owners, who had never seen such paintings. "We could hardly tear our eyes away from the gleaming spirals, the dreams of strange cities, the subtly composed festival of colours," recalled Jeanne Facchetti, adding: "In those days we lived among Dubuffet's 'chocolates' and the 'nuagiste' deserts; here suddenly was a meadow of lyricism that we found delightful." Compared to prevailing painting's lack of specific compositional commitment, Hundertwasser was a challenge to current taste and wisdom. The Facchettis' instincts were augmented by Kurt Valentine, who visited the gallery and, on seeing Hundertwasser's work, expressed unalloyed enthusiasm.

Vienna, 1952, with the watercolours "The Border" and "Coloured Linear Structure with a Gray Centre"

53

SPIRALS

In the post-War period, the international art scene was dominated by Abstract Expressionism in general and by the American artist Jackson Pollock in particular. Hundertwasser was swimming against this current, and also against other native styles which made the Paris art world anathema to him: "abstraction froide", the coterie of "art autre" around Michel Tapie, and other splinter groups. It was a world of vying interests and beliefs. And into that world Hundertwasser introduced a set form capable of infinite variation: the spiral.

Spirals first appeared in his work in 1953. At the University of Vienna's medical school, Hundertwasser saw the French documentary film "Images de la Folie", which presented the creativity of schizophrenic patients at Saint-Anne, the main psychiatric hospital in Paris. The film showed paintings done by the insane, and Hundertwasser saw some patients making spirals. The spiral seemed to embody both life and death. It was an intersection of living and inanimate matter, able to express all of nature, all of creation.

Possibly Vienna's Jugendstil (i. e. art nouveau) tradition predisposed Hundertwasser to respond to the spiral form. The Jugendstil was still manifest all around him, in posters and paintings, in architecture, in typography and book design, in graphics, in textiles, even in stamps, and of course in all the decorative arts. The spiral was given substantial form in Hermann Obrist's 1902 project for a monument (which remained unbuilt), a project which presaged Vladimir Tatlin's *Monument for the Third International* (1919–1920), an imposing and impossible work with a spiral motif. Hundertwasser's own architectural expression of the spiral appeared years later in his *Integrative School, Church, Office and Dwelling Complex* in Frankfurt, 1987 (p. 49). Despite its capricious appearance, by the time Hundertwasser attempted such an ambitious (though eminently sensible) structure he had spent years exploring the spiral and thinking about buildings. The sweeping ramps that come spiralling back upon themselves are all grass-covered; when seen from the air, the building disappears.

One of the first pictures in which the spiral occurs as a motif is *Blood Flowing in a Circle and I Have a Bicycle* (p. 50). The figure standing at the left of the picture has a round yellow head, a red and yellow body, and blue feet, and is echoed at the right by a stack of shapes within vertical divisions. These verticals flank both sides of the picture. The central rectangle contains the painting's major element – a great spiral. The compositional division into a horizontal with two outer verticals resembles Jackson Pollock's *Guardians of the Secret*. The gravely symmetrical composition – animated by the rotating spiral line fiercely throbbing at the work's core – resurrects European pre-history. Something unspoken lurks at the picture's centre. The spiral is alive, not geometrically predictable, and its colours seem organic, as if they were alive inside the bands.

In *The Garden of the Happy Dead* (p. 59), also from 1953 the spiral motif (the constant against which Hundertwasser's invention played) reappears as a broad path consisting of motifs inside cartouches. In this strange painting, the surrounding fringe separates the graveyard from the (surprisingly blank) world. The comparison is not the usual sort of living/dead contrast. In Hundertwasser's sense, in an ecological age (as in traditional Jewish custom), the dead continue to "live" (decomposing with the help of anaerobic humus bacteria) in trees and in fecund nature. What other artists thought of such issues at the time? From the picture's core, the realm of the dead, surprisingly happy colours shine. Green faces and red features characterize the "Happy Dead".

166 *On the Sunny Side of the Street – Maison-Invasions – Auf der Sonnenseite der Straße*, St. Maurice/Seine, July 1953
Oil on plywood primed with chalk zinc white and fish glue, surrounded by a "baguette électrique", 51 x 71 cm

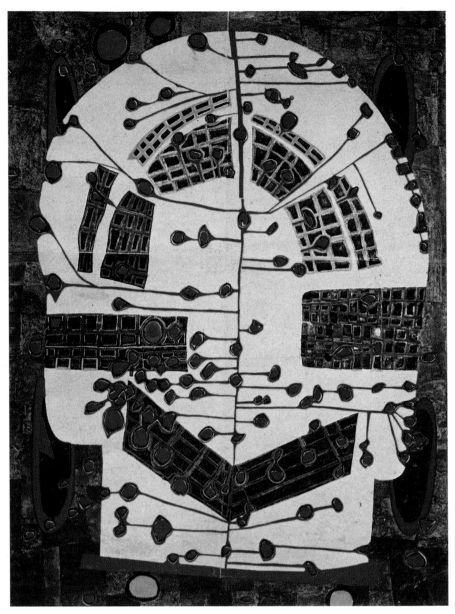

154 *Automobil mit roten Regentropfen – Car with Red Raindrops*, 1953,
completed 1957
Watercolour, 85 x 65 cm

numbers. This inventory did not merely record the sequence in which works were produced; indeed, often the Hundertwasser opus numbers are not accurate in their sequence. Instead he was concerned to record the whereabouts of every painting and its development – the titles, localities of execution, for how long he worked on each picture, what materials he used, the subsequent histories of each work, how many times each had changed hands and to what homes it went. For Hundertwasser, this record imbues each work with a life-history not unlike that of a living creature.

H. R.: Why did you start serially numbering and keeping precise dossiers of your work?
F. H.: Otherwise you don't know what you have done. It is important that you have some record. So I have a certificate which accompanies the painting like a birth certificate, like a passport, so the painting is to be considered as living. It has to be considered like a child of mine, like a living being.
H. R.: Are there favourite pieces that you yourself regard as key?
F. H.: Yes, of course, there are key works, important works.

One of the watercolours of this period, *Ein Kopf mit Erdfenstern (A Head with Earth Windows)* (p. 57) is a strikingly simple design: a face (with three pairs of eyes) gazes from a brilliant purple background. Dominant brown passages feature patterned leaf-shaped areas, the interstices filled with blues shining against the browns. Few artists have mastered watercolour so as to give such keenly vivid colours. *A Head with Earth Windows'* shapes too are suggestive. They recall North Africa, or Matisse's South-Sea forms, and these half-remem-

OPUS NUMBERS

The Garden of the Happy Dead (p. 59) was painted in Brô's house, in August 1953. In September and October 1954 Hundertwasser was confined to Rome's Santo Spirito Hospital for two months fighting severe jaundice. Once his strength returned he diligently painted watercolours, creating a substantial body of work in the hospital. While hospitalized, Hundertwasser began to number all his works sequentially. Modernist artists submerge artworks' specificity within the Impressionist idea of "serialism". Hundertwasser, on the other hand, saw every work as individual, yet woven into the uniform procession of his opus

Ill. p. 56: 186 *Il Sole Pesante – Die Schwere Sonne – The Heavy Sun*, 1954
Watercolour and indelible pencil on crumpled wrapping paper primed
with chalk white and fish glue, 44 x 29 cm

Ill. p. 57: 191 *Ein Kopf mit Erdfenstern – A Head with Earth Windows*,
September 1954
Watercolour and indelible pencil on white drawing paper, 18 x 27 cm

170 *Le jardin des morts heureux – Der Garten der glücklichen Toten – The Garden of the Happy Dead,* St. Maurice/Seine, August 1953
Oil on wood fibreboard primed with chalk zinc white and fish glue, surrounded by a "baguette électrique", 47 x 58.5 cm

bered recollections heighten Hundertwasser's colour effects. A seemingly unpremeditated painting shows off Hundertwasser at his best, unshackled to a larger programme. Viewers were immediately won by this art's non-rhetorical, decorative vivacity that (while growing from Viennese tradition) foreshadowed much popular painting of the 1970s.

Hemdärmelschnitt, Manica Di Camicia (A Tailor's Shirtsleeve-Cut)* (p. 61) was also painted during this period. This picture is divided horizontally, with its lower half predominantly bright yellow. Touches of red in rectangular passages suggest architecture – a town, and its streets and lanes. The rooflines were not laid out by a cityplanner or Bauhaus architect, and they end where a line bisects the picture. On the left a brilliant green column, flecked with golden yellow, rises from a solid black base like a marvellous monument that glows in the darkness around it as if lit from within:

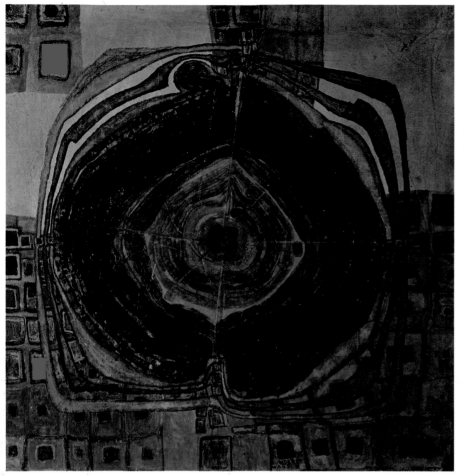

227 *Ein Regentropfen, der in die Stadt fällt – A Raindrop Falls into Town*, Paris, August 1955
Watercolour on primed, crumpled wrapping paper with indelible pencil, 42 x 41 cm

painted in 1955, records the rain's downward-looking glance. But this ideographic landscape view found its full expression in Hundertwasser's work in the ecological circuit of the *Spiral House*. The *Spiral House* was conceived as a mainly self-sufficient eco-dwelling to radically reduce liquid and solid waste pollution to the environment. Waste water would be drawn to the roof by a windpump, and it would then flow down a grass-covered spiral. The power of the grass to trap pollutants would be augmented by aesthetically pleasing plants and flowers on the spiral ramp. Water that travelled all the way to the bottom of the ramp would be much cleaner and ready for re-use. The water cycle apears in many forms in Hundertwasser's art.

From the irregular blue pool at the centre of *The Great Way* (pp. 6–7), a small stream flows. The great spiral begins. Ragged at times, flowing swiftly or slowly, it courses past "islands" in a pseudo-narrative journey. As it proceeds towards the outer edge we are pulled along by a force akin to, but different from, inexorable narrative time. Once begun, the spiral cannot

a pillar of precious stone erected in a peaceful village. We wander in a dream-world with its own rationale and, to the degree that we can enter this reverie, Hundertwasser has succeeded in his early Schiele-inspired goal of providing the entrance to a world akin to musical realms.

A Raindrop Falls Into Town (above),

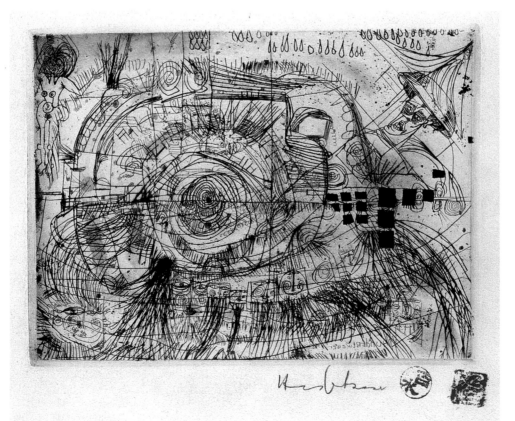

stop, and like the telling of a story, a beginning must lead us onward. Every story is different, and every spiral is different, but each contains the element of time. (Years later Hundertwasser tried to communicate something like this to his students, with disastrous results.) A series of irregular squares, like stepping stones across a stream, lead through *The Great Way*. Such rustic suggestions carry a pastoral tone,

and, simultaneously, move the eye across the work, rather than into depth. These incidents rivet the picture's surface against a flow that would otherwise overwhelm. The artist's signature is outside the work. In deep red on the frame, Hundertwasser's signature indicates that the pattern is complete without conventional declarations of authorship.

Left: 529 *Spirale mit Neuffer-Köpfen – Spiral with Neuffer Heads,* Paris, 1957/59, Vienna, 1962
Etching, 32 x 18.5 cm (14 x 19)
Edition of 50 signed. A few proofs without Neuffer Heads. Printed by G. Leblanc, Paris. Published by Enrico Magalio de Micheli, Paris 1962

Top: 201 *Manica Di Camicia – Hemdärmelschnitt – A Tailor's Shirtsleeve-Cut,* Florence, October 1954
Watercolour on primed wrapping paper, 61 x 73 cm
Ill. pp. 62/63: 274 *S.S. Bauta,* painted on board the S.S. Bauta in the port of Stugsund, near Söderhamm, September 1956
Watercolour on white wrapping paper, 34 x 50 cm

61

FURTHER TRAVELS

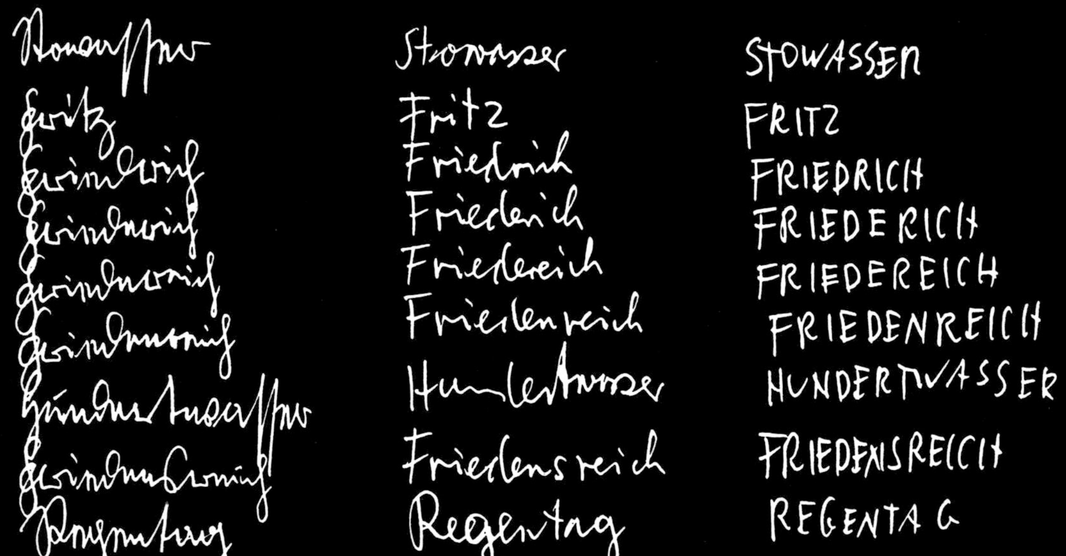
Stowasser
Fritz
Friedrich
Friederich
Friedereich
Friedenreich
Hundertwasser
Friedensreich
Regentag
Dunkelbunt
STOWASSER
FRITZ
FRIEDRICH
FRIEDERICH
FRIEDEREICH
FRIEDENREICH
HUNDERTWASSER
FRIEDENSREICH
REGENTAG
DUNKELBUNT

305 *Frisch gefundenes Labyrinth – Freshly Found Labyrinth,* Paris 1957
Lithograph in red and green, 62 x 46 cm (51 x 45)
Poster for the exhibition in the Galerie H. Kamer
Edition of 50 unnumbered, unsigned. Printed by Pons, Paris

255 *Montagne – Berg – Mountain,* St. Maurice/Seine, May 1956
Mixed media: egg tempera on white primed canvas with horizontal seam at bottom, 85 x 116 cm

Right: 278 *Paysage au soleil violet – Landschaft mit violetter Sonne – Landscape with Violet Sun,* Paris, 1956
Mixed media, 51 x 25 cm
Bottom: 254 *Le petit repos gazon – Die kleine Rasenruhe – Small Meadow Repose,* St. Maurice/Seine, May 1956
Mixed media: egg tempera and watercolour, varnished, on white primed canvas with vertical seam, 63 x 90 cm

In the mid–1950s Hundertwasser wrestled with a cluster of ideas that he moulded into a personal statement for his theory of "transautomatism", published in the May 1956 issue of "Cimaise" as "La visibilité de la création transautomatique". Later, this material was expanded, becoming "The Grammar of Seeing", which evolved through 1957. (In 1956, Hundertwasser worked incongruously as a dishwasher in Stockholm, while "Cimaise" and "Phases" published his article.) That summer, Hundertwasser and a friend, Hans Neuffer, worked as deck hands on an Estonian ship under Liberian flag from Söderhamm to Hull. Neuffer, who died in 1973, collaborated with Hundertwasser on a print – Hundertwasser's first joint effort since the 1950 murals at St. Mandé that he and Brô had undertaken. In 1962 Hundertwasser issued an etching with Neuffer's additions of some grotesque heads.

At the stern of the *S. S. Bauta* (pp. 62–63) a flag flies beneath a glowering moon or sun. The ship and its contents appear in x-ray view. In red against the white bulkhead, the exterior steps and supports of the outer iron structure are legible; blue highlights flash from the ventilators. Through the opaque forecastle and stern, lights gleam hopefully in portholes and normality seems to reign. Peacefully, running lights

glow at the tops of the masts. In reality the S. S. Bauta was apparently a murderous hell of violently depraved sailors, hallucinating that they were in the grip of Goebbels, who meant to continue the war. These drunken, homeless men were half -desperate refugees from Communism, with no countries to which they could return. The rest of the crew were criminals, some of them murderers, who, not daring to come ashore, attacked the others on board with iron bars. None of this is expressed in Hundertwasser's beautiful little work.

Reports of the political suppression of Hungary depressed him – as have few political situations since. Only the Chinese invasion of Tibet and the Dalai Lama's flight to India similarly moved Hundertwasser to devote many paintings to an event – four or five works on the topic of the Dalai Lama's escape. Later events in Budapest occasioned a painting titled *Budapest*, while the 1968 Warsaw Pact invasion of Czechoslovakia affected Hundertwasser profoundly.

POLITICS AND THE IMAGINATION

H. R.: Your images issue from your imagination?

F. H.: I don't know where they come from. It is something which I witness. Forms develop and grow by themselves. Really, sometimes some houses, some colour interests me and I want to have it as a starting point, but then the work develops into something else. Sometimes I start with a theme, but always it gets out of hand – I go the easy way.

It is just as if you had a donkey, a beautiful donkey. You like the donkey and you want to take him up the hill, but the donkey does not want to go to the hill and he turns toward the river. Of course you follow him to the river – what is the use of pushing him, pulling him up the mountain [. . .]? It would give you a bad feeling to beat him all the time to force him into a way that he does not want to go. So I go the easy way, I follow him and it is always right.

Top: 304 *Si la vague aime deux soleils – Wenn die Welle zwei Sonnen liebt – If the Wave Loves Two Suns*, St. Mandé/Seine, March 1957
Watercolour on wrapping paper primed with chalk, 12 x 22 cm

Right: 325 *Le fleuve jaune – Der gelbe Fluß – The Yellow River*, Vienna, September-October 1957, repainted Paris, 1960, completed and varnished La Picaudière, March 1963
Mixed media: egg tempera and oil on primed white material with visible horizontal seam at centre, 48 x 63 cm

311 *L'œuf de l'ancien Japon précolumbien – Das Ei des alten präkolumbianischen Japan – The Egg of the Old Precolumbian Japan,*
St. Mandé/Seine, June 1957
Mixed media: egg tempera, oil, watercolour, wax on cardboard on wooden frame, one half finished with a wax coating, 97 x 146 cm

H. R.: Who is the donkey?

F. H.: The donkey is the subconscious, this outside power which I follow. It is very easy to follow. In fact, it is the easy way, the lazy way, and the lazy way leads to success. The diligent way, the forceful way leads to disaster. If it is forced you see it in the painting. You see in so many paintings that the man who made it wanted to fulfil a task, but in the meantime he suffered so much and sacrificed so much that the result is not so important any more.

H. R.: What happens when the "donkey" starts going to some place that you don't want to go?

F. H.: Most of the time I feel comfortable in the place where the donkey wants to go.

The mechanics of Hundertwasser's art have not changed much over the years. He often starts painting from the edge of a sheet and gradually works towards the centre. There is no reason for him to change.

H. R.: Do you sketch in the composition before you start painting?

F. H.: Yes, I do, but very quickly. I make a

HUNDERTWASSER'S LETTER TO MINICH

MY DEAR FRIEND MINICH,

THANK YOU FOR YOUR LETTER OF 25 MAY, RE THE SPITTELAU DISTRICT HEATING STATION.

I FULLY UNDERSTAND THAT YOU ARE AGAINST IT, JUST LIKE MYSELF AND MANY OTHER CONCERNED PEOPLE. I PERSONALLY GREW UP IN THE BRIGITTENAU AREA, IN OTHER WORDS VERY CLOSE BY.

BUT YOUR LETTER LACKS A PRACTICAL ALTERNATIVE FOR TODAY.

WE OURSELVES, ALL OF US, EVERY VIENNESE CITIZEN, ARE RESPONSIBLE FOR OUR OWN REFUSE. IF WE PRODUCED NO REFUSE, THERE WOULD BE NONE TO BURN. LET US BOYCOTT WASTE-INCINERATION PLANTS BY SIMPLY NOT SUPPLYING THEM WITH REFUSE. IS THAT FEASIBLE IN PRESENT-DAY VIENNA? REFUSE SHOULD BE MADE A CRIMINAL OFFENCE.

REFUSE PRODUCERS, PACKAGING INDUSTRIES, REFUSE CAUSERS, REFUSE MAKERS, I.E. ALL OF US, SHOULD BE SEVERELY PUNISHED IN ORDER TO INDUCE A RADICAL AVOIDANCE OF WASTE.

I SPENT A YEAR AGONIZING OVER THE SAME ARGUMENTS FOR DECLINING THE PROJECT AS YOURS, BEFORE FINALLY DECIDING TO ACCEPT THE COMMISSION FOR THE VISUAL REDESIGN OF THE PLANT. AS YOU KNOW, I AM VEHEMENTLY AGAINST ALL ENVIRONMENTAL POLLUTANTS AND HAVE ALWAYS USED ALL MY MEANS TO PROMOTE A WASTE-FREE SOCIETY.

I AM A REALIST, HOWEVER.

WE CANNOT CLOSE OUR EYES TO REALITY.

ALL MY UTOPIAS AND DREAMS CAN BE REALIZED, AS I AM CONTINUALLY DEMONSTRATING.

HAVING MADE A DETAILED STUDY OF WHAT WOULD HAPPEN IF SPITTELAU DID NOT GO INTO OPERATION, I.E. BY THINKING IT THROUGH TO THE END, I DECIDED THE NEGATIVE CONSEQUENCES ARE FAR WORSE.

WE WON'T HAVE A WASTE-FREE SOCIETY TOMORROW.

BUT HOPEFULLY THE DAY AFTER TOMORROW.

I WILL FIGHT VEHEMENTLY FOR IT, AND WE MUST ALL WORK DAILY TOWARDS IT.

THE NEGATIVE POINTS:

1. REFUSE INCINERATION IN A BUILT-UP URBAN AREA WITH THE FEAR THAT TOXINS WILL ENDANGER PEOPLE IN THE CITY.

2. SKIPPING THE HUMUS PHASE BY INCINERATING.

THE POSITIVE POINTS:

1. EXTENSIVE, ALMOST COMPLETE NEUTRALIZATION OF TOXIC SUBSTANCES IN REFUSE THROUGH INCINERATION IN NEW (STATE-OF-THE-ART) DENOX FILTER PLANTS.

2. HEAT EXTRACTION: IT WILL HEAT 10-15% OF VIENNA.

3. FOLLOWING MY REDESIGN THE WORKS WILL LOSE THEIR UGLINESS, AND THUS THE PSYCHOLOGICAL DISTRESS CAUSED BY THE EARLIER SIGHT OF ITS IMMENSE AND VISIBLY THREATENING POLLUTION OF THE ENVIRONMENT WILL BE RELIEVED.

I AM CERTAIN THAT PEOPLE WILL EVEN FEEL PRIDE AT HAVING THIS NEW SYMBOL OF VIENNA IN THEIR NEIGHBOURHOOD, AND THIS WILL INCREASE THE SELF-CONFIDENCE AND JOY IN LIFE OF AN ENTIRE CITY DISTRICT. PARTICULARLY WHEN THE FILTER PLANT AND TECHNICAL SECTION ARE SETTING EXAMPLES TO THE WORLD.

HOWEVER PARADOXICAL IT SOUNDS, I SEE THE SPITTELAU STATION AS A FIRST CALL FOR A MORE ATTRACTIVE, WASTE-FREE ENVIRONMENT. I AM ALSO PROUD THAT AUSTRIA IS SETTING THIS EXAMPLE.

THE AUTHORITIES, THE BUREAUCRATS, THE POLITICIANS AND RESPONSIBLE TECHNICIANS HAVE DONE ALL THEY COULD. WE MUST ACKNOWLEDGE THAT.

IT IS NOW UP TO US TO PROVE THAT WE CAN DO EVEN BETTER AND EVEN MORE. PROTESTS ALONE ARE OF NO HELP HERE.

ONLY A NEW SOCIETY, RESPECTING THE TRUE ECOLOGICALLY-CREATIVE VALUES WHICH WE ESTABLISH OURSELVES, CAN BRING ABOUT GRADUAL CHANGE.

IN DETAIL:

COLD INCINERATION (ROTTING IN REFUSE DUMPS) HAS THE SAME EFFECTS AS HOT INCINERATION:

1. THE SAME OXYGEN IS CONSUMED, I.E. REMOVED FROM THE AIR, SIMPLY OVER A LONGER PERIOD OF TIME.

2. THE AIR IS ENRICHED WITH THE SAME AMOUNT OF C02, OVER A LONGER PERIOD OF TIME.

3. APPROXIMATELY THE SAME TOXINS AND POLLUTANTS ESCAPE INTO THE AIR AND WATER; IT SIMPLY TAKES LONGER.

4. THE SAME HEAT (ENERGY) IS PRODUCED, ALBEIT UNEXPLOITED. E.G., A PIECE OF WOOD HUMIFYING AND MINERALIZING OVER SOME 3-5 YEARS RELEASES THE SAME ENERGY AS WHEN BURNT IN AN INCINERATOR IN JUST ONE MINUTE.

5. THE SAME ASH (RESIDUE) IS PRODUCED FROM A PIECE OF WOOD IN ONE MINUTE (HOT INCINERATION) AS OVER 3-5 YEARS OF COLD INCINERATION.

HOWEVER: IN REFUSE DUMPS, TOXINS ARE NOT RENDERED HARMLESS AND ESCAPE UNCHECKED. THIS APPLIES PARTICULARLY TO HEAVY METALS, WHICH IN SPITTELAU WILL BE RECOVERED.

SHOULD REFUSE HAVE TO BE REMOVED FROM THE CITY BY LORRY, WHETHER TO A DUMP OR AN INCINERATION PLANT, LET US SAY 30 KM OUTSIDE VIENNA, THE EXHAUST FUMES AND TOXIC EMISSIONS FROM THE LORRIES' INTERNAL COMBUSTION ENGINES WOULD POSE A MUCH GREATER AND REAL DANGER TO THE POPULATION THAN THE SPITTELAU DISTRICT HEATING STATION, AND AN ADDITIONAL ONE AT THAT. CONSIDER THIS: SOME 2000 TONS OF REFUSE PER DAY, TRANSPORTED IN SOME 300 LORRIES, EACH LORRY EMITTING SOME 5 TIMES THE TOXIC FUMES, UNFILTERED, AS AN ORDINARY CAR. AND THAT IN THE STREET AT BREATHING LEVEL! NOR COULD THE REFUSE BE EMPLOYED FOR VIENNA'S DISTRICT HEATING SYSTEM. VIENNA'S ALREADY POTENTIALLY DANGEROUS REFUSE DUMPS ARE ALMOST FULL AND CAN TAKE NO MORE.

THE EARTH'S AIR LAYER IS A COMMUNICATING SYSTEM. WHETHER A SMOKESTACK STANDS IN VIENNA OR ALASKA, THE EFFECTS ARE VIRTUALLY THE SAME FOR ALL OF EARTH'S INHABITANTS.

THUS THE DETERIORATING QUALITY OF OUR AIR CAN BE CONFIRMED ANYWHERE IN THE WORLD, WHETHER IN EUROPE, THE SAHARA DESERT OR NEW ZEALAND.

OUR PRESENT UNGRADED REFUSE IS SO TOXIC THAT THE COMPOST OBTAINED FROM IT CANNOT EVEN BE USED FOR GARDENING OR AGRICULTURE. HORRIFYINGLY, NOT EVEN FOR FORESTS.

ACCORDING TO MEASUREMENTS AND CALCULATIONS, THE LEVEL OF DIOXIN EMISSIONS FROM THE SPITTELAU STACK WILL TOTAL LESS THAN 0.0000000004 (9 ZEROS) PER M^3 AIR. THE AMOUNT OF DIOXIN OR FORAN ACTUALLY INHALED PER M^3 AIR WILL BE MAXIMUM 0.00000000000002 (13 ZEROS). I DO NOT BELIEVE THESE FIGURES TO BE FABRICATED. EVEN IF THEY HAD FEWER ZEROS, THEY WOULD STILL BE IMPRESSIVE.

PROPORTIONAL TO THE DISTANCE BETWEEN EARTH AND MOON (380,000 KM), THE POLLUTANT VOLUME WOULD COVER A DISTANCE OF 1.2 MILLIMETRES! SPITTELAU'S FUTURE FILTERING CAPACITY IS QUITE INCREDIBLE.

IN PARTICULAR, UP TO 99% OF THE TOXIC HEAVY METALS CADMIUM, LEAD, ZINC, CHROME ETC. WILL BE FILTERED OUT AND WILL REACH NEITHER OUR AIR NOR OUR GROUND WATER.

THE SLAG AND FLUE DUST PRODUCED WILL BE RENDERED HIGHLY INNOCUOUS BY THE DENOX SYSTEM AND EFFECTIVELY FULLY NEUTRALIZED. THIS IS ONE OF THE MOST OUTSTANDING FEATURES OF THE NEW PLANT. MOREOVER, A LARGE PART OF THE SLAG IS BOUND IN GLASS. THE HEAVY METALS ARE RECOVERED FROM THE FILTERS. THE CONCENTRATION OF HEAVY METALS IN THE FILTERS IS FAR HIGHER THAN IN MINES. AND THEIR RECOVERY IS VERY MUCH MORE SIMPLE AND ENERGY-EFFICIENT. HIGH LEVELS OF HEAVY METAL ARE RECOVERED WHICH WOULD OTHERWISE NOT ONLY BE LOST BUT WOULD ALSO POISON US.

CIGARETTE SMOKE AND CAR EXHAUSTS ARE FAR MORE DANGEROUS IN TERMS OF DIOXINS, CARBON MONOXIDES, NITROGEN MONOXIDES AND SO ON. JUST HOW MANY (UNFILTERED) STACKS THAT EQUALS IS UNIMAGINABLE. AND POSING A VERY REAL HAZARD DOWN HERE AT BREATHING LEVEL!

INHALING THE EXHAUST FUMES OF A SINGLE CAR WILL KILL A PERSON IN ONE MINUTE. THERE ARE, I BELIEVE, 600,000 CARS REGISTERED IN VIENNA! BUT STILL WE ALL DRIVE CARS, EVEN THE ENVIRONMENTALISTS AMONG US. WHAT ARE THE LEVELS LIKE HERE, I WONDER? STILL A POINT FOLLOWED BY SEVERAL ZEROS?

THE OBSTACLES TO AN (EXHAUST-FREE) MOTORIZED SOCIETY ARE SIMILAR TO THOSE FACING A WASTE-FREE SOCIETY.

NOTHING CAN BE ACHIEVED OVERNIGHT. BEFORE I DECIDED TO ACCEPT THE COMMISSION, LÖTSCH HELPED ME TO FORMULATE A LETTER OF REFUSAL.

BUT HE SUBSEQUENTLY ARRIVED AT THE OPINION THAT OBSTRUCTING THE NEW INCINERATION PLANT WITHOUT SUPPLYING A REALISTIC PRESENT ALTERNATIVE WOULD CAUSE GREATER ECOLOGICAL DAMAGE THAN ITS ACTUAL COMMISSIONING, AND LEFT THE DECISION REGARDING ITS ARTISTIC REFURBISHING UP TO ME.

IN-DEPTH STUDIES ON A GLOBAL BASIS REVEAL WHAT I ALREADY KNEW. REFUSE SEPARATION OFFERS NO LONG-TERM ESCAPE FROM THE ECOLOGICAL IMPASSE. COMPOSTABLE, LARGELY NON-TOXIC SUBSTANCES WOULD HAVE TO BE ALLOWED TO DECOMPOSE SEPARATELY.

THE ONLY ANSWER IS TOTAL REFUSE AVOIDANCE BY THE ENTIRE HUMAN RACE: A WASTELESS SOCIETY. AND THIS TOTAL REFUSE AVOIDANCE COULD ONLY BE ACHIEVED THUS: NO FOSSIL FUELS, NO NOXIOUS OR RADIOACTIVE MATERIALS TO BE EXTRACTED FROM THE EARTH'S UPPER CRUST AND BROUGHT TO THE SURFACE! ONCE MATERIALS SUCH AS OIL, COAL AND TOXIC SUBSTANCES HAVE BEEN BROUGHT TO THE EARTH'S SURFACE, IT MAKES NO DIFFERENCE WHETHER THEY ARE BURNT OR DUMPED IN HOT OR COLD INCINERATION, WHETHER THEY ARE TURNED INTO SYNTHETIC MATERIALS, PLASTIC ETC. OR RECYCLED, WHETHER THESE PLASTIC AND OTHER SYNTHETIC GOODS ARE INCINERATED OR NOT INCINERATED, RECYCLED OR DUMPED.

THE FINAL RESULT IS ALWAYS THE SAME. AN ATMOSPHERE UNBALANCED BY EXCESS TOXIC SUBSTANCES AND A WORLD OF POISONED HUMUS, WATER, AIR, PLANTS, ANIMALS AND PEOPLE.

THUS IF THE ENORMOUS CONCENTRATION OF FOSSIL FUELS, FORMED OVER MILLIONS OF YEARS, IS INCINERATED AT ONCE, EITHER HOT OR COLD, I.E. BY DUMPING, OR IF THE PRODUCTS OF OIL AND COAL ARE INCINERATED OR NOT INCINERATED, THE CATASTROPHIC RESULT IS THE SAME, WITH INEVITABLE CONSEQUENCES FOR THE NEXT GENERATIONS.

THERE IS ONLY ONE WAY OUT. TO EXTRACT NO FURTHER FOSSIL FUELS FROM BELOW GROUND AS FROM NOW.

NATURE HAS TAKEN MILLIONS OF YEARS TO COVER THE TOXIC SUBSTANCES ORIGINALLY COMPOSING THE EARTH'S SURFACE WITH A LAYER OF HUMUS, VEGETATION AND OXYGEN.

BY RETURNING THESE TOXINS TO THE EARTH'S SURFACE, WE ARE VIOLENTLY RE-

CREATING THOSE ORIGINAL CONDITIONS OF MILLIONS OF YEARS AGO, WHEN MAN COULD NOT YET LIVE UPON THE EARTH.
I HOPE YOU APPRECIATE THE PROBLEM IN ITS ENTIRETY.
IMMEDIATE NECESSITIES DEMAND THAT WE CHOOSE NOT MERELY THE LESSER EVIL BUT THE ONLY POSSIBLE CURRENT SOLUTION, AND THAT WE FIGHT DAILY FOR A BETTER FUTURE.
IN THE SPIRIT OF FAIRNESS AND IN THE INTERESTS OF THE ECOLOGICAL DEBATE WHICH AFFECTS US ALL, PLEASE PUBLISH THIS LETTER ALONGSIDE YOUR OWN IN THE "WIENER NATURSCHUTZNACHRICHTEN".

CORDIALLY, HUNDERTWASSER
VIENNA, 3 JUNE 1988

CLEANING MANIA

THE CLEANING PSYCHOSIS IS A SYMPTOM TYPICAL OF OUR CIVILIZATION. FIRST IT WAS DIRT AND INADEQUATE HYGIENE WHICH BROUGHT SICKNESS AND DEATH. TODAY SICKNESS AND DEATH ARE CAUSED BY EXCESSIVE STERILITY.
THE ORGANIC, THE SEEMINGLY CHAOTIC, VARIETY, THE UNCONTROLLED AND IN-DIVIDUAL CREATION OF MAN AND THE SPONTANEOUS VEGETATION OF NATURE ARE CONSIDERED DIRTY, CHAOTIC AND DANGEROUS.
EXCESSIVE STERILITY BRINGS DEATH. THE DETERGENT INDUSTRY AND THE AERO-SOL LOBBY CANVAS FREELY ON TELEVISION AND IN THE MEDIA, WITH UNTRUTHS AND BRAIN-WASHING REMINISCENT OF THE MOST UNSCRUPULOUS POLITICAL PROPAGANDA. THEY APPEAL TO THE MOST BASIC INSTINCTS OF SIMPLE PEOPLE AND CHILDREN: YOUR SHIRT MUST BE WHITER THAN YOUR JEALOUS NEIGH-BOUR'S. THE FACT THAT DEADLY TOXINS THEREBY KILL OUR LOVED ONES AND NATURE IS NOT MENTIONED. WE ARE ENCOURAGED TO POISON AND COUNTER-POISON.
THE COUNTER-POISONS ARE INCREASINGLY MORE DANGEROUS THAN THE POI-SONS. WASTE IS INCREASINGLY MORE DANGEROUS THAN THE PRODUCT.
IN OUR UGLY, STERILE SATELLITE TOWNS THERE IS A WOMAN WITH A CLOTH AT EVERY FIFTH WINDOW, POLISHING AN ALREADY PERFECTLY CLEAN WINDOW.
IT IS A DEPLORABLE AND A DANGEROUS MANIA.
IF A BLOT APPEARS ON A WALL, THE ENTIRE FACADE IS REPAINTED TO PREVENT ANY ENRICHMENT OF THE UNIFORM, STERILE FACADE.
WOE BETIDE THE MARK WHICH APPEARS ON A CLEAN SHIRT WASHED WITH NOR-MAL SOAP. IT WILL IMMEDIATELY BE REMOVED WITH EVEN MORE DANGEROUS TOXINS, INSTEAD OF BEING WELCOMED AS AN UNHOPED-FOR GIFT WHICH ELE-VATES THIS SAME SHIRT FROM THE ANONYMOUS MASS OF IDENTICAL SHIRTS.
WOE BETIDE THE GRASS WHICH GROWS IN CRACKS IN THE PAVEMENT, WOE BETIDE THE TREE WHICH SPONTANEOUSLY SPRINGS UP, UNPLANNED AND UNPLANTED BY HUMAN HAND. SUCH THINGS MAY NOT BE AND ARE BRUTALLY SUPPRESSED AND WEEDED OUT.
THESE ARE TYPICAL SYMPTOMS OF THE SICKNESS OF OUR PERVERSE CIVILIZATION. EXCESSIVE STERILITY BRINGS DEATH. INTELLIGENT PRESERVATION OF UNCON-TROLLED ORGANIC GROWTH AND VARIETY BRING LIFE.
WE NEED BEAUTY BARRIERS.
BEAUTY BARRIERS ARE NON-REGULARIZED IRREGULARITIES.
HUNDERTWASSER   DECEMBER 1989, FROM NEW ZEALAND

FOR A WASTE-FREE SOCIETY

IF MAN WISHES TO HAVE A CLEAR CONSCIENCE, HE MUST STRIVE FOR A WASTE-FREE SOCIETY. WE ARE GUESTS OF NATURE AND MUST BEHAVE ACCORDINGLY. A DIS-POSABLE SOCIETY MUST NOT BE TOLERATED. MAN MUST RECOGNIZE THAT HE HIMSELF IS THE MOST DANGEROUS PARASITE EVER TO HAVE RAVAGED THE WORLD. MAN MUST PUT HIMSELF BACK IN HIS ECOLOGICAL PLACE TO ALLOW THE EARTH TO REGENERATE. NATURE HAS TAKEN MILLIONS OF YEARS TO COVER THE SLUDGE, THE TOXIC SUBSTANCES WITH A LAYER OF HUMUS, A LAYER OF VEGETATION AND A LAYER OF OXYGEN, SO THAT MAN CAN LIVE ON EARTH. BUT UNGRATEFUL MAN THEN FETCHES THE SLUDGE AND THE TOXINS, COVERED WITH SUCH PAINSTAKING COSMIC CARE, BACK UP TO THE EARTH'S SURFACE. THUS THE ATROCIOUS ACT OF IRRESPONSIBLE MAN MAKES THE END OF THE WORLD THE SAME AS THE BEGIN-NING OF TIME. WE ARE COMMITTING SUICIDE. OUR CITIES ARE CANCEROUS UL-CERS.
WE ARE ALL RESPONSIBLE FOR OUR REFUSE. REFUSE SHOULD BE MADE A CRIMINAL OFFENCE. REFUSE PRODUCERS, PACKAGING INDUSTRIES, REFUSE CAUSERS, REFUSE MAKERS, I.E. ALL OF US, SHOULD BE SEVERELY PUNISHED IN ORDER TO INDUCE A RADICAL AVOIDANCE OF WASTE.

WE DO NOT EAT WHAT GROWS IN OUR OWN COUNTRY, BUT IMPORT OUR FOOD FROM FAR AWAY, FROM AFRICA, AMERICA, CHINA AND NEW ZEALAND. NOR DO WE KEEP OUR SHIT. OUR WASTE IS WASHED FAR, FAR AWAY. WE THEREBY POLLUTE RIVERS, LAKES AND OCEANS. SHIT NEVER RETURNS TO OUR FIELDS. NOR TO THE PLACES WHERE OUR FOOD COMES FROM.
WE SAY GRACE BEFORE AND AFTER MEALS. NO ONE SAYS GRACE WHEN THEY SHIT. WE THANK GOD FOR OUR DAILY BREAD, WHICH COMES FROM THE EARTH. BUT WE DO NOT PRAY FOR OUR SHIT TO BE TRANSSUBSTANTIATED. WASTE IS BEAUTI-FUL. THE GRADING AND REINTEGRATION OF WASTE IS A BEAUTIFUL AND JOYOUS ACTIVITY.
HUNDERTWASSER   18 DECEMBER 1989

NATURE HAS NO DEFECTS. ONLY MAN HAS DEFECTS.

WHENEVER MAN FEELS HE HAS TO CORRECT NATURE, HE IS MAKING AN IRREDEEM-ABLE MISTAKE. IT SHOULD NOT DO A COMMUNITY CREDIT TO DESTROY A LARGE AREA OF NATURE; IT SHOULD RATHER BE A MATTER OF COMMUNITY PRIDE TO PROTECT AS MUCH OF ITS NATURAL ENVIRONMENT AS POSSIBLE.
WE MUST TREAT STREAMS, RIVERS, MARSHES, RIVER MEADOWS IN THEIR PRE-OR-DAINED STATE AS HOLY AND SACROSANCT.
REGULATING STREAMS ONLY BRINGS PROBLEMS FOR WHICH WE PAY DEARLY: LOWERING OF THE GROUND WATER, LOWERING OF THE FOREST LINE BY UP TO 100 METRES, DESSICATION OF LARGE AREAS OF LAND, NO REGENERATION OF WATER WHICH IS FLOWING AWAY TOO RAPIDLY. THE RIVER MEADOWS CAN NO LONGER FULFIL THEIR SPONGE FUNCTION - THE ABSORPTION OF EXCESS WATER AND ITS SLOW RELEASE IN PERIODS OF DROUGHT, LIKE A GOOD SAVINGS BANK IN DIFFICULT TIMES.
REGULATED STREAMS BECOME SEWAGE DRAINS. FISH DIE AND THERE ARE NO FISH IN THE STREAMS, SINCE THEY CANNOT GET THROUGH REGULATED CHANNELS.
REGULATION LEADS TO FLOODING WITH DEVASTING CONSEQUENCES, BECAUSE TOO MUCH WATER IS FLOWING TOO QUICKLY AND IN TOO LARGE VOLUMES TO BE SOAKED UP AND CAPTURED BY THE EARTH AND VEGETATION.
ONLY A FULL, IRREGULARLY-FLOWING STREAM WITH TREE-LINED BANKS CAN PRO-DUCE PURE WATER, REGULATE THE WATER BALANCE AND SUSTAIN FISH AND ANI-MAL LIFE FOR THE BENEFIT OF MAN AND HIS AGRICULTURE.
NOW, ALMOST TOO LATE, WE ARE GRASPING THIS ANCIENT WISDOM, BREAKING UP THE STRAIGHT CONCRETE LINES OF REGULATED STREAM AND RIVER COURSES, IN ORDER TO RECREATE THEIR ORIGINAL, IRREGULAR STATE. HOW IRONIC.
WHY REGULATE A STREAM ONLY TO DEREGULATE IT AGAIN AFTERWARDS?
HUNDERTWASSER   MAY 1990

Before renovation

Chimney with mosaics

Model

Detail of completed façade

Model

Large steel sculpture above the loading bays

INCINERATOR, SPITTELAU

View of the model from all four sides

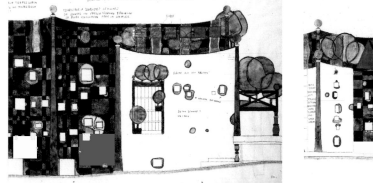
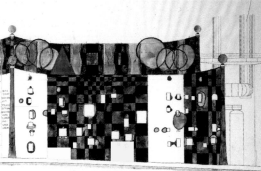

quick sketch that takes only one minute; that is enough to paint for several months. I do it with a pencil, very simple, very naïve, some lines, a face, a house. Then I fill it with colours and the work starts. Even if it looks too simple, criminally simple, when it is filled with colours you can hardly imagine that a simple drawing was the basis. The simpler the drawing, the more open and free I am with the colours. If I were to make a very elaborate and sophisticated drawing I would have a hard time matching it with colours, but I cannot paint directly on the canvas without any lines.

A clean surface frightens me so I make it dirty somehow. Generally before I draw I already have two or three canvases ready. I paint on one and use the other white canvases as a palette. Instead of smearing it away on a paper I smear the extra colours which I don't use on the other paintings. I use the other paintings as a paint-rag. I do this for two reasons. First, I save the colours; I don't throw away any colours. I dirty the paintings before I start and it gives me a start. When I have finished the painting I have two or three other prepared backgrounds. Then I make a quick drawing on one of the backgrounds and have a very strong starting point. There is always life in it. The paintings that I use as paint-rags are always better. I'm a painter without garbage; everything is used in the painting.

Hundertwasser gives this account of his sense of the sanctity of the calling and its sacramental materials: "Another reason why I don't like modern art of the Rauschenberg-Pollock type is that they splash around colours. When you come into the studio everything is full of colours, full of splashes, and only some of it is on the painting. Most of it is on the walls, on the floors, on their clothes and in the garbage can."

An example of how colour can be used carefully, methodically, is *Die Kleine Rasenruhe (Small Meadow Repose, p.66).* Piled in ascending order, the colours are layered from the deep liquid blue at the bottom of the picture to light green. The

same colour-graph ascends on the left, but more rapidly; the picture's lower third traverses the range from blue to yellow. Then, exiting from the fixed colour scale, Hundertwasser has introduced greys with subtle tones of mother-of-pearl. Atop these stacked shapes is a blazing red rectangle and some pink suffuses the forms below it. As in so many Hundertwasser works, the contrapuntal complexity of these two vertical passages, despite their intricate relationships, does not detract from the work's overall impression of placidity. A feeling of gentleness is conveyed.

ECOLOGY

H. R.: Your idea of ecology long preceded the mass movement.

F. H.: I started a long time ago. In 1957, and even before, in 1953, I attacked the straight line. Humans wanted to kill, not only our brothers but everything that grows organically. This is possible for a while as long as there are resources left, but then you have to put things back, and now we are in this position. This term ecology was introduced, and the word ecology can be considered a mistake, because ecology means nature and the cycle of nature, but one important factor is left out by the ecologists, and that is the feeling of being creative.

Without creation and creativity, nothing works, especially not in ecology. We switch from producing cars to building new generators, bicycles, purification plants, catalytic converters and solar cells. Instead of producing weapons and machine guns, the same factory, the same people, the same mentality, wages, and materials are used to produce solar heaters. We use the same technical know-how. This simply does not work, because if you enter a new age you cannot do it with the old mentality. You must start from scratch; everybody must share the responsibility. It is very hard but it is the only way.

Hundertwasser was given the chance to demonstrate the rebuilding of industrial so-

ciety by means of one example and he triumphed. A disused Viennese incinerator was transformed by Hundertwasser. He took up the challenge only because this particular installation was the cleanest, state-of-the-art model (and therefore ecologically acceptable as a project). Also it was a chance to show how a Hundertwasser building could enliven any function. With its gleaming golden ball floating like another sun in the sky and its dazzling patterns of applied colour, the harsh rigour of the underlying structure dissolves.

H. R.: If "ecology" means a closed system, does creativity replace religion?
F. H.: There is always a system of superior order, of creative intelligence, and you have to fit into this system. Only the one who is a creative intelligence will survive. That means we are a congregation of Gods. This is our normal status.
This is very easy to say for an artist, who is a creator; the others say, "It is easy for you, Hundertwasser, but we – factory workers, housewives, prisoners – are not allowed to create, have no creative power and cannot do it." And that I think is wrong of them. People are very different from one another. They are already different at birth. Everyone can and must be creative. That is a law of nature. The beggar becomes a king and the king a beggar. What matters is what you are and what you make of yourself. It is your creative power. It is very easy, no problem.

Nature stands at the centre of Hundertwasser's painting *Mountain* (p. 66, top). The landscape in *Mountain* heaves like the sea. Falling and surging, sky and ground follow the same lines. Even the deep midnight of space moves in the same rhythm. While van Gogh's *The Starry Night* animates a churning landscape, Hundertwasser's *Mountain* suggests a benign motion. Van Gogh's manic pathology is completely absent and Hundertwasser's work seems genuinely to be about nature, not about a psychological state. For him, nature is neither oppressive nor unresponsive.

More closely than any other Hundertwasser work, *Landscape with Violet Sun* (p. 67) approaches the intense colour schemes of Marc Chagall. Perhaps their similarities as Eastern European artists predispose their works to congeniality. Chagall is not a direct influence on Hundertwasser; but, like Chagall, Hundertwasser prefers saturated colours and amazing vistas. Their works share a sense of the everyday quality of magic.

Without the breathtaking embellishments of the Surrealists, Chagall and Hundertwasser step aside from their imagery to become mere reporters of enchanted events. Chagall's fantasies often rely on generally known myths, Jewish or otherwise, and his love-paintings are similar to Hundertwasser's, through the latter's affections are fiercer and more varied. These artists attest to love of women, and the idealization of the beloved in a fabled landscape.

DUNKELBUNT

In March of 1957 Hundertwasser mounted a show at the Paris Galerie H. Kamer (with whom he worked for the next three years) and he produced an exhibition poster – his first use of spirals in the print media. It proved a pathfinding experiment. From his first days as a printmaker, Hundertwasser disliked graphics that mechanically reproduce an image and blunt its intimacy. He felt each print ought to be an "original". Years later he took this notion to its monumental conclusion in huge and varied editions.

In *Freshly Found Labyrinth* (p. 64) he found a solution: each sheet (of the fifty to be printed) Hundertwasser primed with an egg tempera coloured with brick dust; he applied this underpainting with a palette knife somewhat differently to each sheet before printing the lithographic image. A combination of printing and painting, every sheet was a unique image of a red and green spiral through which the earth-coloured underpainting showed.

Artistic ventures into unexplored territory need not be treacherous or inhospitable going. Beauty, which has been held suspect for some time, is a legitimate destination. No less a Modernist than Matisse envisioned art as a respite, "devoid of troubling or depressing subject matter, an art which might be for every mental worker, be he businessman or writer, like an appeasing influence, like a mental soother, something like a good armchair in which to rest from physical fatigue." ("Notes of a Painter", 1908.) Hundertwasser does not suggest, but states. His torrent of formal, iconographical motifs and his highly saturated colour schemes seem unfettered. His colour (like the wings of Jan van Eyck's angels) provides samples of a world unlike all but corners of our own.

H.R.: To you colours are very significant, but what do the colours mean?
F. H.: Colours mean nothing in themselves. Colours can mean something when they are well put together in certain quantities surrounded by other colours. When juxtaposed they can effectively form a kind of visual music. The ones who can impress you with

real visual music are the great painters, and the others who cannot do it are bad painters. I thought that everybody could do it when I started to paint. Many years later I found out that people don't want to, or they cannot, or there is something that prevents them from doing the most basic and simple things. There must be some power that prevents people from doing these things, like an invisible barrier.

In 1957 he summered in St. Tropez and took part in the São Paulo Biennale. Hundertwasser bought his home, "La Picaudière", in rural Normandy. That autumn, on the advertising pillars and tram stations of Vienna, one of Hundertwasser's posters appeared; it showed him with a red banner headline that proclaimed "My eyes are tired", with a photograph of the artist lying on a path in a park in Cannes surrounded by trees and plants, head raised and chest bared before the camera. The back of the poster served as the catalogue for the show, and the text, one of Hundertwasser's early statements on architecture, provoked a scandal that swept Vienna. Hundertwasser wrote that "it is better to kill people or

Hundertwasser in front of Cathedral Chapter Seckau, Steiermark, July 1958, with his first car, a tomato-red Renault Dauphine, and his Mould Manifesto

abort children in the womb than to put them into mass-produced housing or to have them eat from plates of which there are 1,000 identical examples". The Catholic Church objected to the mention of abortion, and the gallery that mounted the exhibition, Galerie St. Stephen, had to change its name to dissociate itself from the church. (It was re-named Galerie Near St. Stephen's, under which name it has flourished ever since.) The exhibition was a great success and the Viennese flocked to see the young artist's work.

Viennese reviewers (of all the arts) and the audience are notoriously stormy. The last place a Viennese artist will be recognised is in Vienna, and years later Hundertwasser noted that "part of the blame belongs to the art critics, who are traditionally always opposed to anything from Vienna. There is similarity everywhere, we're moving towards a unified culture everywhere: the same influences. If a country has its own independent identity (and this is still the case with Vienna) art critics should recognize this as a positive value". But the Viennese critics are not alone to blame, as they accurately reflect the character of the Viennese. "Everyone thinks he is very important but no one is willing to recognise the greatness of a fellow-citizen. This is the provincial side of Vienna. Every Viennese wants to judge, and believes himself capable of expressing personal criticism in all fields." ("Intervista con Hundertwasser", "Domus", October 1983) With such a public, the critics have to appear even more knowledgeable and intolerant, which has always driven their reviews to wild extremes of irritability.

In *The Egg of the Old Precolumbian Japan* (p. 69, top), the spiral's form reveals its close relation to the circle. Insistent con-

centricity recalls plans of Bronze Age earthwork fortresses (or, more prosaically, targets, or the circular ripples on water). Confirming the impression of antiquity, from the major shape's lower right edge, a series of small yellow houses cluster like dwellings in the shadow of a great castle. This theme varies at the extreme right in a blue and red concentric "hill" whose furrows reach the design's left side.

In *Gas Flames together with the Flames of the Holy Spirit* (p. 79), Hundertwasser takes up a difficult theme, which few artists have attempted to render visually: the flames of the Nazis' crematoria unite with the flames of the Holy Spirit. The activity, the "movement" and its suggestions of rushing sounds, injects a nightmare quality into what was already, for us who did not suffer, a silent horror. If we were uninformed of the title's gas jets that burn

Hundertwasser in Seckau, Steiermark, 1958, on the site of his Mould Manifesto, pointing out the deterioration of iron.

343 *Les deux Sinaï – Die beiden Sinai – The Two Sinais,* Vienna, 1957, La Picaudière, January 1958, Vienna, January 1961
Mixed media: watercolour, polyvinyl, gold foil, egg, shellac on chalk primed paper mounted on canvas, 48 x 63 cm

so brightly at the painting's centre, we should still sense the turbulence in the work. At the left and right flow gaseous torrents of blue flame. This is not Yves Klein's heroic flame of *Fire Fountain;* Hundertwasser's interest in streams of flames was placed in another service.

With its firm, fresh colour, simple folkloric house forms, streets, the flowing river itself, *The Yellow River* (p. 69) shares early Kandinsky's magic. But Hundertwasser avoids narrative, costumes, rearing horses, heroes and other saga dements. Only the precedent of early Kandinsky sanctions *The Yellow River* as high "art". Early in the century the terms of understanding *The Yellow River* were set, but not fully gleaned.

Hundertwasser learnt from the Fauves, from Kandinsky, but he painted with an authority and free spirit won personally for himself. We are the benefi-

ciaries of all these traditions, of Hundertwasser's work and that of his predecessors. The past is revived by Hundertwasser's confirmation and extension of his heritage.

The Two Sinais (below) is a wonderful, dark picture which illustrates this revival of traditions. Darkness represents one of the most difficult kinds of painting. Goya resorted to glowing darkness for his last haunting images, works stripped bare of pretence. Recent artists, especially Franz Kline, remind us that black is not the same as darkness, that black is a vibrant colour fully the equal of any other hue. Darkness, rather, is the depression of the colour scheme to the lowest values (farthest from white). Such depressed hues in proximity depict night itself when augmented by high values – as in the glowing lights aboard the *S. S. Bauta* (pp. 62–63) – but absence of colour is not the same as lack of light. Hun-

321 *Gasflammen zusammen mit den Flammen des Heiligen Geistes – Gas Flammes together with the Flames of the Holy Spirit*, Cannes, August 1957
Mixed media: oil, egg tempera, watercolour, gold foil on white primed paper mounted on canvas, 63 x 98 cm

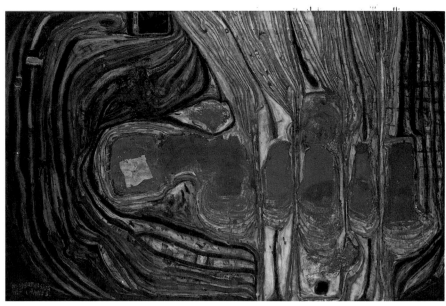

dertwasser calls these dark colours "dunkelbunt", or "dark-colourful": a darkness consisting of the greatest possible concentration of saturated colours, glowing as though out of an endless depth.

Compared to such subtle (typically Modernist) narrowing of means, *The Two Sinais* uses metallic pigments to add contrast. Hundertwasser here unites a great variety of stylistic elements. While he may combine matt and shiny colours, most painters working in oils make everything glisten and in watercolours everything matt. Nothing could have been further from the quasi-scientific exploration of the nature of pigment than this sensuous play. Delightful comparisons and striking oppositions feature in his work. Hundertwasser varies surface textures and includes gold for another dimension.

Gold has a history and mythology that render it almost too powerful, both as symbol and as hue. Until recently there was no metallic substitute for gold; when one saw it one knew oneself in the presence of mystery. Hundertwasser disregards gold's preciousness, and treats it like silver or copper. Though now we possess other metallic colours, only real gold has a special shine. In his paintings and prints, gleaming colours contrast with black. Colours surrounded by black shine from out of the dark (hence "Dunkelbunt"). Used sparingly, metallic colours are precious. Their use is limited not only because of cost. If a whole picture were golden it might feel, paradoxically, monochromatic – something like a completely grey painting, neither rich nor precious.

Though bright, the glimmering metal foils of *The Two Sinais* (p. 78) suggest the night's shimmering sky and air, night's often sourceless light. Similarly, Indian miniatures frequently reveal deep night with stunning virtuosity. Relatively reduced citations of red and yellow are precise as star-points in *The Two Sinais* and these touches of light-and-dark introduce the possibility of light-and-shadow; that the painting essays a nighttime scene should not be taken for granted.

H. R.: Do you set off the colours with black to heighten the effect of the colours?
F. H.: When colours are surrounded by black they glow out of the dark and that gives the colours a special importance. If you put colours on white, in a white frame or in white surroundings, then they appear muddy. White dulls the colours. The same is true for gold. Gold is expensive – which is why you don't cover whole paintings with it – you use it only for certain details or points in gold and that makes these parts precious.
H. R.: Icons were painted with gold backgrounds.
F. H.: Yes, but only certain parts. The halos have gold backgrounds to heighten some colours, for instance a face, the face of Jesus, the face of Mary, and behind there is a big space in gold. What was important was not the gold surround but the face.

THE LIFE OF MATERIALS

	Stowasser	STOWASSEN
	Fritz	FRITZ
	Friedrich	FRIEDRICH
	Friederich	FRIEDERICH
	Friedereich	FRIEDEREICH
	Friedenreich	FRIEDENREICH
	Hundertwasser	HUNDERTWASSER
	Friedensreich	FRIEDENSREICH
	Regentag	REGENTA G
	Dunkelbunt	DUNKELBUNT

348 L'Arnal – Les peines du contretemps dans l'amour – Contretemps I,
La Picaudière, February 1958, Zurich, June 1965, Silvaplana, July 1965, repainted October 1965
Mixed media: egg tempera and polyvinyl over an old painting by Arnulf Rainer on canvas primed
with polyvinyl and casearti, 56 x 46 cm

On Gibraltar, in 1958, Hundertwasser married Herta Leitner, an Austro-Italian (from whom he was divorced in 1960).

F. H.: When I was twenty-five, I met a girl of sixteen and she wanted to marry me. I liked her but I was a little reluctant, so I thought of marrying in Gibraltar and maybe on the way I could get rid of her. I had a car and I used the most difficult roads, so I thought when the car broke down I could say, "I am sorry we cannot reach Gibraltar because the car is finished now."

Once, in a small town somewhere near Barcelona, we passed a vegetable shop and she said, "Stop the car, I will buy you something". There were vegetables, apples, etc. She went into the shop and I thought she would buy me some fruit to eat while we drove. She came out with a big bag of onions. I thought, "Strange, why did she buy a kilo of onions?" She bought it like you would buy two pounds of apples, or grapes, or plums or bananas, but she only got onions. I drove and she took this big sack with about two pounds of big onions and gave me an onion to eat. I said, "I don't want to eat an onion like that." She was very astonished and said, "Eat it." "No, I don't want it." "But you are Jewish, Jews eat onions."

Just like if you have a monkey and you give him a banana and the monkey says, "Sorry, but I don't eat bananas." "But you are a monkey, you must eat bananas; it says so in all the books, illustrated in all the children's books you see monkeys with bananas, so you, a monkey, you must eat bananas." Well, I finally understood.

Nazi propaganda had depicted the Jewish people eating onions. When they wanted to see who was a Jew and who was an Aryan you could tell by very simple things, for instance the curved nose, the ears, black hair and one of the decisive characteristics was that Jews eat onions: when you saw somebody eating an onion he was a Jew. Her parents were Nazis; she lived in a kind of Nazi family and heard all the time that Jews eat onions like Germans and Aryans eat apples. As she wanted to marry me and she knew that I was half Jewish, she thought it would be a very nice gesture to give me what I wanted to eat. It is amazing, very amazing. When that happened I thought: this is not the woman for me, but when we arrived in Gibraltar she said that if I didn't marry her she would jump from the rock. I was afraid to have a dead girl there, so I married her but then started a divorce, immediately.

H. R.: Where is she now?

F. H.: I don't know.

In July he read from his *Mould Manifesto: Against Rationalism in Architecture* ("Verschimmelungsmanifest"), at the congress in Seckau monastery; this presentation attracted considerable attention. As if to emphasize recycling, *L'Arnal – Contretemps I* (p. 80) was painted over a work by Arnulf Rainer. Its title refers to "being out of step", the mischance of being out of time with things, events and emotions.

372 *Conséquence de la Terre Allemande – Hommage à Hans Neuffer le Marin*, Saltsjöbaden, near Stockholm, August 1958
Mixed media: egg tempera, China ink, polyvinyl on paper primed with chalk and polyvinyl, 49 x 65 cm

The work reminds us that the "fantastic" is so overused we have forgotten the worlds in which the mind takes refuge and delight. The political implications of fantasy in art make it distasteful to some. Fantasy's exuberant irrationalism undermines discourse, beclouds meanings, and jettisons general denotation. True fantasy, as opposed to commercial fiction, yearns always to be elsewhere, avoiding the here-and-now. All this makes fantasy the enemy of progressive and liberal politics.

The most prominent mixture of fantasy and politics, Surrealism, invented a politics of fantasy which substituted for revolution the imposition of irrationalism. But at root Surrealism was impotent, unwilling to live with its implications. Hundertwasser understands the inherent pitfalls of fantasy and he functions artistically and politically within given situations. What makes fantasy a practical condition for Hundertwasser is Vienna, its heritage, its place in his life and art.

Vienna, politically precarious for much of its history, and the Viennese (at the hub of a continent over which they once had near-hegemony) still think they are at the world's centre and deserve an immensely disproportionate share of world

465 *The Very End of a Weeping King – Das letzte Ende des weinenden Königs,* Ikenoso Ryokan, Ikebukuro, Tokyo, March 1961
Watercolour on wrapping paper primed with chalk and polyvinyl, 32 x 31 cm

414 *Die Flucht des Dalai Lama – The Flight of the Dalai Lama,* Paris, 1959
Lithograph in 2 versions: vermilion, orange, green (red version), red, green, blue (blue version), 47 x 62 cm
Edition of c. 1800 unnumbered. C. 500 signed later. Printed by Patris, Paris 1959. Published by Carl László, Panderma, Basle, 1959

attention. This cruelly refined climate has also allowed Hundertwasser to practise an art of richness, of almost Oriental excess. Luxurious colour and texture are combined in *L'Arnal – Contretemps I.* The painting's two figures – locked within malachite green – present profile and frontal views of simplified figures and faces (without race, country or period). They are timelessly human – people looking past each other.

It is easy enough to call Hundertwasser a painter of spirals. First, though, we should note in passing that in modern times it was the English artist Victor Pasmore who first used the spiral. Before Pasmore systematically rationalized his own abstract art, he painted such works as *Spiral Motif in Green, Violet, Blue and Gold: The Coast of the Inland Sea* (1950). This painting, derived from nature (and specifically from the landscape of Japan, which Hundertwasser too came to admire), relies on the spiral for its overall form and for smaller flourishes. But Pasmore, unlike Hundertwasser, made no definite commit-

ment to the spiral as form or to the spiral as emblem.

Labelling Hundertwasser a painter of spirals ignores the immense variety in his treatment of the motif. The artist has constantly experimented, seeing the form anew, exploring the implications of the motif, feeling his way towards its essential character. By exploiting the utmost of a motif's potential, the true artist (inevitably) makes it impossible for a successor to robe himself in borrowed finery. The seam (so to speak) will have been worked out. In his devotion to a nameable motif, Hundertwasser differed vastly from fellow-artists in, e.g., America, who were involved in indefinable processes. Perhaps unexpectedly, his closest associate was Morandi – endlessly painting a fixed number of forms, each named and defined.

EXHIBITING ART

H. R.: How do you show your work?

F. H.: Paintings should be shown as if they were jewels. They should be displayed to show their precious values, with black frames, floating in space, parallel to the wall but not clinging to it. Another requirement is that you have light from behind you (which is much better than having the light from the sides) – like if you go into a church and you see the altar at the far end and the light is behind you rather than behind the altar, which would have a blinding effect.

H. R.: What is the ideal number of works for people to look at?

F. H.: It depends on what paintings you have. I think ten to twenty is enough. Not more than thirty. If it is more, you get tired, and it has no meaning for you.

The gimmickry characteristic of Hundertwasser's public persona, particularly in photographs, has not endeared him to the ill-disposed. And once his personality became an issue, everything else in his art became subject to contention, too. His meticulous cataloguing of his work struck some as egoistic. The demands on collectors seemed ritualistic in flavour (though Hundertwasser quite reasonably wants his creations to be properly looked after). The artist requires that his work on paper should not be subjected to fluctuations in the humidity level, and insists that collectors provide a humidifier if they live in central-heated accommodation. His works in egg-tempera mixed technique may be varnished with a solution of beeswax and turpentine. Before taking delivery of a painting, a Hundertwasser collector pays to have it photographed for the artist's archive. In all of this, despite the obvious quality of his work, he has provided ammunition for his enemies. His eccentric behaviour, public image and messianic stance have struck many potential allies as impertinent posturing.

In August 1958, Hundertwasser was working near Saltsjøbaden near Stockholm. There he painted *Conséquence de la Terre Allemande; Hommage à Hans Neuffer le Marin* (Consequence of the German Earth; Homage to Hans Neuffer the Mariner) (p. 82). The overall composition is a view of groined vaulting with black windows. We see a Gothic chapel as if we were on the floor staring up (the reverse of a raindrop's view). The lower part of the work is strongly accented with blue and green; the upper part is mainly red and yellow; and through the middle float wispy green forms. An eerily glowing building surrounded by darkness, this somber chapel scene was dedicated to his deceased friend Hans Neuffer.

Another powerful composition dating from 1958, *The Tongue of Lucifer I* (p. 86), recalls Rothko's basic compositional format, with its three horizontal bands. Hundertwasser's choice of vibrantly smoky yet luminous colours suggests an aerial perspective akin to the abstract grandeur similarly achieved by Franz Kline (using kindred methods); but Hundertwasser's exaltation avoids Rothko's self-conscious dolefulness. Red flows through the centre like a tongue of lava, pooling here and there amid the upper and lower green, melting into oceanic blue. While suggestions of the natural world abound, they would not suffice to account for the painting's appeal. The source of the painting's energy must surely be something more – though natural metaphors are of course suggested as the picture communicates the scale and implied force of natural wonders. But more than nature attracted the artist's attention. When the Chinese occupied Tibet in 1959, a Swiss art dealer, Carl László, supervised the publication of Hundertwasser's colour lithograph, *The Flight of the Dalai Lama* (p. 83) in the periodical "Panderma". The plight of the Dalai Lama, and of the Tibetans exiled with their theocratic ruler, stunned Hundertwasser. This print – along with a group of fifteen other works on the subject – came from the artist in a period of real agitation between April and July 1959.

In 1959, at the Fifth São Paulo Biennale in Brazil, Hundertwasser took a prize, but that was far from the year's most celebrated activity for him. That autumn he served as the guest lecturer at the Hamburg College of Art. He gave only one lecture. To his astonished pupils he announced that "it is certain that many of you have no real talent for art, and should therefore not be here. It is equally certain that a few of you are born artists, and therefore in no need of my instruction. In the one case as in the other you would do well to return to your homes and get on with the business of developing your unique individual creativity, as I intend to do. That is the sum of my advice and teaching." (Although he has given advice, contrary to this statement, Hundertwasser has maintained a similar philosophy of teaching ever since.) Instead of lecturing, he organized his students to "make the longest line in the world" – which, naturally, attracted considerable attention. For two days and nights Arab music played; the class drew a ten-mile long uninterrupted spiral line in pencil, ink, and oil paint. The line extended across the floor, walls, windows, and ceiling, eventually covering a good bit of the classroom.

After five days of work on the *Endless Line* the College Director, fearing ridicule to his school, halted the experiment. A scandal resulted, and Hundertwasser resigned the lectureship (see pp. 94–95).

ON TEACHING

(Hundertwasser taught master classes twenty-five years later at the Academy of Fine Arts in Vienna.)

F. H.: Physical absence is a precondition for my spiritual presence. If I were present in a master class it would influence people and frighten them out of expressing themselves. Of course, the students influence each other. In the classroom there are plants and trees. They take my place, they are the teachers. Sitting between plants and trees in a room and being creative is very interesting because the students immediately compare their own creativity with the creativity of nature. Nature grows according to very stable laws and patterns, and nature is always right – how the leaves come out and how the trunk grows and how the bud comes out. Plants influence people, but when an artist is influenced by a plant's creativity then the artist's own creativity will be almost perfect; he cannot fail – he follows the laws of vegetation in creating paintings.

H. R.: Do you tell your students this or do they figure it out from being around the plants?

F. H.: I tell them nothing. I just put the plants there and I leave them alone together. I am hopeful that some sparks will reach them.

Though it is a single tree, the top of *Raintree* (p. 87) is completely occupied by foliage, as are Klimt's "Park" pictures. Filling the sky, this is the enormous mythic world-

Ill. p. 86: 377 *La langue de Lucifer (I) – Luzifers Zunge (I) – The Tongue of Lucifer (I)*, La Picaudière, October 1958
Mixed media: egg tempera on wrapping paper primed with chalk, mounted on canvas, 92 x 66 cm

Ill. p. 87: 422 *Arbre de pluie – Regenbaum – Raintree*, Hamburg, December 1959
Watercolour on wrapping paper primed with chalk, 64 x 50 cm

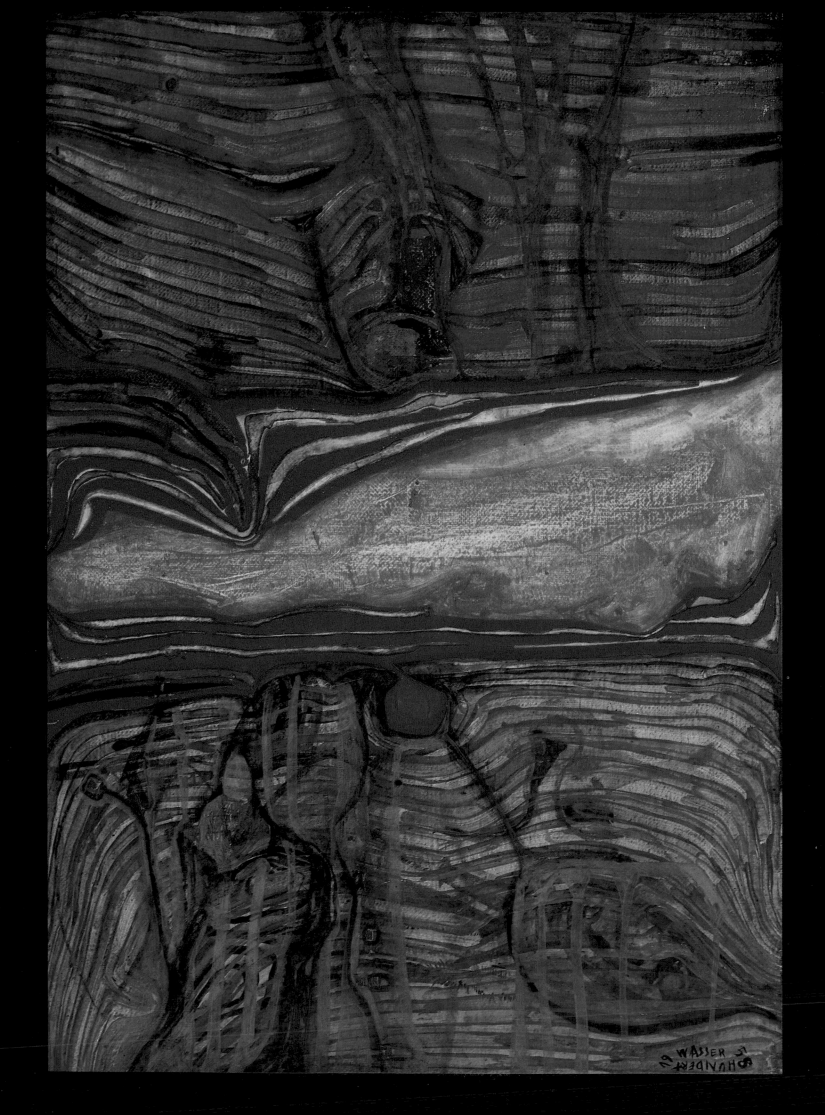

tree. Hundertwasser, prone to a complex mixed-media technique, instead chose an unencumbered watercolour for this painting. The choice of watercolour prohibited significant reworking. Hundertwasser augmented the pattern with opaque paints and metallic foils, and the absence of re-worked paint matches direct presentation to the giant subject. Simplicity contributes monumentality. Grandeur frequently distinguishes Hundertwasser's work. For this subject monumentality was appropriate, as we know this awe before nature to be one of our most basic, primitive emotions. "Raintree" salutes our conscious recognition, our humility and deference, to the elemental requirements of life's sustenance.

H. R.: Is compromise possible in art?
F. H.: Of course, all the time. Every piece of art is a compromise between what is feasible and what is wanted. The aim to achieve is never reached in art but it is more or less close to what the artist wanted to do. I think I have a solution: just let things happen. I let things happen, and it is so astounding that I astound myself. I always say a painting is good when the artist is surprised by his own painting. A house is good when the architect is surprised by the reality of his own house, as though a dream of his had become real.

TACHISME

Culminating the spiral pictures is the expansive *Homage to Tachisme, Hommage au Tachisme* (p. 90), which may represent Hundertwasser's closest approach to the restless spirit of "Jugendstil". Its throbbing, ever-moving line sweeps through an upper blue section, contrasted with a particularly arresting black edging. In the picture's lower centre twelve squares of gold foil provide an opaque screen, distantly recalling the iconostasis of the Eastern church or the choir screens of the West. This hieratic note permeates the work, amplifying and growing more potent until the whole seems alive with spiritual fervour. The pillar of

gold at the bottom seems an altar, from which smoke, the red spiral, rises. This haunting image was central to Anti-Tachisme, of which Hundertwasser may be said to be the leading figure. It was a dialectical response to Modernism from within its own ranks.

As the dominant form of post-War European painting, Tachisme bore the full brunt of Hundertwasser's antagonism. Tachisme embodied all he abhorred: it was sloppy and non-representational. So Hundertwasser's attack appeared self-serving. As an alternative to Tachisme, Hundertwasser replied with an avant-garde of his own invention. If he repelled American spectators, he infuriated the Europeans.

Hundertwasser has always ensured himself a place in the limelight. Undeniably he has an attractive personality. He has become the subject of a private myth and is supported by a clique of admirers and friends. His provocative though silent appearances in caftan or kimono, bathing trunks, burnous or velvet jacket, with or without a beard, sandals and furcap, have given rise to astonishment, distaste and positive annoyance. The same reaction has been provoked by the slogans and catch-phrases printed in his catalogues, for instance: "My eyes are tired!" (Galerie St. Stefan, Vienna, 1957), or "Hundertwasser is a Gift to Germany!" (Galerie Anne Abels, Cologne, 1963). Just as Georges Mathieu became the Dali of the Tachists, Hundertwasser soon became the Dali of the Anti-Tachists. (Hanns Theodor Flemming, "Hundertwasser: Narcissus Reflected in Spirals", "Studio International", November 1964.)

Though it initially does not intimate its concern for space, *Homage to Tachisme* aptly describes a huge volume. It gives a sense of nearby space, that shared with the spectator through the picture plane at the extreme bottom of the work; it indicates a fictive depth as great as any in Western art. (We might compare Altdorfer's plummeting views.) Glimpsed through the spiral's maze is a landscape. Initially unavoidable, the spiral recedes from prominence as we gaze through it into the picture. This labyrinth is the measure of all things within the painting; it establishes the picture plane, and (like our visual field) it softens as it approaches the edges.

H. R.: Does the French version of surrealism, Breton's, hold any interest for you?
F. H.: Breton's, no. I don't think so. I did not study him but some people who were around him, they are very skilful, like Dalí, Magritte, Delvaux.
H. R.: If an avant-garde artist should be ahead of society, is it more important for the artist to anticipate general behaviour or artistic style?
F. H.: A style does not mean anything. The style is only an empty tool to express yourself. A true artist has no style. What he does doesn't fit into any existing styles, so it will be named later on.

There are great untapped potentials in art. Morandi reinvented Cezanne and thereby violated what lesser minds would regard as historical necessity: that Modernism's telos and inherent agenda be pursued without any backward glances. But to return to the origins of an art is not primitivism (or even archaism), but a search for first causes. Hundertwasser's rich ornament is neither primitive nor synthetically trans-cultural, but a logical re-emergence of the richness of visual experience. Only through lavish ornament and decoration, embellishment that exceeds every possible definition of modern good taste, can the marvel and "otherness" of the art object be re-attained. That has been Hundertwasser's goal.

THE LIFE OF PAINT MATERIALS

H. R.: Do your materials play an important role in the choice of media?
F. H.: Yes, of course. With ready-made materials you cannot work well because it is like a dead material. If it is manufactured by somebody else or by a machine, it loses creativity. Before, there were colours from many different sources. Now there are many paint factories, but they are in competition with each other and one day there may be only one paint factory somewhere, maybe in America or Germany, that provides colours for all the artists in the world. When you ask a young painter, where do your colours come from, he will say: "The colours come from the paint shop", or "It probably comes from a paint factory". He does not know where the origins of his colours are.

As recently as a few generations ago artists knew the sources of their pigments – blue from lapis lazuli, earth browns and blues from Bohemia or Italy, yellow from India, etc. There was romance in these colours from faraway places. Every artist understood how paints were manufactured. In the past, caravans shipped specific exotic pigments; certain colours came only from unique locales, special forests, certain plants. Now, paint comes uniformly in tubes. Alienated from his materials, the artist is ever more disadvantaged. Also, since each pigment can only absorb a specific amount of binder, having pigments made by huge machine lots – except for very expensive colours, out of the reach of most artists – leads to uniform density. In Old Master paintings each colour has a different density, a different degree of elasticity, a different texture. The modern situation constitutes visual loss for us. But these properties still exist in Hundertwasser's paintings.

H. R.: Do you think that it harms artists not to know anything about the source of their colours?
F. H.: Yes. If they don't know where the colour comes from it is just like somebody you don't know distributing candy on the

Ill. p. 90: 460 *Hommage au Tachisme – Homage to Tachism,* La Picaudière, January 1961
Mixed media: egg tempera, oil, gold leaf on wrapping paper primed with chalk and polyvinyl, mounted on jute, 195 x 130 cm

Ill. p. 91: 468 *A Rain of Blood is Falling into a Garden with a Weeping Church – Blutregen fällt in einen Garten mit weinender Kirche,* Tokyo, March 1961
Mixed media: watercolour, egg tempera, oil, gold leaf on rice paper primed with chalk, mounted on jute, 54 x 42 cm

467 *Garden without Bottom – Garten ohne Grund,* Shinkomatsu Ryokan, Tokyo, February 1961
Mixed media: watercolour, egg tempera, oil, gold leaf on rice paper primed with chalk, mounted on jute, 60 x 73 cm

what is modern and what is "in" today and what is fashionable today. Even the application of the paint is psychologically ready-made, so he does not do the painting – materially or spiritually. I try to step back as far as possible and put myself into the process as early as possible, but I cannot do everything.

H. R.: Brueghel and Dürer had studios in which assistants prepared panels. Would you ever consider having assistants who would help you make stretchers and prepare surfaces?

F. H.: Yes, that would be fantastic, but I think it would be quite impossible to find young people who would just prepare the colours so that I could paint, and that for twenty years.

H. R.: Because you wring the very last bit of colour from your paint-box, perhaps you use too little colour?

F. H.: When you have thinner paint you

street – it can be poison candy. So when I make the materials myself I am there from the start. You cannot adopt a child when it is twenty-five years old. You can adopt a child when it is three years old, or when it is a baby – you can step into the creative process any time. You can very well take a ready-made thing and declare it is a piece of art. You can take a chair – or a urinal, as did Marcel Duchamp and others – sign it and have a piece of art. Or you can take pieces of ready-made things and glue them together. Then you have something that contains a little more of you. Most of it is ready-made but the glue and how you glue it together is you, or you can make the forms yourself and it is still more of you. The same is true of the painter. If he takes the paint ready-made and the materials ready-made, a big part is prefabricated. You don't have to grind pigments anymore, but this grinding process, this manufacturing process, is very important for the artist, because it is the starting point. A painter cannot miss out on the build-up of the painting. Then something is wrong.

Many things are wrong in modern art because it is ready-made. The conceptions are ready-made because the artist copies from

Hundertwasser in Tokyo, 1961

have more feeling of the colour, you can put more layers on top. I found out that the more colour you put on in a transparent way, the richer the painting gets. But if you use the colour sparingly, very little colour, the painting gets richer. If you use the colour thickly, as in pastose painting, the painting gets poor. Once I met (Karel) Appel, a painter in Holland, he paints thick. I visited him and he showed me his whole house, which was filled with shelves along the walls. They were filled with big, huge tubes. In each tube maybe one pound of paint – one-pound colour tubes stacked like firewood along the whole wall. About 500 blues, 500 yellows, 500 greens, 500 blacks – and he was very proud of that. He said he had a special contract with the paint factory that provided him the colour wholesale because when he paints he is in an ecstasy of painting; he pulls the cap off with his teeth, and then he squeezes out the one pound of paint in one go and throws the tube away. That is how he paints and I was very shocked, but he was very proud because in fact these colours were very expensive. You can imagine what it costs — a pound of genuine cadmium!

I want to say that though such a mass of colour is thickly applied, the effect is poor. It does not give you the effect of richness; lots of gold does not mean richness.

H. R.: You sometimes use found materials to make colours. Are you worried about colours fading and disappearing, about the permanence of your colours?

F. H.: I try not to use materials from plants and animals, they fade. What I use is inorganic, like bricks, volcanic sand, earth, soil and coal, burned charcoal, grey and white lime, and bricks, which you can find in yellow, red, almost black – these are the best colours. There is quite a wide range of colours. These are all very lasting and I grind the colours and mix them with oil or with egg or with acrylic or polyvinyl or with wax.

H. R.: Why do you find these colours yourself rather than buying them?

F. H.: Because I don't depend on the stores. To a high degree I want to be independent even where paint is concerned, and, secondly, the colours you buy in the store are not so good. They are so finely ground that they don't have any soul anymore. When I grind them myself they are much rougher and have a texture you can see and feel. There are no colours you can buy which have a feeling and a life. This is one of the secrets of my paintings. Some colours you cannot make – a very strong red, a very strong blue, and a very strong yellow you cannot make yourself. The colours you can make yourself are all brownish-black

Hundertwasser as guest lecturer at the Kunsthochschule Lerchenfeld, Hamburg, 1959.
The canopy over his desk is meant to show that he is the best in the masterclass.

FROM: THE HAMBURG LINE (DECEMBER 1959). A CONVERSATION WITH PIERRE RESTANY (FEBRUARY 1975)

I WANTED TO DRAW A SPIRAL CLIMBING HORIZONTALLY UP THE WALLS LIKE SEDIMENTARY LAYERS OF ROCK.

AT THE DESIGNATED MOMENT I BEGAN DRAWING A LINE COUNTER-CLOCKWISE AROUND THE ROOM, STARTING ABOUT ONE CENTIMETRE FROM THE FLOOR. WHEN I ARRIVED BACK AT MY STARTING POINT, I BEGAN ANOTHER LINE ABOUT ONE CENTIMETRE HIGHER AND LOOSELY PARALLEL TO THE FIRST. THUS THE SPIRAL GREW. I CONTINUED THE LINE ACROSS ALL THE INTERVENING OBSTACLES, ACROSS DOORS, RADIATORS AND THE LIKE. SOME OBSTACLES WERE AVOIDED AND LEFT FREE. I HAD MOVED ALL THE FURNITURE AWAY FROM THE WAY SO THAT I WOULD HAVE PLENTY OF SPACE. THUS I DREW MY LINE ON HANDS AND KNEES, CRAWLING BETWEEN THE LEGS OF THE SPECTATORS, AND ONLY A VERY FEW COULD SEE WHAT I WAS DOING. PEOPLE HAD PROBABLY EXPECTED A CONVENTIONAL DEMONSTRA-TION FROM THE FRONT OF THE ROOM, WITH ME TALKING FROM A PODIUM AND SO ON, AND NOT FROM DOWN BETWEEN THEIR FEET. THEY WERE PROBABLY EX-PECTING A SHOW, AN EXPLOSION, AND NOT THIS SILENT EVOLUTION. AND SO THEY LEFT THE ROOM AFTER AN HOUR BECAUSE AS FAR AS THEY COULD SEE NOTH-ING WAS HAPPENING. IT WAS STRANGE: THEY WERE IN THE CENTRE OF A DEMON-STRATION WHICH WAS SURROUNDING AND ENVELOPING THEM, AND NOBODY NOTICED.

I BEGAN THE LINE IN BLACK, AND LATER RED, FIRST WITH DARK PENS AND THEN WITH PAINT AND BRUSH. WHEN I GREW TIRED, I HANDED THE BRUSH TO BAZON BROCK, WHO TOOK OVER FROM ME AS IN A RELAY RACE. I WENT DOWN TO THE HALL TO RELAX AND FOUND A GROTESQUE SITUATION: HERE WERE ALL THE PEOPLE WHO HAD RECEIVED AN INVITATION TO THE DEMONSTRATION AND WANTED TO COME UPSTAIRS. THE HUNDERTWASSER CLASS WAS ON THE UPPER FLOOR, BUT THE VISITORS WERE BEING PREVENTED FROM GOING UP BY A GROUP OF FIVE CARETAKERS. IN PERFECT FIGHTING FORMATION THESE WERE PUNCHING THE CROWD OF VISITORS BACK DOWN THE WIDE STAIRCASE, JUST LIKE THE FA-MOUS FILM BY EISENSTEIN. A NUMBER OF PEOPLE WERE BLEEDING. IT DEGENER-ATED INTO A PROPER FIGHT. ON THE INSTRUCTIONS OF THE DEPUTY RECTOR, EVERYONE WAS BOXED OUT OF THE BUILDING, AMONG THEM A HIGH-RANKING JUDGE WHO DEMANDED COMPENSATION. A POSTER WAS RAPIDLY PUT UP ON A STAND WITH THE INFORMATION: "NO MEMBERS OF THE PUBLIC SHALL BE AD-MITTED TO THE HUNDERTWASSER EXPERIMENT." BUT THE PRESS WERE PRESENT, AND THE INCIDENT BECAME PUBLIC. THE RECTOR OF THE UNIVERSITY, WHO WAS IN ROME AT THE TIME, LEARNED OF WHAT HAD HAPPENED FROM THE NEWSPAPERS AND TOOK THE NEXT PLANE TO HAMBURG.

MEANWHILE I CONTINUED THE LINE. THE LINE PASSED ACROSS THE INSIDE OF THE DOOR. EVERY TIME THE LINE REACHED THIS POINT, THE ENTRANCE DOOR HAD TO BE CLOSED. IT TOOK ABOUT TWENTY MINUTES TO DRAW ONE SPIRAL CIRCLE AROUND THE ROOM, AND ABOUT ONE MINUTE TO COMPLETE THE SECTION ACROSS THE CLOSED DOOR. WITH THE EXCEPTION OF THIS BRIEF MINUTE, THE DOOR WAS ALWAYS OPEN. AT JUST ONE SUCH MOMENT, WHEN THE LINE WAS CROSSING THE DOOR, THE DEPUTY RECTOR APPEARED OUTSIDE DEMANDING IM-MEDIATE ENTRY. I CALLED OUT FROM WITHIN: "WAIT A MINUTE, I CAN'T OPEN THE DOOR NOW, THE LAW OF THE LINE FORBIDS IT. WAIT A MINUTE UNTIL THE LINE HAS LEFT THE DOOR." HE WAS FURIOUS AND FLUNG HIMSELF AT THE DOOR TRYING TO FORCE HIS WAY IN. HE UNDERSTOOD NOTHING. I CALMLY CON-TINUED THE LINE, AND ONCE IT HAD PASSED THE DOOR I OPENED UP.

IT WAS LIKE BEING ON THE MOUNT OF OLIVES. I WAS ALONE WITH THE TWO POETS. OUR ELECTRICITY WAS CUT OFF DURING THE NIGHT. I WENT OUT TO GET CANDLES FROM A NEIGHBOUR. WE TOOK TURNS: ONE PERSON DREW THE LINE,

Hundertwasser at the Kunsthochschule Lerchenfeld, Hamburg, taken with delay timer, 1959

ANOTHER SLEPT ON THE SOFA AND THE THIRD WENT OUT TO GET FOOD AND DRINK AND CANDLES AND TALK TO THE PRESS. WE WORKED UNTIL DAWN. IT WAS LIKE BEING ON A SHIP IN HIGH SEAS: WE EACH HELD WATCH IN TURN. THE LINE WAS RED AND GREW LIKE THE RED SEA, THE RED SPIRAL SEA. AND THEN CAME THE SECOND DAY. THE NEWSPAPERS REPORTED EVERYTHING IN DETAIL. THE SCANDAL WAS COMPLETE.

THE CATHEDRALS OF TRUE FAITH, THE CATHEDRALS OF CREATION, CANNOT BE BUILT WITH STRAIGHT LINES, BECAUSE THE STRAIGHT LINE IS GODLESS.

MY "EXPERIMENT" WAS ACTUALLY SUPPOSED TO END AT A POINT SOMEWHERE ON THE CEILING. THE LINE WOULD THEN BE A SPIRAL WHICH COMES FROM OUTSIDE, FROM A DISTANCE, SEEMS TO GROW NARROWER AND NARROWER AND SEEMS TO END AT A CENTRE, SIMILAR TO THE PEAK OF A PYRAMID OR THE SPIRE OF A CATHE-DRAL, OF A FAITH, WHICH ARE ALSO CHARGED WITH SPECIAL ENERGIES. IN RE-ALITY, HOWEVER, THE SPIRAL CONDENSES ITSELF INTO A CENTRE WHICH SIGNIFIES LIFE AND DEATH SIMULTANEOUSLY AND CONCENTRATES IMMENSE FORCES FOR A REBIRTH INTO ANOTHER PLANE. UNFORTUNATELY, I WAS NOT PERMITTED TO FIND THIS POINT. THAT I WAS NOT TO ATTAIN.

oto: Hundertwasser. Photographing the line was forbidden by the Rector

1958 H UNDERTWASSER 1963

colours which shade into yellow or red. They are lying around on the street. If you have them as a background and the industrially manufactured colours are in-between it heightens the effect. If you have manufactured and hand-made paints side-by-side they complement each other so you don't know which is more precious, the home-made colours or the industrial colours.

Hundertwasser's painting directly opposes Tachisme's profligate use of materials. He concerns himself with the conservation of small and large resources. "Colour is precious." Our use of daylight and artificial light are another concern: "In modern cities we waste a lot of electricity for nothing. There is no point in having electricity on all night. Plants lit by electric light inside a house change the atmosphere, they give moisture – you don't need a vaporizer or moisturizer spray – you have a softer throat than when you're in dry air.") Perhaps paradoxically to non-painters, thin colours supply a greater sense of a specific hue, as in the works of the American "stain painters" (Morris Louis or Kenneth Noland, for example), or in Henri Matisse's painted papers. Layered colours – in stained glass, or Flemish Renaissance painters' glazing – intensifies hue and depth, and creates the finest differentiations. To master his glowing mixed media, Hundertwasser sacrificed

the developed effects of oil paint, which more readily locates the picture plane with raised "facture".

The AVANT-GARDE

Modern art arguably began with Gericault, whose work epitomized the qualities associated with the avant-garde ever since. His most famous painting, *The Raft of the Medusa*, was a massive, insistently political indictment. Gericault's painted protest exhausted his action on behalf of the sailors and the navy. (The dichotomy between the artist as an aesthetic worker and as a citizen and political animal has always vexed artists.) But Gericault never – after unveiling his enormous canvas – published a plan for the reorganization of the French navy. Such actions are not the province of the modern artist as we envision that calling (except, briefly, in post-revolutionary Russia). Yet such advocacy is precisely what Hundertwasser does.

Which prominent modern artist would deign to beautify an unsightly highway restaurant, built of prefabricated parts years ago and designed by someone else? Such work is selfless and, being ornamental, contrary to the spirit of Modernism in art and architecture. What painter other than Hundertwasser would redesign a museum to glorify the colours of other painters – by working in black and white on the exterior?

Ill. pp. 96/97: 358 *Sole Ligure – Ligurische Sonne – The Ligurian Sun*, Liguria, April 1958 – La Picaudière, June 1963

Mixed media: watercolour on chalk-primed wrapping paper, laid down on canvas with polyvinyl in 1963 and repainted with oil, egg tempera and watercolour, 38.5 x 55.5 cm

Top left: Wigast Service Area, Bad Fischau, before renovation

Top right: Wigast Service Area, Bad Fischau with Hundertwasser's suggestions for improvement painted onto original photo

After years of drafting images of a paradisiacal world, he busied himself with thoughts of sewage, traffic, architecture, diet, urban planning, humus toilet, the foresting of roofs, a waste-free society, clothing, energy, identity, and the other notions that undergird modern life. Such activities reduce his respectability among Modernist critics who regard Hundertwasser's extra-artistic activities as anathema. Fundamentally, it is not his varied attentions that offend Modernists, it is the social activities themselves. These practices lie at the core of his rejection by the international Modernists. Once we understand the substance of that rejection, the mutual anger of the protagonists stands clear. Hundertwasser does not regard the "avant-garde" as an external critique of society, but uses the phrase in its original sense of a military vanguard, culture's shock-troops.

F. H.: A painter should be avant-garde, should be in advance of the needs of our society and ecology — which is in a state of crisis. A painter should act as an example against the consumer society. He should be an example of how to live in a wasteless society. And what does the painter do? He does the contrary. He splashes around and wastes the paint. He is worse, wasting valuable stuff. I consider painting a religious activity; the substance of paint is a sacred material. It should be cared for like gold. It should be used wisely and intelligently. At least as bread was used in the war. That is why in the Academy, in my master class, I try to keep everything in order. Most of the Academy buildings that you see are very nice buildings designed by architects in former times, classic architecture with statues right and left, steps going up, columns, like a Greek temple, mosaics, like the Vienna

Academy of Fine Arts – the same as the Paris Ecole des Beaux-Arts, and the American Schools of Arts. They tried to make something beautiful, and when you go in front there is a garden, a kind of Versailles. People who pass by, for instance the people of the town, show this to foreigners and say, "This is the Academy of Fine Arts" as they would say, "This is the Parliament" or "This is a palace". When they pass in front of the Academy they think, there is the fantastic world of Raphael, Rembrandt, van Gogh, and Picasso, the whole fantastic world of art. You go up the steps thinking you are about to enter into a paradise of art, a Garden of Eden of the arts. Then you go into an open classroom and you step into shit. Immediately you smell shit and urine and dust and you walk on rags and garbage cans and beer-bottles and sausages. You can't distinguish between the contents of the garbage cans and the stuff that is not yet garbage. It is more incredible than a pissoir in Paris or a third-class waiting room in Naples. There is something wrong with the arts. Being an artist is a way of being, it's not just what you produce.

Hundertwasser's "way of being" became apparent in 1960 on the occasion of the happening "Les Orties" which took place in the gallery "Quatre Saisons" in Paris and was organized by the art critic Alain Jouffrey.

Model of the Wigast Service Area, Bad Fischau

KUNSTHAUS, VIENNA

Before renovation

Model of the Kunsthaus

Above and right: Façade of the Kunsthaus

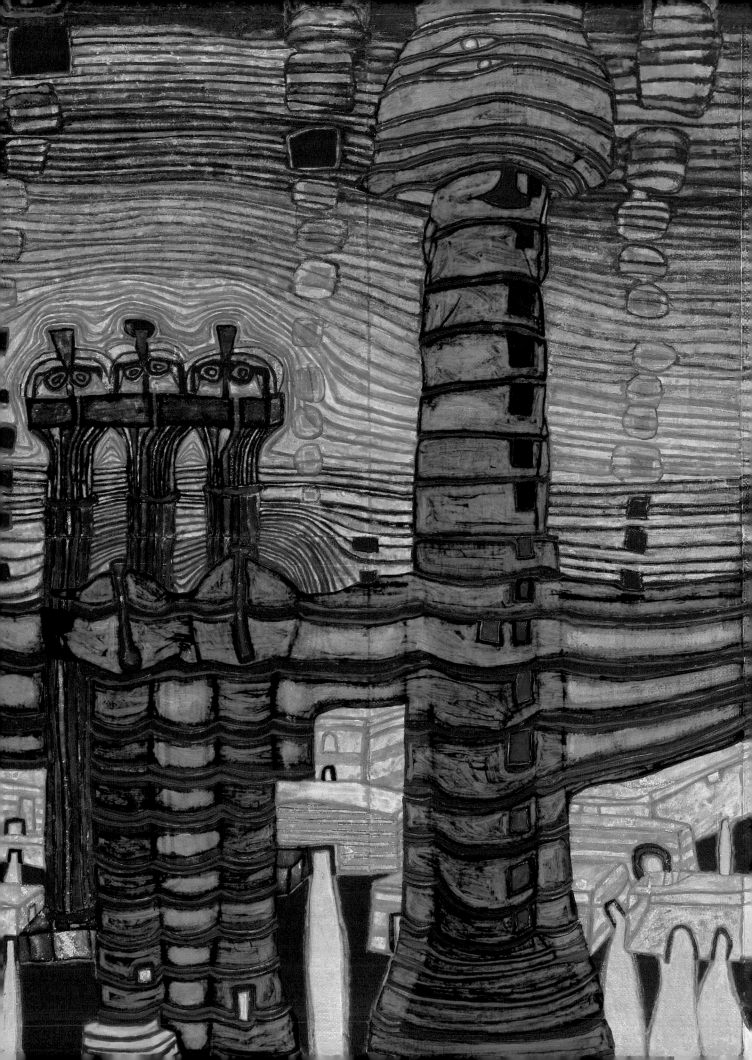

A PAINTER'S LIFE

(handwritten signatures)	(handwritten signatures)	(printed)
	Stowasser	STOWASSER
	Fritz	FRITZ
	Friedrich	FRIEDRICH
	Friederich	FRIEDERICH
	Friedereich	FRIEDEREICH
	Friedenreich	FRIEDENREICH
	Hundertwasser	HUNDERTWASSER
	Friedensreich	FRIEDENSREICH
	Regentag	REGENTAG
	Dunkelbunt	DUNKELBUNT

585 *Das Ende Griechenlands – The End of Greece,* Delphi, Heraklion on the S.S. Delos, Santorini, My-
konos, September 1963, Venice, October 1963, Hanover, February 1964
Mixed media: first watercolour on drawing paper primed with chalk and polyvinyl, then stuck onto
hemp with polyvinyl and finished with egg tempera, oil, polyvinyl and watercolour, 67 x 48 cm

The Eastern church's onion dome imparts an Oriental tone to *A Rain of Blood is Falling into a Garden with a Weeping Church (Blutregen fällt in einen Garten mit weinender Kirche)* (p. 91). No denomination is indicated by the onion dome, neither Greek nor Russian Orthodox. The purple onion dome only suggests we look away from the Mediterranean world, that we think of a location north of the Alps and east of Alsace; this is the church Hundertwasser had always known. And into this landscape comes horror. From the sky, in great globules too massive to be "drops", blood falls. Using a technique the Impressionists borrowed from Japan – having a major pictorial element only partially included within the frame – Hundertwasser presents a reservoir of blood extending beyond the borders of the picture. This was not an image Realism of any sort could have created. Recalling *The Tongue of Lucifer's* compositional structure, three strong horizontals divide the design. Blue sky, grass-covered earth, and, in the middle, rising from earth to heaven, rows of yellow houses. These houses form between them a narrow street – a typical Eastern European village. (This theme did not remain dormant but was re-examined in *Rain of Blood is Falling into an Austrian Seven River Side* (p. 93).) This is Hundertwasser's generous historical statement.

F. H.: I think the onion shape means richness and happiness and wealth and opulence and fertility. The onion shape is like a woman with a big stomach. The Byzantine empire extended east to Russia. The

Hundertwasser with Yuko Ikewada, Tokyo, 1961

Left: 474 *Part of the Yellow River – Teil des gelben Flusses*, Ikenoso Ryokan, Ikebukuro, Tokyo, March 1961
Watercolour on rice paper primed with chalk and CH-3, 12 x 31 cm

Kremlin is one of the most fantastic buildings, with its ten onion-shaped towers, all different from one another, gold and silver with different kinds of shapes – it is a dream out of the Arabian Nights. I wonder how the Kremlin towers can be in Moscow – they should be nearer Jerusalem.

I feel very attached to onion domes and I do them everywhere. I put them in my paintings and on my buildings. On the buildings I have troubles, the intellectuals don't like onion domes, although they cannot explain why they are against them.

H. R.: Do you think associations with the Church bother them?

F. H.: Yes, but Vienna is the gateway to the Balkans anyhow. It is the gateway to the East, the easternmost city of the German-speaking realm. It is a symbol which somehow relates to the spiral. The onion is not a symbol of any state – like lions, hawks, trees on flags.

H. R.: An onion is related to a spiral because its cross-section describes concentric circles, but when you draw or build a tower, do you really think of an onion or of an onion-shaped dome?

F. H.: I think of it as a shape, not so much as an onion. When I put it in my paintings it is the promise of a good land, the holy land, the beloved land, the promised land, paradise. It is something like paradise, the Garden of Eden, earthly gardens, fairy tales, and the holy land, something very beautiful which is on this earth. That is what I am doing all the time – showing the way to this land. This is part of my Jewish blood – wanting to show beauty and the way to go there. That is why I paint onion towers, because this is the very symbol of paradise in architecture. The architecture of paradise. The architecture of the holy land must have onion-shaped towers.

Then Hundertwasser built his onion domes, his ideal church, his paradisiacal community. In 1948 the Catholic church of Saint Barbara was built in the town of Bärnbach, in the province of Styria, Austria. Forty years later Hundertwasser trans-

133 *Pissender Knabe mit Wolkenkratzer – Pissing Boy with Skyscraper*, Obere Donaustraße, Vienna, January-June 1952, woven by the artist himself
Material: coloured wool; thread/cm: 6 strands, 280 x 140 cm

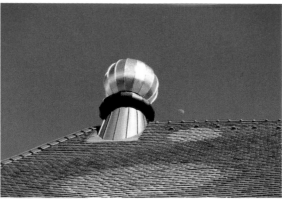

CHURCH, BÄRNBACH

Hundertwasser designed the first model in April 1987. Work began in October that same year. On Sunday, 4 September 1988, the redesigned St. Barbara's Church was consecrated.
"I am very happy - the best present ever given to me in my whole life was to be allowed to design this church."
Hundertwasser, 27 July 1988.

Ill. p. 108/109:
Pillars in the church, Bärnbach

484 *Häuser im Blutregen – Bild, das einen österreichischen Juden weinen macht – Houses in Rain of Blood – A Picture which Makes an Austrian Jew Weep,* Hyakusen Ryokan, Higaschi Nagasaki, Tokyo, April 1961
Mixed media: egg tempera, oil, pieces of blue cloth, brick dust on rice paper primed with chalk and mounted on jute with CH-3, 97 x 130 cm

formed this building from a nondescript parish church into a marvel. The steeple became a gleaming onion dome. Here, all faiths are recognized and respected. Along a circular path, ceremonial gates colourfully honour the major religions, with the various emblems – Cross, Crescent, Star of David, etc. The variegated roof's unexpected design can be seen from afar. The building's details are joyful.

Circumstance offered Hundertwasser a great experience, but the path was not straightforward. In 1961 he travelled to Japan. There he visited Hokkaido before going on to Siberia. At this time he accepted the Mainichi Prize at the 6th International Art Exhibition in Tokyo and his at-

tachment to Japan grew stronger. His first exhibition in Paris had been reviewed by the Japanese critic Shinichi Segui who, in 1960, together with Yves Klein, brought Hundertwasser to the attention of the owner of a gallery in the Ginza, Tokyo's main thoroughfare. The dealer, Mr. Yamamoto, invited Hundertwasser to visit Japan, where Hundertwasser arrived in February 1961. There Hundertwasser painted with remarkable fervour, savouring Japanese culture, producing a show that hung at the Tokyo Gallery from May to June and sold out to Japanese collectors. Before leaving Japan he met his second wife, Yuko Ikewada, a Japanese art student.

Hundertwasser also became fascinated by traditional Japanese "ukiyo-e" printing, which, though it had flourished for centuries, was practised in a dwindling handful of workshops. Hundertwasser determined to produce an "ukiyo-e" print. Though the woodcarvers who transfer the artist's preparatory materials to the cherrywood blocks were reluctant, eventually some senior craftsmen consented to work on *Houses in Rain of Blood,* a project that required over thirty carved blocks. The print is based on his mixed media painting, *Houses in Rain of Blood – A Picture which Makes an Austrian Jew Weep.* The process, by which an artist's designs are cut by others, belies modern notions of authenticity. While not especially a "modern" approach, it preserves a precious and irreplaceably beautiful method of printing – a technique whose resulting radiance has no equal. Just before leaving Japan in August 1961, Hundertwasser worked with craftsmen on the colour separations with which rice paper would be imprinted with "blood" that drops from the sky upon Austria, striking fields and houses alike.

488 *Rain in the Meadow – Gefangener Regen in der Wiese,* Hyakusen Ryokan, Higashi Nagasaki, Tokyo, June 1961
Mixed media: egg tempera, watercolour on rice paper primed with chalk and CH-3 and laid down on jute with CH-3, 73 x 92 cm

A SOLITARY OCCUPATION

F. H.: You are a lone master; paint and canvas and you in a room. No other art can do that. If you do graphics, you have to deal with printers, editors, and technicians. When you make a film, you need a developer. Building a house you have to deal with many people. It is less noble when you have to deal with other people – it gets less pure; you use machines. When you make a tapestry you can hardly do it alone. Weaving is such a slow process that after one year of weaving you get a piece like one square yard, and this is not very finely woven. If Dürer or Brueghel, instead of painting ten fantastic paintings like *The Tower of Babel* or *The Blind Leading the Blind,* had been a weaver, he would have employed all his energy doing only one tapestry, and this tapestry would be so clumsy that you would not see Brueghel's hand at all.

H. R.: What do you think of working flat, about painting that is a surface arrangement?

F. H.: The true proportions in this world are the views to the stars and the views down to the surface of the earth. Grass and vegetation in the city should grow on all horizontal spaces – that is to say, wherever rain and snow falls vegetation should grow, on the roads and on the roofs. The horizontal is the domain of nature and wherever vegetation grows on the horizontal level man is off limits; he should not interfere. I mean taking away territories from nature, which human beings have always done.

H. R.: Humus is a Latin word, dirt; if you want to make somebody low you force him to the ground, you *hum*ble him, you *humil*iate him. To be humble is to sit upon the ground, not a throne, etc. Humus has lots of associated words.

F. H.: Humanity too has the same origin – humus – humanitas.

H. R.: Yes, the concept is the same in German, Old English, Greek, and even in Hebrew; the name Adam means "of the soil". And in Spanish too, "hombre".

F. H.: Very interesting. I've worked a great deal with grass roofs, putting soil on top and having things grow, but there is something strange in this, more than ecological. It is a religious act to have soil on your roof and trees growing on top of you; the act reconciles you with God, with nature, maybe not Christian or Jewish monotheism, but something wider, older – a very ancient wisdom.

493 *Greenfield Bluelake Goldlane – Grünes Feld, blauer See, goldener Pfad,* Eisankei, Hokkaido, July 1961
Mixed media: egg tempera and watercolour on rice paper primed with chalk and CH-3 and mounted on canvas with CH-3, 33 x 24 cm

A painter who puts his canvas flat on the table has the basic conditions for doing things right. In fact if he works vertically on his canvas on the wall he basically starts wrong because it is an illusion. When he paints flat, what he does are facts, are real, but when he paints vertically the conditions are wrong, and what he does will be wrong because it is a lie and a distortion by perspective. The egoistic thing about perspective is that what is nearer is more important and bigger than what is farther and seemingly less important.

Aerial, or high-angle, views were congenial to Hundertwasser's theory of images, which were confirmed by Japanese ideography. Japanese culture contrasted with the prevailing trends of Western evolution.
Beginning in the late Middle Ages,

Western art strove to free itself of such conceptualization as Japan and other cultures maintained. The Renaissance was a "rebirth" of naturalistic observation, which grew in importance until Impressionism directed our attention to the very means of perception. Since the Renaissance, both the glory and limitation of Western painting has been its transcription of perception. In Japan, Hundertwasser encountered a culture that had not completed this transition, in which much that we consider "modern" had long been a feature of daily life. *Greenfield Bluelake Goldlane* (p. 111) displays a colourfully ideographic "aeroplane view".

H. R.: Your notions, and some of your artistic practice, might be called traditional; as an artist and environmental thinker you would not be considered as technologically "modern" as Buckminster Fuller or Paolo Soleri.
F. H.: One reason for my success is that I will not fight the elements. Anybody who fights the elements is a fool. If you want to be active when it is raining or when it is snowing, at night, or if you want to be active when you are sick – these are all times when nature wants you to be calm. Some crazy stupid architect (Buckminster Fuller) wants to build a glass dome over all of New York. Inside you have daylight night and day, you have no wind, no rain. But this is completely crazy because when you really cut off nature you have a kind of spacecraft, and man is not born to live in a spacecraft.

HOMECOMING

In 1962 Hundertwasser and Yuko Ikewada were married in Vienna (the marriage was dissolved in 1966). He established his studio in a palazzo on the Giudecca, Venice,

605 *Landschaft am Silberfluß – Landscape with Silverstream*, Giudecca, October 1964
Mixed media: watercolour on wrapping paper primed with polyvinyl, later mounted on hemp with polyvinyl and partly repainted with oil, 50 x 57 cm

opposite San Marco, and that summer Hundertwasser was featured in a one-man show at the Austrian pavilion at the Venice Biennale. His return to Vienna had prompted Hundertwasser's adoption by the Austrians for their 1962 Biennale; at the time, this support was seen as part of a trend, a tide of artistic internationalism. His presentation at the Biennale was a great success Giacometti and Manessier were awarded the major prizes. (Hundertwasser's works were very well received. However, Austria was too insignificant to make any inroads against the powerful French art dealers and the French government's policy of massive support for culture. It was this that prevented him from winning the first prize. By way of consolation, Hundertwasser received the unofficial "Prix de la Critique".)

In September, Hundertwasser participated in the opening exhibition of the Museum des 20. Jahrhunderts in Vienna. His success in Japan brought this Austrian painter attention at home. Only after his worldwide recognition started to form did Vienna accept him. Since nationality seemed so fickle, the tradition of art offered a glorious ancestry to replace his own family. Hundertwasser's art became his native country.

Hundertwasser began the *Jew's House in Austria* (p. 112) at Radschink, Waldvier-

Left: 610 *Narrenhaus – Mausoleum der Maler – Bethäuser – Die Maler haben Bethäuser und benützen sie nicht – Fool's House – Mausoleum for Painters – Houses to Pray – The Painters Have Houses to Pray and Do Not Use Them,* Venice, November 1964, finished January 1965
Mixed media: polyvinyl acetate, watercolour, oil and egg on drawing paper primed with chalk and polyvinyl, mounted on jute with polyvinyl, 61 x 73 cm.

Right: 603A *Sonnenuntergang – Sunset – Raku Yoo,* Venice – Tokyo, 1966
Japanese woodcut in about 20 colours, 26 x 34 cm (25 x 33)
Portfolio "Nana Hyaku Mizu". Edition of 200, all signed. Cut and printed by Nakamura Hanga Kobo, Tokyo 1966. Coordinator Yuko Ikewada. Published by Gruener Janura, Glarus

tel in December 1961 and finished it on the Giudecca in Venice on 4 June 1962. The windows of a *Jew's House in Austria* glow yellow, as if darkness surrounded all. Amid richly sonorous colour the backyard is a pool of blood. Over the house the sky rains blood, and the windows reveal red dots inside the house. The centre drainspout is red with blood. Blood everywhere. In several pictures of the mid-1960s Hundertwasser pondered what had happened in Austria in the Nazi period. Expanding on the motifs of *Jew's House in Austria,* Hundertwasser also painted *Blood-Garden-Houses with Yellow Smoke* (p. 114).

In *Castle of the Survivors of László with Silverstreet XVIII–XXIV* linear perspective sharply converges in depth. Hundertwasser also employed descriptive perspective (when opaque shapes partially obscure those behind them in a series of planes whose nearest surfaces have the least obscured edges). Such doubly articulated spatial depth accommodates Hundertwasser's fantasy world. As the careful spatial construction shows, Hundertwasser is not a pure fantasist. His works acknowledge and obey natural law.

An environmentalist does not transgress the laws of nature, as would a Surrealist. The universal rules that organize substances and living things are precisely what Hundertwasser reveres. *Castle of the Survivors of László with Silverstreet XVIII–XXIV* included parts of the collage "La Lune en Rôdage" cut into seven pieces. These fragments appear as vignettes in the lower portion of the new ensemble. A two-eyed sun floats in a panoramic sky above a city with a vast square and massive "triumphal" arch on a street lined with windowless houses.

The splendour of *The End of Greece* (p. 102) features a grid-space construction of open and closed (transparent and opaque) architectural volumes familiar since the work of late Renaissance or Baroque masters. Here rational space again supports the fantastic: columns whose design inherits "Jugendstil's" dormant magnificence. The foreground of the picture is encased in powerful green and lavender bands pierced with blue; this eruption weaves background and foreground together. (The title refers to Greek civilization's polychromed world, now washed off

611 Heimweh der Fenster – Heimweh ins Meer – The Windows' Homesickness – Homesickness into the Sea, Lausanne – Montreuil, October 1964, Venice, November 1964
Mixed media: polyvinyl, watercolour, oil and egg tempera on drawing paper primed with chalk and polyvinyl, mounted on jute with polyvinyl, 70 x 97 cm

116

by centuries of rain; originally the Greek marble temples were painted in brilliant colours.)

During certain periods Hundertwasser has tended to reconsider every adjustment and detail of colour and formal balance. Often laying a painting aside numerous times over a period of years, he named his protracted re-working the "vegetative method"; his answer to automatism, "trans-automatism". Without losing his hold on commonplace reality, Hundertwasser performed a slow-motion version of Abstract Expressionism. He reacted to – then reconsidered, then adjusted again – what emerged in the painting. His model for this prolonged act of painting was not Freudian, not based on an exploration of personality; rather, it derived from supra-individual nature itself.

F. H.: I believe my painting is totally different because it is vegetative painting. One reason why other people don't want to paint vegetatively is because it starts so inconspicuously, without any éclat or drum rolls. Instead it develops quite slowly and steadily, and that doesn't suit our social order – people want immediate results, achieved through exploitation.

Hundertwasser uses the notion of "exploitation" in the sense of a selfish and unethical rape of resources for publicity. At the time he began to work this way his procedures were not only without precedent, but have never since been adopted by others.

H. R.: What does a work of art gain by being done slowly?
F. H.: It gains time. The help of time is in-

Ill. p. 114: 564 *Blood-Garden-Houses with Yellow Smoke – Blut-Garten-Häuser mit gelbem Rauch*, Vienna, 1962, Giudecca, summer 1962, La Pi-caudière, January-April 1963
Mixed media: egg tempera, oil, watercolour, wax crayon on wrapping paper primed with with chalk and polyvinyl, mounted on jute with polyvinyl, 81 x 65 cm

Ill. p. 115: 623 *End of the Night – Die waagerechten und senkrechten Tränen des Mannes, auf den die Sonne und der Schatten fällt – The Horizontal and Vertical Tears of the Man onto Whom Sun Shines and Shade Falls*, Giudecca, March 1966
Mixed media: watercolour, egg tempera, polyvinyl and oil on drawing paper, mounted on jute with polyvinyl and cellulose, 92 x 65 cm

117

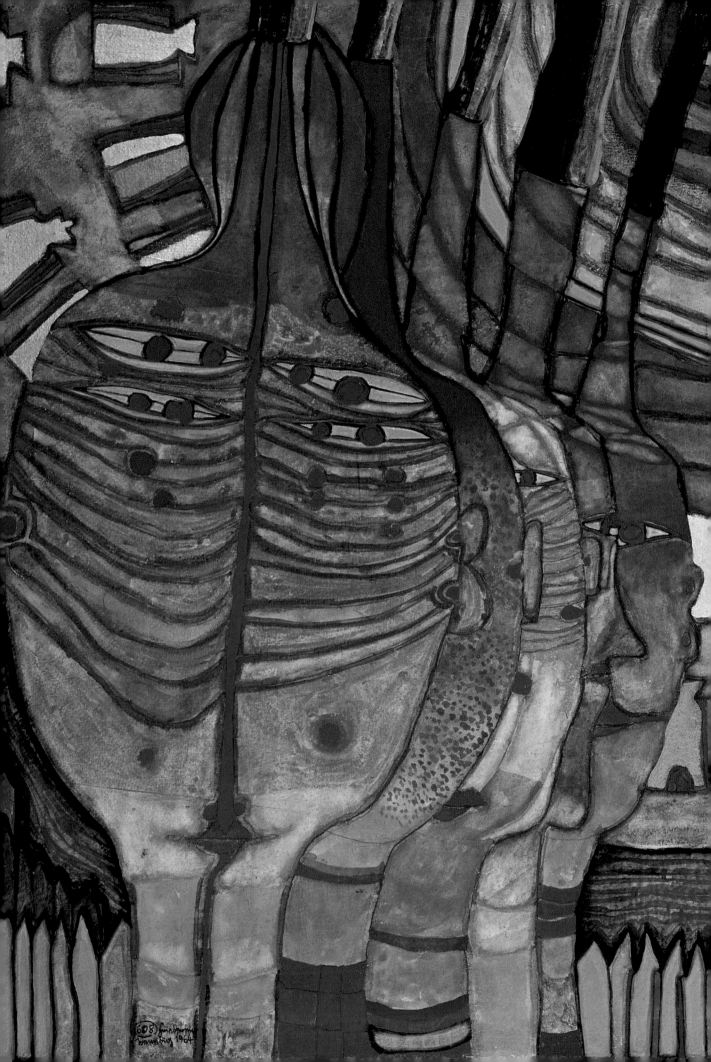

credible in art. Something grows; then it can't fail. Only the quick things fail. You feel that they do not have that patina, the mark of evolution, the mark of age. Slow-growing trees are better than fast-growing, the wood is better, they look better.

Creation takes time and art which does not involve evolution is going to disappear quickly. The longer it took to create it the longer it will live later on. This is a basic rule, but there are exceptions to it.

In 1964 he stayed in Hanover for a long time in preparation for his exhibition arranged by the Kestner-Gesellschaft as its 100th exhibition since the war. Here were the fruits of Hundertwasser's longing to free himself from both the exhausted rigours of factual representationalism and the worst transgressions of irresponsible Surrealism. He wanted an art that was reliable as the expression of his growing environmental concerns, notions that were far in advance of his day, and the Hanover show did establish Hundertwasser's independent identity from contemporary movements. The exhibition and beautiful catalogue documented what was already apparent to all:

"After this tour Hundertwasser will be one of the best known painters in Europe. This can be predicted with confidence, as his paintings are different from all others and engrave themselves without effort upon the memory. They belong to none of the current movements. Hundertwasser seems to be as little in sympathy with geometric abstraction as with action painting, and he certainly has nothing in common with pop art or three-dimensional constructions which can only be brought to life by an electric switch . . . He covers his picture surface completely, from edge to edge, but as he often paints on pieces of packing paper or any other bit of paper he can lay his hands on, these edges are by no means smooth; in such cases he sticks his painting on a black background which completes the pictures . . . and there is a certain amount of automation or compul-

sion in his work, although one should not overstress this point, a more controlled art can hardly be imagined . . . Hundertwasser has a refined sense for his medium, his transitions are sophisticated, and his application of colour is delicate." (Edith Hoffmann, "The Burlington Magazine", December 1964)

His viewers soon noticed that Hundertwasser was unallied to prevailing trends. His art shared nothing with geometric abstraction; he was more serious than Dada; more restrained and humanly scaled than Abstract Expressionism (of any form); Hundertwasser was never as sly or "camp" as Pop Art; the makers of technologically animated constructions, or Op Art (so named the following year) were anathema to him. Hundertwasser stood almost alone. His deliberate painting of recurring themes distinguished him from automatist-Surrealism and its sympathizers: "There is no doubt of Hundertwasser's genuine artistic inspiration. Yet I do not think that he has an interior simplicity and has retained his own childlike world, as his friends assert. No, every step forward that he makes in his pictures and in his own life is much too intellectual, conscious and calculated." (Hanns Theodor Flemming, "Studio International", November 1964.)

At about the time of his 1964 Hanover exhibition, Hundertwasser took a climbing tour of the Tyrolean Alps and his mother bought Hahnsäge, an old wood mill in Lower Austria, where Hundertwasser now often retires to paint. Rural images are prominent in his art. The *Landscape with Silverstream* (p. 113) celebrates the endless sky, clouds, sunlight, mountains, high meadows and pastureland, broken by glaciers (applied as metallic silver). Clouds drift below in the valley, seen from his favourite high-angled viewpoint. The setting sun lights a landscape and below the mist a town perches on a shoulder of the mountain that rises in the extreme left foreground to supply the platform from which we observe the vista. Through this countryside, viewed from a high angle, a great river flows silver, sun-raked with light on water. The land's rich green furrows bespeak agriculture, a human presence depicted as lovingly as nature.

Hundertwasser does not advocate man's absence from landscape, only that humanity coexist with nature. Just as Hundertwasser is not a vegetarian (but understands that life is sacred), he believes that the land can be used, but only with good cause; for him, unlike some environmentalists, humanity is present in paradise. Among Hundertwasser's haunting fantasies, *The End of the Greeks, Ostrogoths and Visigoths* (pp. 118–119) features multiple eyes, far up on the head. These figures are shown within a dome-like vault. This odd structure might be a monolithic roof, such as that atop Theodoric's tomb, or a beehive, or even the sky beyond city walls with windows behind.

THE PAST AND FUTURE OF BEAUTY

Hundertwasser is rarely a painter of whimsy, though humour and wit are mainstays of his art. Even in his most clever invention, *The Windows' Homesickness* (p. 116), mere caprice does not rule. Hundertwasser pictured windows migrating over the countryside. They fly over a city park, out into deep blue night and far space. Years later, Hundertwasser re-encountered "Window Rights", but now the windows are protagonists in an amazing painting. The image puns on the idea of the window as the channel of open space craving the great ancestor, space itself.

H. R.: The images and shapes in your work have great complicated meanings, very rich meanings. Do the colours have meanings for you also?
F. H.: The question should be the other way round. The colours have a meaning because the shapes are not so important. In my paintings the forms are not rich at all, the colours are rich. The forms are very poor.
I cannot draw. I cannot sculpt. I am very weak in the colourless arts. I am not very

good as far as shading is concerned – light and shade are not my strong point. My strong points are the colours, and there I am quite good. (Lately I have had some doubts about what I am doing because a colourful world, as I conceive it, might be very unnatural.)
Manmade colours will quickly disappear. A poem lasts longer; for instance, Homer has lasted for 3000 years and you can always read him, always repeat it, but the colours put down 3000 years ago would not have lasted to today. Of course, you could paint for immediate use, more or less like a singer, a performer who makes people happy for a day, and next day only a memory remains. A painting lasts longer; it lasts a generation. It lasts at least as long as one man lives. But then it starts to fade, to get strange, and disappears. Not only because of the colours, but also because fashion changes and the painting becomes unsightly. The paintings which have been done before are starting to get interesting again, Jugendstil paintings and things that are older. That's how it is. I am sure that the paintings which we are doing now will soon be completely out of fashion, so completely out of fashion that it will be inconceivable even to have them or to discuss them.

Hundertwasser notes the banality of art fostered by zeal, and his own position on kitsch impinges on the issue of academic realism: "When you look at pictures sponsored by the Nazis they have no concentration camps, no feeling that people are being forced into something. Painting during the Hitler era was completely harmless. I know that in America, in France (especially in France), and in Italy they did exactly the same kind of painting. It is painting that is forced to idealize, painting without purpose."

Ill. pp. 118/119: 608 *Das Ende der Griechen, Ost- und Westgoten – The End of the Greeks, Ostrogoths and Visigoths,* painted on board the S.S. Philippos Rhodes-Daphne, Venice, 1964
Mixed media: watercolour on drawing paper primed with polyvinyl, mounted on hemp with polyvinyl, partially repainted with watercolour, polyvinyl and oil, 49 x 68 cm

MATURE STYLE

(signature)	Stowasser	STOWASSEN
(signature)	Fritz	FRITZ
(signature)	Friedrich	FRIEDRICH
(signature)	Friederich	FRIEDERICH
(signature)	Friedereich	FRIEDEREICH
(signature)	Friedenreich	FRIEDENREICH
(signature)	Hundertwasser	HUNDERTWASSER
(signature)	Friedensreich	FRIEDENSREICH
(signature)	Regentag	REGENTAG
(signature)	Dunkelbunt	DUNKELBUNT

622 *Der Nasenbohrer und die Beweinung Egon Schieles – The Nose-Picker and the Mourning of Egon Schiele*, Paris, October 1965, Vorchdorf, Lugano, between Christmas and New Year 1965
Mixed media: polyvinyl acetate, watercolour, oil paper primed with chalk, mounted on jute with polyvinyl, 116 x 73 cm

In January 1965 Hundertwasser journeyed to Stockholm, then went on to Vienna; he wrote his essay "35 Days in Sweden", and exhibited at the Moderna Museet, Stockholm – a show that drew a record attendance. His work had now found its audience. In 1966 Hundertwasser's marriage to Yuko Ikewada ended in divorce. She continued as a liaison to Japanese printers so that Hundertwasser could continue woodblock printing. Thereafter, Hundertwasser produced about one Japanese woodblock print a year.

The proofs were sent between Europe and Japan; Hundertwasser communicated his desires to the printers, each proof carrying some slight modification and working notes. Hundertwasser kept a careful and clearly enumerated dossier about each print – using coloured dots or a square to identify the woodcutter's and printer's or artist's contribution.

656 *L'expulsion – The Expulsion,* Paris, 1967
Lithograph in many colours, 71.5 x 90 cm (68 x 80)
Signed edition of 154, a further 700 posters for exhibition in Geneva unsigned. Printed by Mourlot in cooperation with "Serge", Paris. Published by Galerie Krugier und Moos, Geneva 1967

124

Ill. p. 126: 639 *Seereise I – Journey I*, Giudecca, Sardinia, Paris, 1966/67
Copperplate engraving in four colours: yellow, red, green and blue,
38 x 28 cm (32 x 24)
Signed edition of 107. Printed by Lacourière, Paris. Published by Lazar-Vernet, Paris 1967

Ill. p. 127: 652 *Seereise II – Reise zur See und mit der Bahn – Journey II – Journey to the Sea and by Rail*, Paris 1967
Lithograph in 5 colours: yellow, green, red, black and blue, 66 x 50 cm
Signed edition of 267 and 5 proofs, 2 colour versions: with black or blue portholes. Printed by Michel Gasse, Paris. Published by Galerie Krugier und Moos, Geneva 1967

In a self-portrait, *End of the Night – The Horizontal and Vertical Tears of the Man onto Whom Sun Shines and Shade Falls* (p. 115), multiple suns have become red tears. A terrific wind lifts the artist's hair. The same wind storms away his tears and blows back his shirt. The storm was real enough in his life. Apparently eschewing the possibility of ever marrying again, he travelled and was attracted to several women. In August and September of 1967 he undertook a journey to Uganda and Sudan. He immersed himself in printing technique, doing graphics in colours using metallic imprints for the first time.

Hundertwasser exhibited at galleries in Rome, Paris, London, Geneva, and Berlin. It seemed that the reviewers aligned on national lines than on aesthetic ones. Sometimes his work was received warmly, while in other places it raised more questions than praise. Still, an overall pattern began to form. Most spectators admired Hundertwasser's bright colours, his quality of line and imaginative spaces. This consensus reflected his own thinking.

COLOUR PARADISE

For Hundertwasser, paradise is colourful, while purgatory, if there is such a thing, must be a grey or monochromatic world. The pardisiacal colours of heaven are not bound together or dictated by abstract concepts.

F. H.: Paradise is not just colours at random, but certain creative colours. Colour is only the outer appearance of wealth and diversity. The more different things there are, the richer the world. It approaches paradise: many different things living next to each other.

686 *Good Morning City – Bleeding Town*, Giudecca, 1969–70
Phosphorescent edition of 2000, in ten colour versions each of 200, 85 x 55.5 cm
Coordinator Alberto della Vecchia. Printed by Studio Quattro, Mestre 1970. Distributed by Ars Viva, Zurich 1971

Before humans domesticated plants and animals, and long before industrialization, the earth teemed with a fantastic variety of life. Primitive societies lived on this abundance and knew what we are discovering as we catalogue the world. Yet already we see a diminution; this endless number of species is shrinking rapidly, and humanity is to blame. The earthly paradise we found will eventually become hell as this variety of life shrinks. We are on the way already, and we are digging our own grave.

XXV/XXV   Hundertwasser

690 *Green Power,* Venice, 1970–72
After the work 625 *Wintergeist* (see ill. p. 131)
Serigraph in 19 colours with metal embossing in 2 colours and 2 phosphorescent colours, 83 x 64 cm (77 x 58)
Signed edition of 249 and 36 proofs. Coordinator Alberto della Vecchio.
Printed by Serialgraphic, Venice. Metal embossing by Studio Quattro, Mestre. Published by Gruener Janura, Glarus

ours, often on small canvases rich with princely patterning. His artistic ancestors showed him the way. The Vienna Secession artists rather than the School of Paris furnished his warrant, but few have tapped this same resource, which constitutes an alternative tradition to the mainstream. The gaudy delight of the Viennese offered as rich a vein of material as any in modern art. Inevitably, Hundertwasser has seemed a loner on the international scene. Critics accustomed to a reductionist aesthetic – Modernist abstraction, the Bauhaus, de Stijl, romantic Minimalism, etc. – must be disappointed. (Then there are his public appearances, Hundertwasser's two "Nude Demonstrations" in Munich and Vienna against architecture's inhuman environment. These actions have only further antagonized the Establishment.)

ARTISTIC HERITAGE

H. R.: Do you think of yourself as an extension of Jugendstil?
F. H.: Yes, but I cannot answer that question clearly. It's as if you were to ask somebody, "Do you consider yourself the son of your father?", and he will say "Yes". Who could say, "No, I don't consider myself the son of

F. H.: A colourful world is always a synonym for paradise. A grey or monocoloured world is always a synonym for purgatory or hell. Hell is only red: everything is red, fire, faces, blood – it is horrible. Just as horrible is a world which is only blue. If you live in a hell of vegetation, in the middle of the jungle where everything is green all the time, you go mad. You have the green hell, the blue hell, the red hell, the black hell, the grey hell. In cities you have it grey. It is strange that architects continue to build more grey. The diversity of colour brings betterment, brings paradise.

Hundertwasser strives to make his art rich in effects; he never preaches that "less is more". He successfully animates many col-

691A *Irinaland über dem Balkan – Irinaland over the Balkans,* Lengmoos, 1971
Serigraph in 29 colours with metal embossing in 5 colours and 2 phosphorescent colours, 67 x 50 cm (62 x 44)
Total edition of 3000, 300 copies ending with the number 7 are signed.
Printed by Dietz Offizin, Lengmoos. Published by Ars Viva, Zurich

625 *Wintergeist – Tableau d'hiver – Winterbild – Polyp – Winter Painting,*
Giudecca, April 1966
Mixed media: watercolour, egg tempera and polyvinyl on paper, glued on
hemp and mounted on canvas, 92 x 60 cm

my father"? There is a relationship between me and Jugendstil, but I know nothing about the philosophy of Jugendstil. Just that my paintings resemble Jugendstil, but if you put my paintings next to Jugendstil paintings there is a big gap.

Today the names of Klimt and Schiele, Otto Wagner and Josef Hoffman, Mahler, Hoffmannsthal, Strauss, Schnitzler, Altenburg and Gerstl are celebrated (and Viennese culture's contribution to modernity's tenor is recognized). Yet when Hundertwasser began as an artist they lacked worldwide acclaim. "I was born so much later. I was born 10 years after they died, so I am 2 generations younger. By the time I was born their fame was established, maybe to a lesser extent worldwide than in Austria."

For a 1967 print Hundertwasser re-examined an idea he first tried in a painting of 1958, *Nostalgia for the beyond – a spiraloid* – so-called because the subject was a solitary magnified spiral. The print, *The Journey I* (p. 126), adapted the painting's theme. Hundertwasser modified the letterpress blocks with drypoint and he reworked sections, creating smooth areas of high contrast. The etching's rich print quality could be achieved no other way.

A new period began when Galerie Finker, in Paris, assumed the management of Hundertwasser's affairs. The *Journey II* (p. 127) was the first project commissioned by Galerie Finker.

The colours of *Journey II* are more saturated than anything Hundertwasser had undertaken before; perhaps his visit to the Sudan and Uganda had lent an African strength to his hues. The insistent rhythm of the railroad ties and engine smoke appear as part of the imagery, while ocean waves lap at the bottom – recalling Japanese prints.

Ill. pp. 128/129: 659 *Zwolle,* Zwolle, August 1967
Mixed media, 44 x 62.5 cm

H. R.: If you could regard your work from the vantage of the future, how would you like it to be compared with other contemporary manifestations?
F. H.: I would like to be estimated as Klimt and Schiele, as an innovator, to have my right place in the history of art – which is not the case now. I am not regarded seriously for what I do because I am an outsider. The museums of today and contemporary critics see me as a publicity hound and money-minded artist who makes decorative kitsch. They are a handful of intolerant people who practise cultural and intellectual terrorism against anything that is not propagated by this group.
Artists are rarely considered what they want to be, but considered something completely

Ill. pp. 132/133: 691 *Irinaland über dem Balkan – Irinaland over the Balkans,* Rome, November 1969
Mixed media: watercolour, egg tempera and oil on aluminium foil primed with chalk and polyvinyl, on Schöllerhammer cardboard, 36.5 x 51 cm

719 *Funchal,* Madeira, Corsica, 1973
Mixed media: watercolour egg tempera and oil on aluminium cardboard,
44 x 63 cm

an example. Painting is only an exercise towards that aim – a kind of prayer.

In 1968 the University of California, Berkeley, organized an exhibition of Hundertwasser's works that toured the United States. (On that occasion Hundertwasser toured northern California.) The Berkeley retrospective contained eighty works from 1950 to 1968. The American press, unprepared for this work, provided bad reviews but the public thronged to the show anyway. Journalists thought Hundertwasser's art unfashionable. Those who saw the show in New York (and could compare it with the international art world) reacted more favourably. Unexpectedly, the exhibition was a turning-point; as one of the catalogue's two co-authors wrote:

"In truth, a Hundertwasser retrospective at this time is premature, for the paintings are not yet uniquely his own: they are Karel Appel, Rene Brô, child art, Delaunay, Dubuffet, Feininger, Gaudí, Walter Kampmann, Klee, Klimt, North African and Oriental ethnic, Joseph Pickett, the Ravenna mosaicists, Simon Rodia, Schiele, Saul Steinberg, the Wiener Werkstätte – ad infinitum. At Hundertwasser's age and stage of development (having painted only since 1950), it would be extraordinary only if this were not so. It is also not surprising that Hundertwasser himself fails to see all these elements in his work – his innate innocence and freedom of expression have been sorely tested by the dealers and collectors pounding at his door. Ironically, the most recent painting in the exhibition, *Rainy Day before the Rainy Day*, done in May 1968, shows the first signs of a new development." (Brenda Richardson, "College Art Journal", Fall 1970.)

Thus only after a large retrospective

else. Arthur Conan Doyle, for instance, wanted so much to be considered as a serious writer; he wrote historical novels. Instead everybody remembers him as a detective story writer, the creator of Sherlock Holmes. This same fate befalls many other artists. What they really are and achieve is not recognised at all, but they are known by side effects, by by-products.

H. R.: Are you afraid that will happen to you?

F. H.: It is happening to me now. I am famous because I took my clothes off, I am famous because my paintings are expensive and not so much because of what they are.

H. R.: Besides the paintings – which you send as a message to the future – what instructions would you offer about how your paintings ought to be regarded?

F. H.: I would like to have them seen as an incentive for a creative world. I want to set

718 *Franz-Josef-Hospital,* Vienna, September 1972, Auckland, May 1973
Mixed media: watercolour, egg tempera, oil, and quartz sand on cardboard primed with polyvinyl, with 1 mm aluminium, 51 x 73 cm

674A *Heavy Grass Wind – Schwerer Wiesenwind*, 1968
Mixed media, 132 x 177 cm
Weavers: Hilda Absalon and Marga Person, Vienna, 1973

endorsement did Hundertwasser's mature style emerge. Despite his maturing as an artist, many of Hundertwasser's subsequent reviews remained hostile.

REGENTAG

Hundertwasser bought a twelve-ton wooden freighter in Palermo, the "San Giuseppe T", a sixty-year-old single-masted ship that had been plying the waters between Sicily, Africa, and France carrying cargoes of salt and sand. Hundertwasser began to fulfil his boyhood dream of long-distance travel. He spent two months in Sicily getting a licence. Then, from April to June, sailing along the coast of Dalmatia, stopping at Split and Krk, he navigated his way from Sicily to Venice. Over the next four years "San Giuseppe T" was given a thorough refit. Her hull was cut through the middle in two places, another mast was added in the ancient boatyard at Palestrina in the Venice lagoon, and this vessel became the barque "Regentag" (Rainy Day). (Hundertwasser signed this name as early as in 1966 – in the woodcut *Sunset* (p. 117); but he was constrained from changing the ship's name by nautical law until it was registered in Panama in 1972. (This refit has a plausible title to be considered Hundertwasser's first architectural venture.)

Heavy Grass Wind resuscitates something of Romanticism. Like Caspar David Friedrich's mountain views, *Heavy Grass Wind* exalts the immensity of a clear open space. Architecture shrivels before a wind that blows ceaselessly through an unresisting landscape. As in previous paintings, Hundertwasser enlisted the wind to animate space and connote mood. (In a tame, silent world, De Chirico's distant banners and pennants did the same thing.)

663 *Zwollener Eikolonie – Sweet Sea Colony on the Salt Sea Voyage*,
Zwolle, July 1967, Hahnsäge, August 1967
Mixed media: watercolour, oil, egg tempera, lacquered gold leaf and
bronze powder on drawing paper primed with chalk and polyvinyl,
mounted on jute, 72 x 91 cm

Hundertwasser has remarked that his state of mind while working is an absorption akin to dreams. "Once the dream is over, I can't remember what I have dreamt. But the picture remains. The picture is the harvest of the dream." That Hundertwasser is not a Surrealist must be stressed, since Surrealists "usurped" dreams in the Twenties. For Hundertwasser, dreams are mankind's general longings. Artists who rely on dreams throw into question accountability for the work of art which issues from the "unconscious", over which the artist purports to have no control. Thus no liability inheres in the result. For Hundertwasser, however, the meditative revery that accompanies creative work is not to be con-

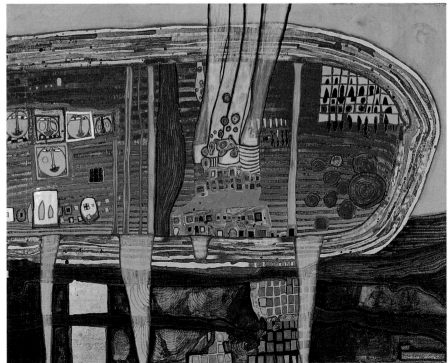

fused with an abandonment of one's duty as a social being. (To that end Hundertwasser can approach such "practical", but essential, projects as the "Village, Einkaufszentrum, Vienna".) Hundertwasser could not paint a politically, ecologically, or morally distasteful painting, as the "dream" in which he wanders while he works includes the super-ego. In the deliberate "vegetative" method, repellent images would not survive translation from his subconscious. If he were to transform factories, or industrial sites, it would be done beautifully – as the transformed Spittelau incinerator in Vienna (pp. 72–73) shows.

F. H.: I have painted skyscrapers, I don't like skyscrapers, but a skyscraper like the colourful one in *Good Morning City* (p. 125), if it existed, would not have the negative effect of skyscrapers.

It is very hard for an owner of a subconscious to beat his own subconscious in his subconscious. I am sure, for instance, that in the Nazi years everybody was acclaiming Hitler and running after him crying "Sieg Heil". I am quite sure that they felt there was something wrong, but they lied to themselves – they cried out "Sieg Heil!" louder than ever, "Heil Führer!", to convince themselves – but somehow they felt it. I think people are not so stupid when it comes to their feelings.

H. R.: If other artists work for something completely different from what you work for, can they be good artists?

F. H.: Yes, of course . . . it depends. They can be bad artists from my point of view. There are many artists whom I appreciate although they do things I don't like. The conversations between artists are always very strange. Artists have the strange habit of trying to shock other artists. For example, I fight for trees and against nuclear power, so another artist might say, "I hate trees, I love nuclear power, I don't have a single tree but I hate them and want to kill all trees". That happens many times in conver-

Hundertwasser's boat "Regentag"

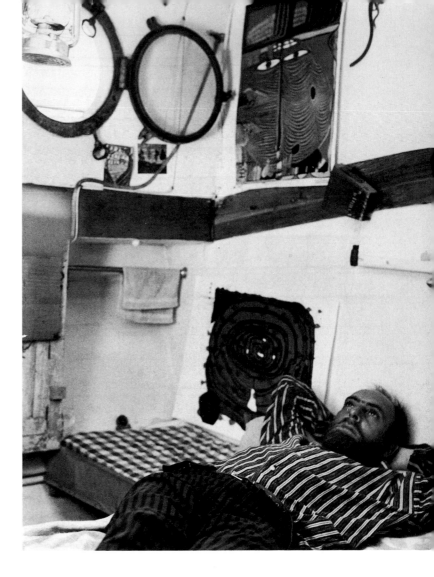

sation. I have the feeling that they want to provoke me even though that is not their real opinion, and generally I find it silly. Or others will say," I have such a strong distaste for Hundertwasser, so, if he is against nuclear energy, then I am for it!". That is not a joke, it really happens.

IMAGE

Certain musicians are melodists (Tschaikovsky), some are orchestrators (Mahler), others are polyphonists (Bach); similar characterizations hold true of visual artists. In such a reckoning Hundertwasser must be counted a poetic rationalist. Beneath his environmentalist's urgency, Hundertwasser's titles suggest something slightly flippant (though not Dada), as do his irreverent images. In general his proven consistency of optimistic outlook and determination distinguish him from Dadaism.

His nude demonstrations in Munich (1967) and Vienna (1968) (pp. 138–139) against the inhuman conditions of sterile modern architecture were heartfelt, if theatrical. These attention-getting events – while Hundertwasser himself remains proud of them – grated on observers who felt their shock value unnecessary.

KITSCH AND THE WINDOW RIGHTS OF TENANTS

Hundertwasser's search for beauty identifies two arts, and, in Tolstoy's words, one of these "has separated itself from the art of the rest of the people". In "What is Art?", Tolstoy salutes spontaneous recognition of the beautiful as the true aim of art:

"The assertion that art may be good art and at the same time incomprehensible to a great number of people, is extremely unjust, and its consequences are ruinous to art itself . . ."

"There is nothing is more common than to hear it said of reputed works of art that they are very good but very difficult to understand. We are quite used to such assertions, and yet to say that a work of art is good but incomprenensible to the majority of men, is the same as saying of some kind of

LOOSE FROM LOOS
A LAW PERMITTING INDIVIDUAL BUILDING ALTERATIONS
OR
ARCHITECTURE BOYCOTT MANIFESTO
(1968)

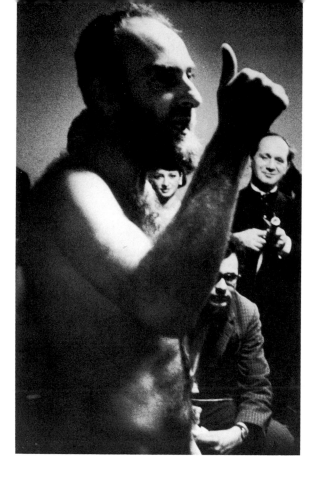

DEAR FRIENDS,
PEOPLE ASK ME WHY, AS A PAINTER, I MEDDLE IN MATTERS OF ARCHITECTURE. BUT AS A PAINTER I AM ALSO JUST A MAN. BEFORE YOU SIT DOWN ANYWHERE, YOU FIRST WIPE THE CHAIR IF IT IS DIRTY. SO IF I GO INTO DIRTY ARCHITECTURE, I MUST CLEAN THAT FIRST, TOO. AND THE DIRTIER THE ARCHITECTURE, THE MORE STRONGLY AND EFFECTIVELY ITS DIRT MUST BE COMBATTED.

I ENTER A HOUSE AS A FREE MAN. NOT AS A SLAVE. ONLY THEN CAN I DO ANYTHING ELSE, SUCH AS PAINTING OR SAYING SOMETHING. THERE IS ANOTHER, VERY IMPORTANT REASON WHY I CHOOSE VIENNA TO ATTACK THIS EVIL BOX-PRISON MISCHIEF, NAMELY BECAUSE I AM AUSTRIAN. WHICH GIVES ME A MORAL OBLIGATION TO DO SO. FOR IT WAS FROM AUSTRIA THAT THIS ARCHITECTURAL CRIME WAS LAUNCHED INTO THE WORLD. IT IS THUS FROM AUSTRIA THAT REPARATIONS MUST COME.

THE AUSTRIAN ADOLF LOOS BROUGHT THIS ATROCITY INTO THE WORLD. IN 1908, CLEVERLY, WITH HIS MANIFESTO "ORNAMENT AND CRIME". NO DOUBT HE MEANT WELL. ADOLF HITLER MEANT WELL TOO. BUT ADOLF LOOS WAS INCAPABLE OF THINKING FIFTY YEARS AHEAD. THE WORLD WILL NEVER BE FREE OF THE DEVIL HE INVOKED.

IT IS THE DUTY OF MYSELF AND ALL OF US IN AUSTRIA TO BE THE FIRST TO CONFESS AND COMBAT THE CATASTROPHE UNLEASHED HERE SIXTY YEARS AGO. EXACTLY FIFTY YEARS LATER, IN 1958 IN SECKAU, I READ OUT MY "MOULD MANIFESTO AGAINST RATIONALISM IN ARCHITECTURE". I AM NOW NO LONGER ALONE. THERE ARE ARCHITECTS WHO HAVE TAKEN IT TO HEART. GERMANY HOLDS CONFERENCE UPON CONFERENCE OF ARCHITECTS WITH A CONSCIENCE, FOR WHOM THE RESPONSIBILITY FOR WHAT THEY ARE DOING IS A FEARFUL BURDEN. BUT THEY KNOW NO SOLUTION. I HAVE NEVERTHELESS SEEN SOME NEW BUILDINGS WHICH WERE NOT PRODUCED ON THE DRAWING BOARD. THAT'S GOOD. BUT IT IS FAR FROM BEING ENOUGH.

BACK TO LOOS. OF COURSE IT IS TRUE THAT STENCILLED ORNAMENTS WERE LIES. BUT THEY WERE NOT CRIMES. NOR DID THE REMOVAL OF ORNAMENT MAKE HOUSES ANY MORE RESPECTABLE. LOOS SHOULD HAVE REPLACED STERILE ORNA-MENT WITH LIVING GROWTH. BUT HE DID NOT. HE VALUED THE STRAIGHT LINE, THE IDENTICAL, THE SMOOTH. NOW WE HAVE THE SMOOTH. EVERYTHING SLIPS OFF SMOOTHNESS. EVEN GOD. FOR THE STRAIGHT LINE IS GODLESS. THE STRAIGHT LINE IS THE ONLY UNCREATIVE LINE. THE ONLY LINE WHICH DOES NOT CORRESPOND TO MAN AS THE IMAGE OF GOD. THE STRAIGHT LINE IS A TRUE TOOL OF THE DEVIL. WHOSOEVER USES IT IS AIDING THE DOWNFALL OF MANKIND. "LA LIGNE DROITE CONDUIT A LA PERTE DE L'HUMANITÉ."

WHAT WILL THIS DOWNFALL BE LIKE? WE HAVE ALREADY HAD A PRELIMINARY

138   Nude demonstration for "The Right to a Third Skin" with Rainer and Fuchs, Munich, 1967

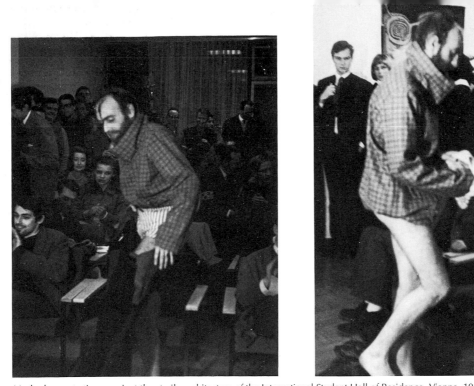

Nude demonstration against the sterile architecture of the International Student Hall of Residence, Vienna, 1968

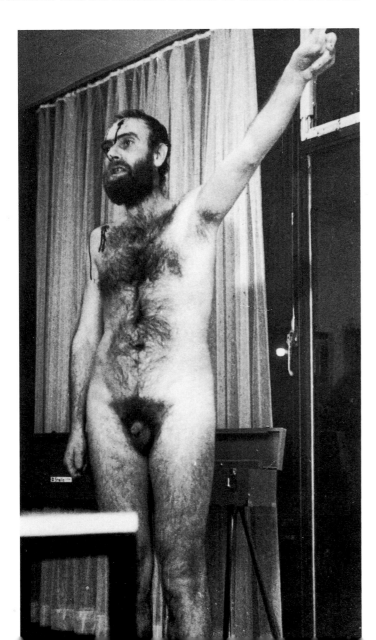

TASTE OF IT: TEN TO TWENTY PSYCHIATRISTS IN EVERY APARTMENT BLOCK IN NEW YORK. OVERFLOWING CLINICS, WHERE THE INSANE CANNOT GET WELL BECAUSE THE CLINICS ARE ALSO BUILT IN THE STYLE OF LOOS. THE DISEASES OF PEOPLE INTERNED IN STERILE ROW HOUSING FLOURISH IN THE DEADLY MONOTONY. RASHES, ULCERS, CANCERS AND STRANGE MANNERS OF DEATH ALL APPEAR. RECOVERY IN SUCH BUILDINGS IS IMPOSSIBLE. DESPITE PYSCHIATRY AND HEALTH INSURANCE. THERE ARE INCREASING NUMBERS OF SUICIDES IN THE SATELLITE TOWNS. AND COUNTLESS SUICIDE ATTEMPTS. THESE ARE WOMEN WHO CANNOT GET OUT DURING THE DAY LIKE THE MEN. WE COULD SPEND HOURS LISTING THE MISERIES WHICH BEGAN WITH LOOS. THE NIHILISM OF THE INTERNED EXPRESSES ITSELF THROUGH A DECLINE IN THE DESIRE TO WORK, A DECLINE IN PRODUCTION, AS PSYCHIATRISTS AND STATICIANS CAN SURELY CONFIRM. FOR UNHAPPINESS, TOO, CAN BE QUANTIFIED IN FIGURES AND MONEY. AND THUS THE DAMAGE CAUSED BY RATIONAL BUILDING METHODS EXCEEDS SEVERAL TIMES OVER ANY APPARENT SAVINGS MADE. THIS SUPPLIES THE PROOF THAT RATIONAL BUILDINGS TURN CRIMINAL WHEN LEFT AS THEY ARE. I AM NOT AGAINST SERIAL PRODUCTION AS SUCH. FOR THE PRESENT, UNFORTUNATELY, WE STILL NEED IT. BUT TO LEAVE SERIALLY-PRODUCED PRODUCTS IN THE STATE IN WHICH THEY REACH US IS AN INDICATION OF PERSONAL BONDAGE, PROOF THAT ONE IS A SLAVE.

HELP ANNUL THE CRIMINAL LAWS SUPPRESSING CREATIVE BUILDING FREEDOM! PEOPLE DO NOT YET EVEN KNOW THEY HAVE A RIGHT TO DESIGN THEIR OWN CLOTHING, THEIR OWN HOUSING, BOTH INSIDE AND OUT. A SINGLE ARCHITECT OR CUSTOMER CANNOT TAKE RESPONSIBILITY FOR ENTIRE APARTMENT BLOCKS, NOR EVEN FOR A SINGLE HOUSE IN WHICH SEVERAL FAMILIES ARE TO LIVE. THIS RESPONSIBILITY MUST BE CONCEDED TO EACH INDIVIDUAL RESIDENT, WHETHER HE BE AN ARCHITECT OR NOT. ALL RESTRICTIONS IMPOSED BY BUILDING INSPECTION AUTHORITIES, LEASES ETC., WHICH FORBID OR PLACE RESTRAINTS ON INDIVIDUAL HOME IMPROVEMENTS, MUST BE LIFTED. INDEED, IT IS THE DUTY OF THE STATE TO PROVIDE FINANCIAL ASSISTANCE AND SUPPORT TO EVERY CITIZEN WISHING TO UNDERTAKE INDIVIDUAL ALTERATIONS WHETHER TO OUTSIDE WALLS OR INDOORS. MAN HAS A PARTICULAR CLAIM TO HIS ARCHITECTURAL OUTER SKIN. WITH ONE CONDITION: NEITHER THE NEIGHBOURS OF THOSE IMPLEMENTING MODIFICATIONS NOR THE STABILITY OF THE HOUSE MAY SUFFER AS A RESULT. BUT THAT IS WHY WE HAVE TECHNICAL EXPERTS WHO CAN CALCULATE EVERYTHING SO NICELY.

TENANTS AS WELL AS OWNERS MUST HAVE THE OPTION OF MAKING HOME IMPROVEMENTS. ONLY WHERE THE SUBSEQUENT TENANT DOES NOT ACCEPT SUCH ALTERATIONS SHOULD THE APARTMENT BE RETURNED TO ITS ORIGINAL STATE. BUT IT CAN BE ASSUMED WITH 90% CERTAINTY THAT INDIVIDUAL IMPROVEMENTS WILL BE HIGHLY WELCOME TO THE NEXT TENANT, SINCE THEIR AIM WILL HAVE BEEN TO MAKE AN APARTMENT MORE HUMANE. IF SUCH A LAW ON INDIVIDUAL BUILDING ALTERATIONS IS NOT PASSED, THE PRISON PSYCHOSIS OF INTERNED RESIDENTS WILL CONTINUE TO WORSEN UNTIL IT REACHES A TERRIBLE END. THERE ARE ONLY TWO OPTIONS: EITHER ABSOLUTE SLAVERY OR REBELLION AGAINST THE RESTRICTIONS ON PERSONAL FREEDOM.

food that it is very good but most people can't eat it."

Naturally a response to this sort of argument is usually rebutted by positing informed discrimination: a taste refined through experience and comparison, the taste of the connoisseur. Tolstoy responded to the mythology that presently incomprehensible art will be understood when everybody is as well educated as the people of the upper classes who produce it. But this assertion is evidently untrue, for we know that the majority of the works of art which delighted people of the upper classes when they were produced never were afterwards either understood or valued by the great masses of mankind, but have remained what they were at first, a mere pastime for the rich people of their time, for whom alone they ever were of any importance.

The one necessary and unanticipated amendment to the above is that Modernism has become our esoterica. Searching for beauty instead of historical Modernism's ethical and intellectual appeal, Hundertwasser skirts the insidious politics of "kitsch", with its tremendous personal and societal risks. Shallow and pretentious, kitsch is gaudy trash calculated for popular appeal. Kitsch is more like mass-culture, like television than "camp", which is very different and involves the collusion of the cynical spectator.

H. R.: Do you think rationalism in modern architecture and art has supplanted the romance and deep meanings of life?

F. H.: Yes. Something is very sad, for what is the country of Romance and the Romantic? Which country in the world is the centre of Romance? It was Germany.

It is strange that it was Germany which destroyed the Romantic age in architecture and in all fields so decisively. This destruction of Romance started in Germany and went to America. The Bauhaus was one of the major factors in the destruction of Romance in the world. Perhaps the Germans got sick of Romance, and then they overdid

it and created the Bauhaus that left nothing of Romance. That is why Neuschwanstein, a Romantic castle from a Romantic time, is such a success now. Because everything else has been destroyed. So of course people go to Neuschwanstein. The feeling for Romance is in everybody, especially the Austrians. Romance is maybe related to kitsch but it does not matter. The absence of Romance makes our life unbearable, but it is more striking if you say kitsch. People do not consider the longing for Romance as kitsch. It is the negative dogmatic intellectuals who want to make the people feel guilty for something which is natural and positive. This small group of theorists have turned values upside down and consider the people as guinea pigs to be indoctrinated for their absurd educational experiments.

Hundertwasser was largely insulated from disgruntled critics at this time. He spent 1969–1971 living and working aboard "Regentag" in the lagoon of Venice. This isolation, within sight of land, vexed his antagonists, as he was beyond the flurry of their attacks. He used his watery vantage point overlooking an ideal city to wrestle with the seeming incompatibility of human beings with the high-rise environment of cities. That an artist should engage in such extra-artistic contemplation has never seriously been challenged in some circles. Modernist critics find Jacques Louis David's glory enhanced by his politics and some portion of Picasso's vast public found solace in his Communism, just as earlier painters were exponents of Catholicism. To his credit, Hundertwasser began to sense that the very environment was a victim in need of championship. Undoubtedly correct, his insight did little to convert critics who would have lavished praise on him had he embraced a political, not an environmental, cause. (Time will undoubtedly settle that score in his favour, regardless of his final critical position.) On his boat, Hundertwasser struggled with a concept that eventually was given form in his notion of tenants' "Rights to Windows".

The tenant was to have the right to alter the environment within which he or she lived, to change the apartment and the exterior of the buildings as far as his or her arms could reach from the window. To produce a visual equivalent for this notion (and to make it more widely known), Hundertwasser planned a huge serigraph edition.

10,000 – PRINT EDITION

In the event, Hundertwasser created his graphic work *Good Morning City – Bleeding Town* (p. 125) in two enormous editions of eight thousand, then two thousand. Both editions were based on an image that first appeared in his 1952 painting *Bleeding Houses* (p. 42). The second edition of *Good Morning City – Bleeding Town* introduced into graphic printing new techniques such as the use of phosphorescent and fluorescent colours, as well as metal embossing. For serigraphy, this innovation represented a new surface effect. The technical wizardry involved in printing *Good Morning City* went off more or less faultlessly. The critics were scandalized. The vast editions were thought purely mercenary; Hundertwasser, however, insisted that the size of the run was necessary to keep the price down. The two editions were clearly distinguishable, but the numbering revealed the total of prints actually produced.

Hundertwasser's choice of serigraphic technique for this image had a social implication: the prints could be sold inexpensively to those who could not afford paintings or woodblock prints. Silk-screening makes possible almost infinite mechanical reproduction without the least deterioration of the image. The print's complete run took almost two years; the first print and the last were of the same sharpness and quality. A price of 100 Deutschmarks was set, which made the work available to all. Yet even that gesture toward the individual print collector, remarkable as it was, only showed the way toward something unique in the annals of the graphic arts.

In 1984 Hundertwasser issued a print in an edition of 10,002, every sheet of which was different from every other.

H. R.: How is every print of *10,002 nights Homo Humus come va how do you do* different?

F. H.: I use different plates on top of one another. It is a printing process which is much more complicated than the printing process of, let's say, Rembrandt. Because I started when I was young with 3 to 5 different colours, one on top of the other, now I end up with something like twenty or thirty, till I have forty different colours. I have one design in yellow and on top of that a design in blue and on top of that another in black and so on. When I start with the design in yellow I make variations of this yellow. The print is first designed in yellow and in blue, green and black and gold and silver.

For example, the first plate could record seven different colours (and there are ten more plates). The second plate can carry ten other colours, so there are already 70 different prints (10 × 7). The third colour impression – with five new colours in combination with each of the earlier ones – can add up to 350 different prints. The fourth plate may use ten different colours and, when each of the 350 is given a different colour, the number goes from 350 to 3500. The fifth plate of ten more colours provides 35,000 variations, and so on.

But the art is to choose from these 100,000 different prints, because 100,000 is humanly impossible to oversee and to design. Before printing – this is a tedious mental job, choosing a selection of the 100,000 different possible variations – I choose only an edition of 10,000 and eliminate 90,000. I can only do this with the experience I have gained in printing, knowing that this colour is not good against that colour but that colour and that colour would harmonize.

It is a very intensive task, imagining paintings instead of painting, painting the variations in your head. It is just like a master chess-player: he must have ten moves in advance in his head before the next move. I

Hundertwasser's work on transparent film
From the brochure issued by Die Galerie publishers, Offenbach am Main, 1984

4 lithographic colours, light blue, pink, yellow and blue, form the colour basis for subsequent screen printing and metallic stamping.

Seen here are Hundertwasser's four drawings on transparent film I - IV for photo-litho printing. These four lithographic colours do not appear in the colour key, but are recorded above left as colour-separation codes.

I Airbrush basis of light blue (round dot)
II Airbrush basis of pink (round dot)
III Red colour separation after watercolour œuvre 193, *Kopf mit weißen Fenstern* - Head with White Windows, with new drawing by Hundertwasser. This drawing was printed in yellow (colour-separation code "FZ, Fotozinko", reversed)
IV Blue colour separation after watercolour œuvre 193, *Kopf mit weißen Fenstern* - Head with White Windows, with new drawing by Hundertwasser, printed in blue (colour-separation code "FZ")
The litho composite print appears above right.

Hundertwasser's transparent-film drawings for screen printing and metallic-foil stamping, numbered 1 - 8, correspond to the numbers of the colour key. They were each printed in up to 10 colours in colour-key colours A - J. Numbers 1, 2 and 8 correspond to metallic stamping, numbers 3, 4, 5, 6 and 7 to screen printing.

With the aid of the colour key, Hundertwasser was able to select 10,002 from the 100,000 possible colour combinations (10 x 10 x 5 x 2 x 5 x 2 x 2 x 5 = 100,000).

860 *10002 Nights Homo Humus Come Va How Do You Do,* Spinea, 1982/83
Mixed media: zinc photo lithograph in 4 colours, serigraph in 7 colours, metal embossing in 10 colours, 69.5 x 50 cm (64 x 43)
Total edition 10254, 10002 signed and numbered. CCLII proofs signed and numbered. Coordinator Alberto della Vecchia. Printed by Quattrifoglio (lithos), Claudio Barbato (serigraphs) and Giuseppe Barbato (metal embossing), Spinea, Venice 1984

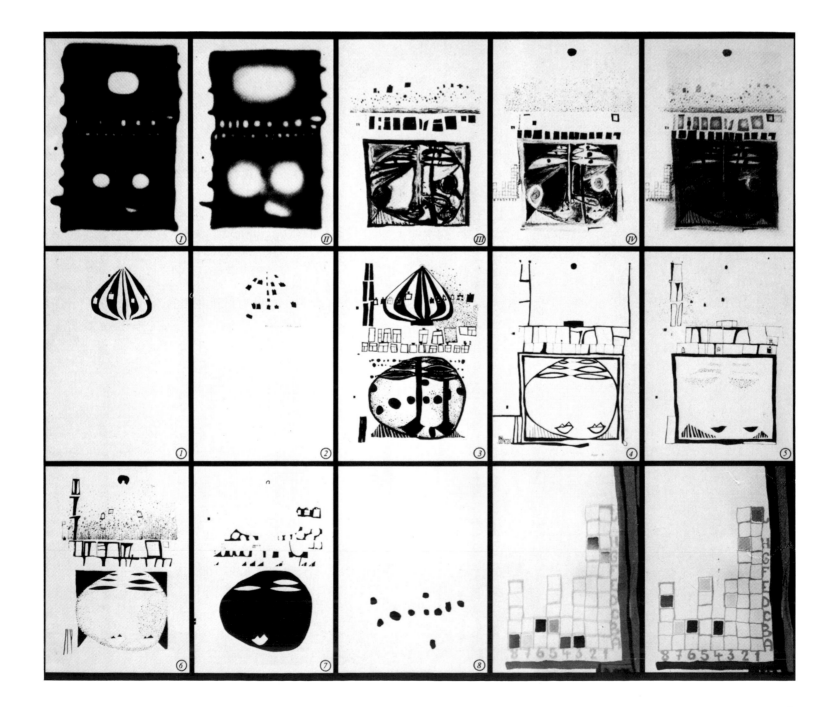

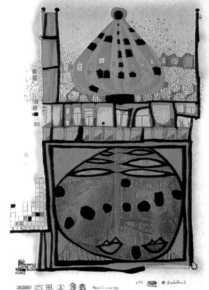

must imagine every possibility, how it would look if printed, and I have it in my mind, and I say "this combination can be printed", and then I go on. So I paint 10,000 paintings in my mind, it is crazy. That is why I am quite sure that nobody could imitate me. Making 10,000 paintings only in your mind and then giving orders to the printer to do it is quite something. It is an achievement.

ART AND RELIGION

H. R.: Why do people become painters?
F. H.: For different reasons. True painters because they want to be priests, because it is a kind of religious activity. If you want to do something worthwhile in this existence, what shall you do? If you don't want to live just for money or profit, if you want to help people, you can become a doctor helping sick people. Being a priest is difficult because the dogmas of many religions have been superseded and don't apply anymore. So it is evident that being an artist gives you an answer; in fact, being an artist does not mean that you must paint. You should paint, of course, but it is a way of living. It is a way to see the world and to recognise the beauty around you and to add beauty. Strangely, the painter is a different breed from other people. If you like him, if you don't like him, his living style, his environment at home, his house, his room, his garden – all is very different from what you see around you.
An artist is more like a priest than a priest, because if you visit a priest at home you will find his environment is just the same as that of any bourgeois. He has a television like all the others; the chairs are the same, and there is nothing – except the Bible – that will tell you there is any difference in the style of the room of a priest or a middle-class worker or a doctor. It is just a clean normal room.
H. R.: If art is a religious activity, and if artists live a special exemplary life as a model to the community, are artists involved in doing good?
F. H.: Unfortunately not. That is the prob-

lem. Some say the world today is ugly and perverse, so art should be ugly and perverse, because it is a mirror of society, and the artist just depicts what he sees. But I say this is rubbish. Because what do artists achieve in that way? They achieve only the disgust of the true spectator of art. He doesn't get a clue because this kind of artist does not show any solution, no way out. He just reflects and exaggerates, amplifies the ugliness and the perversity but does not propose a solution. I think we must fight; if something is horrible we must make it better. If it is ugly we must make it beautiful. If something is perverse we must try to untangle that perversity; if something is complicated you have to try to even it out.

One of Hundertwasser's strongest and most enduring images, *Irinaland Over the Balkans* (pp. 132–133), printed in 1969 was inspired by the Bulgarian actress Irina Maleeva. (The composition recapitulates a painting of 1966 and re-appeared in *Green Power* (p. 130), 1972.) Hundertwasser's print taxed his printers to the utmost. An astonishing thirty-one colours had to register perfectly, and of this number two were phosphorescent (so "Irina's" eyes and mouth shine alluringly), while five metal imprints captured the glitter of the original painting, which had been done on aluminium foil covered with layers of paper. As Hundertwasser heavily revises graphic conceptions derived from his paintings – indeed he re-conceives them – this new work did not merely translate the "Irinaland" image to a print. The silkscreen was a new work, full of marvellous graphic devices. Each version of the theme became stronger, more compositionally focussed; alterations made the image more forceful.

Irinaland Over the Balkans bespeaks love of a woman, the land and art. While modern art entrenched itself in an examination of the "stuff" of which art is created, no noticeable slackening in artists' sensual appetites was noticed. The sexes draw together with the usual magnetic collision; hearty meals appear when artists sell works; wardrobes are updated on the basis of income from art. Yet, without the least hypocrisy one must conclude that these artists have left the public a legacy of art without passion. Artists have become scientists exploring art's assumptions. But that does not mean we ought to scorn the artist who has the courage to declare his emotions, or indeed his specific affections for life, or even a woman. Thus we understand how large emotional and artistic demands can be placed at the disposal of one declarative work. For it the artist mustered deep resources. Through and above the landscape floats "Irina's" face. Her omnipresence recreates our longing for someone who compels memory – even when they are with us: infatuation. The idea of the woman weaves itself into the countryside. When our time is inventoried to reckon those works that speak to the heart, this will be among them. More than a popular success, *Irinaland Over the Balkans* finalizes much of Hundertwasser's previous experimentation. It reaches a new frontier of formal and technical achievement, while distilling an emotional essence. It is a benchmark accomplishment for him.

Hundertwasser has often been accused of a theatricalization of personality for the purposes of publicity. But it is clear that Hundertwasser never betrays his own beliefs about nature, nor does he subvert his art, but modestly, and with the utmost laborious care, constructs his pictures in humble and solitary settings, away from people and certainly from publicity. The problem arises when, as a social creature, his need for an urgent hearing has led him to seek immediate visibility. But such activities have never influenced or set limits upon his art.

Ill. p. 146: Hundertwasser walking through the streets of Vienna with his picture 672 *Blaue Kappen – Guten Tag Herr Kampmann – Blue Caps – Good Day Herr Kampmann,* January 1968

THEORY AND REALITY

Stowasser STOWASSER
Fritz FRITZ
Friedrich FRIEDRICH
Friederich FRIEDERICH
Friedereich FRIEDEREICH
Friedenreich FRIEDENREICH
Hundertwasser HUNDERTWASSER
Friedensreich FRIEDENSREICH
Regentag REGENTAG
Dunkelbunt DUNKELBUNT

724 *Tree Tenants Do Not Sleep – Tree Tenants Wide Awake*, Rakino Island, September 1973, New York, October 1973
Mixed media: oil, egg tempera and silver foil on primed masonite board, 38 x 38 cm

696A *Yellow Last Will – Testament in Gelb,* Giudecca, 1971
Serigraph in 22 colours and gold embossing on silver foil on cardboard,
52.4 x 74.5 cm
Signed edition of 475. Printed by Dietz Offizin, Lengmoos. Published by
Schünemann Verlag, Bremen

Between 1970 and 1972 Hundertwasser worked with Peter Schamoni on the much-lauded film *Hundertwassers Regentag, (Hundertwasser's Rainy Day);* the film, subsequently the title for a book (by painter and photographer Manfred Bockelmann), represents another collaboration since the murals with René Brô. Hundertwasser produced about a dozen prints and one of the Olympic Posters – for the blood-spattered 1972 Munich Games. He had just finished his painting *Testament im Mohn,* 1970, and decided that this image could be more fully explored in a print which became *Yellow Last Will* (above).

His next print resumed the development of a theme that had occupied him intermittently since his youth. In March 1953, Hundertwasser painted a watercolour in preparation for the linocut *Three High Houses* (HW 155). This and another seven watercolours were cut into 240 pieces and somewhat repainted in Paris in order to be included in the deluxe version of *La Lune en rôdage,* published in Basle by Carl László in 1959. Twenty-six of the pieces did not find their way into that edition but were subsequently overpainted at La Picaudière, where he further integrated the elements, finishing the work between January and May in 1963 as *Chateau des*

survivants de László mit Silberstrasse, a watercolour with collage.

A blue-grey paper and sixteen colours were selected for *Street for Survivors, Strasse der Überlebenden, La route de survivants* (p. 153); three metal imprints and a phosphorescent glaze were employed to bring the work to life. Hundertwasser retained a vision of the ideal combination of human habitation and natural surroundings; throughout his life he has worked to create this balance. In his youth he visualized buildings as violent destroyers of habitat and human scale. His hope for the harmony of man and nature took the form of imagined architecture, and, when he could build them, real structures.

In a delightful watercolour dating from the summer of 1951, *Skyscraper and Village Church* (p. 151), a skyscraper of an uncommon Hundertwasser type features with trees on top. Onion dome and bulbous trees occupy the same place on the two buildings. It is a secular and a liturgical paradise, inseparable. He tried once again to give form to his sense of human balance in the world in *The Houses Are Hanging Underneath the Meadows* (pp. 164/165).

Hundertwasser's painting expounded

726 *Conservation Week,* New Zealand, August 1974
Mixed media: oil, egg tempera and watercolour on wood, 73 x 50 cm

Ill. p. 151: 125 *Hochhaus auf Stelzen nach Le Corbusier und Dorfkirche –*
Skyscraper on Stilts in the Style of Le Corbusier and Village Church,
Aflenz, Steiermark, August 1951
Watercolour on wrapping paper primed with chalk, later mounted on canvas, 63 x 45 cm

Right: 553A *Straße der Überlebenden – Street for Survivors,* 1967
Serigraph in 16 colours with metal embossing in 3 colours and 1 phosphorescent colour on grey paper, 67 x 50 cm (63 x 42)
Total edition of 3000, 300 copies ending with the number 2 are signed.
Printed by Dietz Offizin, Lengmoos. Published by Ars Viva, Zurich

two possibilities for buildings based on his formula that "the horizontal belongs to nature, the vertical to man", and he pictured small cars next to the houses – admitting personal mobility within a sane environment. On the left a pyramid or ziggurat sports planted terraces; the building on the right rises on pylons or stilts, with each floor, and the roof, turned into a meadow. Both ideas were feasible, given modern ferro-concrete construction. (If humans invested a landscape with structures such as these an aerial photograph would show unaltered terrain, every horizontal surface having been replanted, however high the vertical buildings. To return territory to nature, plants cannot be displaced by rampant human growth.) These two hypothetical buildings appeared in a print (699 A) based on *The Houses Are Hanging Underneath the Meadows.* And subsequently Hundertwasser created models of the structures. In 1983 a 5-metre-high concrete model was built for the International Garden Show (p. 167) in Munich.

Later Hundertwasser was able to create a benign environment in *Kindertagesstätte,* Frankfurt (pp. 48–49), in which two ramps gently slope like lawns on a hillside, but are in fact the roofs of a building complex. Presaged by his paintings and prints, such structures relied on concepts he had worked on years before.

In 1972 he issued his manifesto: "Your Right to Windows – Your Duty to Trees". It was a busy time. Hundertwasser sailed "Regentag" around Italy to Elba, and he exhibited the model for a building with forested roofs and individually structured façades. Also 1972 saw the beginning of Hundertwasser's friendship with Joram Harel, who has represented the artist since then. When success seemed assured, and his ideas were actually gaining serious support in many corners, the one firm tie to his past and heritage was severed. His mother died.

In 1973, after eleven years of collaboration, Hundertwasser produced the first European works made by Japanese master wood-block cutters and printers, his portfolio *Nana Hyaku Mizu.* At about the same time, he created the *Franz-Josef-Hospital* (p. 134), which relies on a uniformly coherent descriptive perspective. The space proceeds from the lower edge (a street) upward and backward into the distance. Behind the street, two large facial images like billboards rear up – one bordered in red, one in yellow. Using pure colour, the sidewalk's blue enfolds the painting, becoming the sky's deep azure – the last legible part of the painting.

In 1973 Hundertwasser travelled to the Cape Verde Islands and New Zealand where he was having an exhibition of his paintings. At the Bay of Islands, at the far north of New Zealand's North Island, Hundertwasser bought a dairy farm, its green hills used for grazing cattle. On the farm's

Bottle and Grass Roof House, New Zealand, March 1982

Grass-roofed house built by Ivan Tarulevic in the Bay of Plenty, New Zealand, ca. 1975

1100-plus acres (455 hectares), Hundertwasser planted 60,000 diverse trees from throughout the world, purchased from local nurseries. With his neighbours Hundertwasser created his vision of a Garden of Eden, the opposite of monoculture.

He lives in the farmhouse that was on the land. Hundertwasser painted the roof sky blue, and he painted a vivid design on the front window. He planted thousands of trees on the road to the house, which will eventually become a shaded avenue. A nearby stream was turned into a pond where his "livestock" of ducks and geese gather.

Adjacent to his own house is a guest

156

773 Waikato Island and Steamer of Rio – Ile Waikato et vapeur à Rio – Waikato Insel und Dampfer in Rio, Nandi, Fiji, October 1976, Tahiti, August 1976, Rio de Janeiro, August 1977, completed in Vienna, November 1977
Mixed media: watercolour on primed paper, mounted on canvas with polyvinyl and cellulose, 53 x 43.2 cm

house and studio with glass bottle-embedded walls of cement and sawdust (Hundertwasser uses bottles from a local pub). A soil-covered roof, planted with the same kikuyu grass that blankets the nearby hills, merges the house into the landscape (more gently than Frank Lloyd Wright's "prairie" architecture ever managed). The roof also features solar collectors that power the radio, record player, and interior lighting, while also providing hot water. A humus toilet and a rainwater collector help recycle every aspect of human habitation back into the land. There is a functioning water purification system of plants for the kitchen and bath. To guard the two houses Hundertwasser enlists the help of numerous garden dwarfs! In contrast to this low-tech help, Hundertwasser's telephone and a fax machine wait in his sitting room beside the tapes of many different kinds of music. These energy-efficient tools allow him to stay in touch with the world.

On a muddy tidal creek, Hundertwasser keeps a dinghy, which at high tide can navigate to the harbour at Opua, and the "Regentag", now moored there.

TREE TENANTS

In 1974, returning to New Zealand, Hundertwasser aimed to apply for a permanent residency permit. Once again in Europe, as part of the "Triennale di Milano", Hundertwasser conceived and executed one of his most evocative ideas when he planted twelve "Tree Tenants" through windows on the Via Manzoni (p. 171). Where concrete and asphalt displace the run-off water in our cities, the tree tenants help rectify the situation and return greenery to the city. They cleanse the air and purify water, and that is their "rent", which is of real value –

compared to the fluctuating value of currency paid by human tenants. Subsequent tree tenants have been placed in Austria and Germany.

Almost immediately the tree tenants enlisted in Hundertwasser's repertoire of recurring images. The tree tenants appeared as personages in his two-dimensional art when Hundertwasser composed a picture in September 1973, on Rakino Island, New Zealand. In October he visited New York on the occasion of his show at the newly-opened Aberbach Gallery, and while there he continued work on what became *Tree Tenants Do Not Sleep, Tree Tenants Wide Awake* (p. 148); he continued on board the "Regentag". Finally at La Goulette, Tunis, in December 1973, Hundertwasser finished and signed the painting. Done in a square format, *Tree Tenants Do Not Sleep, Tree Tenants Wide Awake* is stri-

737 Box Grass Red Fog Gallery, Rakino Island, April 1974, New Zealand, April 1974, Vienna, May 1974
Mixed media: watercolour, egg tempera, oil and tinfoil glued with UHU onto Schöllerhammer cardboard primed with polyvinyl, 44 x 62 cm

Ill. pp. 154/155: 738 Grass for Those Who Cry, Malta, Crete, Paphos, Tel Aviv and Vienna, 1974
Mixed media: watercolour, egg tempera, oil and tinfoil glued with UHU onto drawing paper primed with chalk and polyvinyl, mounted on canvas with wallpaper glue and polyvinyl, 65 x 92 cm

Kaurinui Valley, 1978

Kaurinui Valley, 1978

Kaurinui Valley, 1978

With rushes for water purification, ca. 1970

NEW ZEALAND

Kaurinui Valley, 1978

Waikiho Peninsula, ca. 1980

Kaurinui Valley, 1978

ated horizontally. At the right edge is a face: the wide-awake tree tenant looking out, the unsleeping conscience. The forces of ecology do not stop merely because we are not thinking about them.

POSTAGE STAMPS

Paul and Jeanne Facchetti's Paris gallery held an extensive show of Hundertwasser's works after a hiatus of eighteen years. In May and June 1974 the exhibition of his juvenilia and graphic works, "Stowasser 1943 – Hundertwasser 1974", appeared at the Graphische Sammlung Albertina, Vienna (It also occasioned the first catalogue of Hundertwasser's juvenilia). He painted the "Conservation Week" poster for New Zealand (p. 150), and revived his childhood hobby of stamp collecting when he designed the "Spiraltree" stamp for Austria.

"I loved postage stamps long before I became a painter. It was a great joy to collect these little coloured pictures, to separate them from the letters which came from far away . . . I corresponded extensively with stamp collector friends the world over, in far and exotic countries such as India, the U.S.A., Switzerland, Morocco, Ireland and many others. For a long time I was unhappy and unsatisfied with myself because the pictures I painted could not stand the comparison with postage stamps . . . The stamps and those who made them were for me the real ambassadors of this earth, the real representatives of the world parliament. The small pictures I can carry with me in small books. They are like venerable objects, like icons." (Hundertwasser in "Drei Briefmarken für Senegal", printed in "Schöne Wege", Munich 1983)

Some thought his four-Schilling postage stamp neither a stamp nor art. "Somebody in Vienna sent a picture postcard with my stamp on it, but it came back 'Refused' by a German postmaster who filled in the reason: 'This is not a postage stamp'. I'm sure he doesn't think it's art either." ("Art News", October 1976) Such an observation from an Austrian postmaster would be less likely, where a tradition of gorgeous stamps has long existed. In 1979 the Austrian State Printing Office ran off three Hundertwasser-designed stamps for the Republic of Senegal (p. 162). These stamps were greeted with the most sincere appreciation by Senegal's poet President, Senghor. (Politician and noted poet, Senghor is perhaps best known as an exponent of Négritude, which he envisioned as the aggregate quality of African culture, which could erase class strife in Africa.)

"In our country, which has the ambition to be a 'Black Greece', we have introduced art everywhere: into our official life, into our festivities, into our religious ceremonies, into our public monuments, and even into our stadiums . . . Now, to underline his friendship for our country, Hundertwasser offered to create postage stamps as original works of art. No further mention is necessary that Hundertwasser is one of the greatest painters of the world

Hundertwasser's visit to Léopold Sédar Senghor, the President of the Republic of Senegal, July 1978

756 *Antipode Island*, New Zealand, October-December 1975
Mixed media: watercolour, egg tempera, polyvinyl, oil, lacquer, tinfoil,
UHU on white primed paper, glued to hardboard with polyvinyl,
48 x 50 cm

today." (Léopold Sédar Senghor, in "Austria Presents Hundertwasser to the Continents," London 1973; 1983)

At the same time Hundertwasser also produced (through the Austrian State Printing Office) a stamp for the Cape Verde Islands – an image recalling his early steam ships. In his postage stamp, *Vapor*, millions discovered the romance of a haunting image and felt what the ocean meant to Hundertwasser. In addition to Austria, Senegal, and the Cape Verde Islands, Hundertwasser designed six stamps for the United Nations (pp. 232/233). Uniquely among modern artists, Hundertwasser has worked on every size of object, creations as big as buildings and as small as postage stamps. Deciding which images fit which pieces is a matter of scale and viewing distance. Large objects can usually be viewed from far away; paintings are normally scanned at the distance of some metres; stamps require a magnifying glass to see the details. Hundertwasser recognises practical considerations in his choice of scale.

F. H.: It would be impossible to fill a building with fine details like a stamp. Every size has its own law.
H. R.: When you look at a stamp and a building from the proper distance, do they share the same degree of detail?
F. H.: Yes. If a huge building is reduced to stamp size it shows exactly the same detail.
H. R.: Is this unity of design typical of all artists?
F. H.: I don't think so. I don't want to flatter myself but I think that I have the possibility to do that and others don't have it – maybe Le Corbusier in modern times; he made buildings and he was a painter. But his paintings did not match his architecture at all. If you see Corbusier's paintings you could not have a clue as to his capacity as an architect.

Hundertwasser carried a painting back to Vienna that he had begun on Rakino Island during April 1974, and completed it in May 1975: *Box Grass Red Fog Gallery* (p. 156). Its basic composition features a series of horizontal stripes in fibonacci ratios, done freehand, ungeometrically. Above this pattern a series of black and white striated stalactites descend into the painting's upper third. Through the centre float "billboards", rising from cubic architectural shapes in the background. The structures, labelled from left to right "2, 1, 4, 5, 3", mock the interchangeability of modern buildings. The red stripes are not just a pattern. Thickening near the bottom of the work, this red represents the fog mentioned in the title. Perhaps this is the sinister red glow in the sky above a modern city at night, the reflected light that comes from millions of signs and street lights.

Ill. pp. 164/165: 699 *Die Wohnungen hängen unter den Wiesen – The
Houses Are Hanging Underneath the Meadows,* Venice, summer 1970,
Hahnsäge, winter 1970–71
Mixed media: egg tempera, oil on Schöllerhammer cardboard primed with
quartz sand and polyvinyl, with 1 mm aluminium inlay, 44 x 63 cm

161

REPUBLIK

ÖSTERREICH

SENEGAL 1 F

SENEGAL

SENEGAL

THE STAMP IS AN IMPORTANT OBJECT. ALTHOUGH VERY SMALL IN FORMAT, IT CARRIES A MESSAGE. STAMPS ARE A MEASURE OF THE CULTURE OF A COUNTRY. THIS TINY, RECTANGULAR PIECE OF PAPER LINKS THE HEARTS OF SENDER AND RECEIVER. IT IS A BRIDGE BETWEEN PEOPLES AND NATIONS. THE STAMP KNOWS NO BORDERS. IT REACHES US EVEN IN PRISONS, ASYLUMS AND HOSPITALS, AND WHEREVER WE MAY BE ON EARTH. STAMPS SHOULD BE AMBASSADORS OF ART AND LIFE AND NOT SIMPLY SOULLESS PROOFS OF POSTAGE PAID. THE STAMP MUST EXPERI-ENCE ITS DESTINY. THE STAMP MUST ONCE AGAIN FULFIL ITS PURPOSE, WHICH MEANS IT MUST SERVE ON LETTERS. A TRUE STAMP MUST FEEL THE TONGUE OF THE SENDER MOISTENING ITS GUM. A STAMP MUST BE STUCK ON A LETTER. A STAMP MUST EXPERIENCE THE DARK DEPTHS OF THE POST BOX. A STAMP MUST SUFFER FRANKING. A STAMP MUST SENSE THE HAND OF THE POSTMAN HANDING THE LETTER TO THE ADDRESSEE. A STAMP WHICH IS NOT MAILED ON A LETTER IS NO STAMP. IT HAS NEVER LIVED, IT IS A SHAM. IT IS LIKE A FISH WHO HAS NEVER SWUM, A BIRD WHO HAS NEVER FLOWN. A STAMP MUST HAVE LIVED AS A STAMP. THE STAMP IS THE ONLY WORK OF ART THAT EVERYONE CAN OWN, YOUNG AND OLD, RICH AND POOR, HEALTHY AND SICK, EDUCATED AND IGNORANT, FREE OR ROBBED OF FREE-DOM. THIS PRECIOUS PIECE OF ART REACHES EVERYONE AS A GIFT FROM AFAR. A STAMP SHOULD BE A TESTIMONY TO CUL-TURE, BEAUTY AND THE CREATIVE SPIRIT OF MANKIND.
HUNDERTWASSER   14 FEBRUARY 1990

729 *Spirale – Spiral,* stamp design I, Tunis, March 1974 Watercolour and opaque ink on primed drawing paper, 29.5 x 22.5 cm

784 *Schwarze Bäume – Arbres noires – Black Trees,* stamp design III for Senegal, Paris, spring 1978 Watercolour on primed drawing paper, 29.5 x 22.5 cm

785 *Regenbogenfenster – Fenêtres arc-en-ciel – Rainbow Windows,* stamp design IV for Senegal, Paris, spring 1978 Watercolour on primed drawing paper, 29.5 x 22.5 cm

782 *Kopf – Tête – Head,* stamp design I for Senegal, Paris, spring 1978

**YOUR WINDOW RIGHT -
YOUR TREE DUTY**

In the television series "Wünsch Dir was" on 27 February 1972, Hundertwasser presented and illustrated the principle of "Window right - Tree duty" by means of practical models. The programme was broadcast simultaneously in Austria, Germany and Switzerland. Three families were invited to spend a day in Düsseldorf, without radio or newspapers, while Hundertwasser redesigned the windows and façades of their houses in Vienna, Bülach and Essen, in record time in a race against the clock. That same evening the three dazed families were shown a film of the successful transformation of their homes. They refused to believe their eyes. "But we don't have the right to change the windows of our houses", they said. "If you've done so, then it's because you're a painter, and a painter can do anything he likes." The three families dismissed the whole affair as a painter's prank, without themselves wishing to exploit their window right.

Model of the "Hochwiesenhaus" ("Highrise Meadow House"), made out of moulded concrete with bonsai trees, mosaics, glass spheres and wooden windows for the IGA (International Garden Show) in Munich, 1983

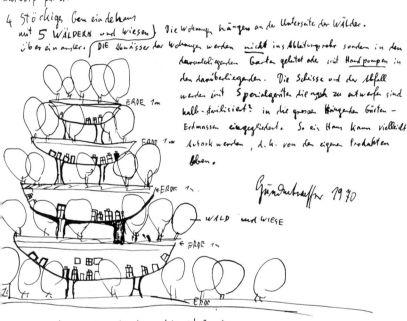

In his model of the Highrise Meadow House, Hundertwasser demonstrates that it is possible to have fields and trees even in the city centre, namely in a series of superimposed storeys. Such houses are cheaper than one might expect, and the main point is that people are happy.

Any soil produced from humus toilets can be deposited on roofs and used to a limited degree to grow food. Sewage can also be treated; waste water can be pumped up and allowed to run down, cleaned, in a spiral.

Cows are transported by lift to the upper storeys, where they eat grass. Apartments hang below the meadows like airship gondolas. The Hanging Houses of Babylon.

The Highrise Meadow House was built for the 1983 IGA international garden exhibition in Munich. Planning by architect Schwanzer, Vienna, engineer Ernst Pfister.

MANIFESTO
YOUR WINDOW RIGHT, YOUR TREE DUTY

THE WINDOW RIGHT
A RESIDENT MUST HAVE THE RIGHT TO LEAN OUT OF HIS WINDOW AND DESIGN EVERYTHING HIS ARM CAN REACH ON THE WALL OUTSIDE JUST AS IT SUITS HIM. IT WILL THUS BE VISIBLE FROM AFAR TO EVERYONE IN THE STREET THAT SOMEONE LIVES THERE.

SECKAU, 1958

WE ARE SUFFOCATING IN OUR CITIES FROM AIR POLLUTION AND LACK OF OXYGEN.
THE VEGETATION WHICH LETS US LIVE AND BREATHE IS BEING SYSTEMATICALLY DESTROYED.
OUR EXISTENCE IS LOSING ITS DIGNITY.
WE WALK PAST GREY, STERILE HOUSE FRONTS AND DO NOT REALISE THAT WE HAVE BEEN COMMITTED TO PRISON CELLS.
IF WE WISH TO SURVIVE, EVERY ONE OF US MUST ACT.
YOU YOURSELF MUST DESIGN YOUR ENVIRONMENT.
YOU CANNOT WAIT FOR THE AUTHORITIES AND FOR PERMISSION.
YOUR OUTSIDE WALLS BELONG TO YOU JUST AS MUCH AS YOUR CLOTHING AND THE INSIDE OF YOUR HOME.
ANY KIND OF INDIVIDUAL DESIGN IS BETTER THAN STERILE DEATH. IT IS YOUR RIGHT TO DESIGN YOUR WINDOWS AND, AS FAR AS YOUR ARM CAN REACH, YOUR OUTSIDE WALLS JUST AS IT SUITS YOU.
REGULATIONS WHICH FORBID OR PLACE RESTRAINTS ON THIS WINDOW RIGHT ARE TO BE IGNORED.
IT IS YOUR DUTY TO HELP VEGETATION TO ITS RIGHTS WITH ALL THE MEANS AVAILABLE TO YOU.
FREE NATURE MUST GROW WHEREVER SNOW AND RAIN FALL; WHAT IS WHITE IN WINTER MUST BE GREEN IN SUMMER.
EVERYTHING HORIZONTAL UNDER THE OPEN SKY BELONGS TO NATURE.
ROADS AND ROOFS SHOULD BE PLANTED WITH TREES.
IT MUST BE POSSIBLE TO BREATHE FOREST AIR IN THE CITY AGAIN.
THE MAN-TREE RELATIONSHIP MUST ASSUME RELIGIOUS PROPORTIONS.
THEN AT LAST PEOPLE WILL UNDERSTAND THE SENTENCE: THE STRAIGHT LINE IS GODLESS.
FRIEDENSREICH HUNDERTWASSER   DÜSSELDORF, 27 FEBRUARY 1972

CALL TO ALL RESIDENTS

THE TIME HAS COME.
THE TIME OF SURVEILLANCE IS PAST.
THE TIME OF WAITING FOR PARADISE IS PAST.
THE TIME OF FRUITLESS TALKING IS PAST.
THE TIME OF ACTION HAS COME.

I GIVE HOUSES BACK TO THE PEOPLE.
NOT MERELY PRO FORMA, BUT IN REALITY.
AS FROM NOW IT IS THE RIGHT AND DUTY OF ALL RESIDENTS
OF SMOOTH, PRISON-LIKE BOXES
TO RESHAPE THEM WITH THEIR OWN HANDS.
OUTSIDE AND INSIDE, WHEREVER THEY LIVE.
WITHOUT INSTRUCTION.
THEY BEGIN
BY PAINTING
THE WHITE ENTRANCE DOOR LEADING ONTO THE CORRIDOR
AND THE WHITE UNIFORM WINDOW FRAMES
IN RED OR GREEN OR WHATEVER THEY LIKE.
IN PARTICULAR OUTSIDE,
SO THEY CAN RECOGNIZE THEIR WINDOWS
WHEN THEY COME HOME TIRED.

WOE TO THE AUTHORITIES
WOE TO LAWS OR ANYTHING
FORBIDDING SUCH AN AUTOMATIC RIGHT.

WOE TO THE ARCHITECTS!
IT IS THE DUTY OF EVERY ARCHITECT
TO DEMAND AND PROCURE
THE TOTAL INDIVIDUAL RIGHT TO BUILDING ALTERATIONS
FOR THE RESIDENTS OF THE HOUSES
HE IS BUILDING OR HAS ALREADY BUILT!
OTHERWISE HIS CONSCIENCE WILL GIVE HIM NO PEACE!

SOS WINDOW RIGHT (VIENNA 1980)

A BRIGADE, CONSISTING OF ONE OF SEVERAL MOTORIZED SITE HUTS, WHICH IS ORDERED - WHETHER BY THE POPULACE OR BY THE
MUNICIPALITY OF VIENNA, THE BUILDING AUTHORITIES OR ANY OTHER BODY - TO WHEREVER IT IS NEEDED, IN ORDER TO REMOVE UNACCEPTABLE, INHUMAN CONDITIONS IN AN APARTMENT BLOCK OR A SATELLITE ESTATE, WITH A RAPID CURE, AS CHEAPLY AS POSSIBLE.
THE SITE HUT DRIVES UP TO AN INHUMAN FAÇADE AND PARKS THERE FOR A WEEK. USING SCAFFOLDING, IN PART HUNG OUT OF WINDOWS OR BUILT UP FROM THE GROUND, A TEAM OF MASONS HUMANIZES THE FAÇADE.
NOT THE WHOLE FAÇADE, BUT MERELY IN THE REGION OF A WINDOW OR THE CORNER OF A WINDOW, IN OTHER WORDS IN STRICTLY LIMITED AREAS. THIS MIGHT BE CARRIED OUT, E.G., ON THE OUTSIDE WALLS OF TEMPORARILY EMPTY APARTMENTS, AFTER ONE TENANT HAS MOVED OUT AND BEFORE A NEW ONE HAS MOVED IN.

WINDOW DICTATES AND WINDOW RIGHTS

SOME PEOPLE SAY HOUSES CONSIST OF WALLS.
I SAY HOUSES CONSIST OF WINDOWS.
WHEN DIFFERENT HOUSES STAND NEXT TO EACH OTHER IN A STREET, ALL HAVING DIFFERENT WINDOW TYPES, OR WINDOW RACES, NOBODY MINDS. THUS AN ART NOUVEAU HOUSE WITH ART NOUVEAU WINDOWS MAY APPEAR BESIDE A MODERN HOUSE WITH UNADORNED SQUARE WINDOWS, FOLLOWED IN TURN BY A BAROQUE HOUSE WITH BAROQUE WINDOWS. BUT SHOULD THE THREE WINDOW TYPES OF THE THREE HOUSES BELONG TO ONE HOUSE, IT IS SEEN AS A VIOLATION OF THE RACIAL SEGREGATION OF WINDOWS.
WHY? EACH INDIVIDUAL WINDOW HAS ITS OWN RIGHT TO LIFE.
ACCORDING TO THE PREVAILING CODE, HOWEVER, IF WINDOW RACES ARE MIXED, WINDOW APARTHEID IS INFRINGED.
THE APARTHEID OF WINDOW RACES MUST CEASE.
FOR THE REPETITION OF IDENTICAL WINDOWS NEXT TO EACH OTHER AND ABOVE EACH OTHER AS IN A GRID SYSTEM IS A CHARACTERISTIC OF CONCENTRATION CAMPS.
IN THE NEW ARCHITECTURE OF SATELLITE TOWNS AND IN NEW ADMINISTRATION BUILDINGS, BANKS, HOSPITALS AND SCHOOLS, THE LEVELLING OF WINDOWS IS UNBEARABLE.
INDIVIDUALS, NEVER IDENTICAL, DEFEND THEMSELVES AGAINST THESE STANDARDIZING DICTATES EITHER PASSIVELY OR ACTIVELY, DEPENDING ON THEIR CONSTITUTION. THUS EITHER WITH ALCOHOL AND DRUG ADDICTION, EXODUS FROM THE CITY, CLEANING MANIA, TELEVISION DEPENDENCY, INEXPLICABLE PHYSICAL COMPLAINTS, ALLERGIES, DEPRESSIONS AND EVEN SUICIDE, OR ALTERNATIVELY WITH AGGRESSION, VANDALISM AND CRIME.
A PERSON IN A RENTED APARTMENT MUST BE ABLE TO LEAN OUT OF HIS WINDOW AND SCRAPE OFF THE MASONRY WITHIN ARM'S REACH. AND HE MUST BE ALLOWED TO TAKE A LONG BRUSH AND PAINT EVERYTHING OUTSIDE WITHIN ARM'S REACH. SO THAT IT WILL BE VISIBLE FROM AFAR TO EVERYONE IN THE STREET THAT SOMEONE LIVES THERE WHO IS DIFFERENT FROM THE IMPRISONED, ENSLAVED, STANDARDIZED MAN WHO LIVES NEXT DOOR.
HUNDERTWASSER   22 JANUARY 1990

LET EVERYTHING OVERGROW (VIENNA 1980)

WHY IS IT A CRIME TO ENCOURAGE GREENERY ON WALLS? WE SHOULD VIEW SUCH GREENING WITH BENEVOLENCE, FOR IT HARMS NO ONE. IT CANNOT HURT AN ANONYMOUS HOUSE OWNER OR HOUSING ASSOCIATION. A BETTER PICTURE CAN ONLY BE GAINED BY POLLING RESIDENTS AND NEIGHBOURS, WITH A VOTE.
LAWS AND STIPULATIONS WHICH ARE HARMFUL HAVE SHOWN THEMSELVES TO BE HARMFUL OR HAVE BECOME HARMFUL (E.G. AS A RESULT OF CHANGES IN SOCIAL STRUCTURE, NEW ECOLOGICAL SURVIVAL NEEDS AND THE NEW CONDITIONS, INSIGHTS AND AIMS OF OUR CIVILIZATION) MUST BE REJECTED AND IGNORED UNTIL NEW LAWS AND STIPULATIONS ARE PASSED WHICH SUIT THE NEW SITUATION. COMPARE, FOR EXAMPLE, THE FAVOURABLE ATTITUDE OF THE AUTHORITIES TOWARDS NUDE BATHING.
WE LIVE IN A STATE OF EMERGENCY IN WHICH GREENING MUST AT ALL COSTS BE GIVEN PRIORITY OVER THE STIPULATIONS OF ANONYMOUS OWNERS THAT OUTSIDE WALLS SHOULD NOT BE GIVEN OVER FOR USE.
OF WHAT USE, OF WHAT HARM IS GREENERY ON WALLS?
EVEN THE NEIGHBOUR UPSTAIRS WHO IS ANTI-GREENING WILL PROFIT UNCONSCIOUSLY:
1. FROM INHALING INCREASED OXYGEN
2. FROM LESS DUST; LIKE A SILENT VACUUM CLEANER, GREENERY TRAPS DUST, WHICH IS THEN WASHED AWAY BY RAIN.
3. FROM LESS NOISE POLLUTION; GREENERY DAMPS NOISE AND VIBRATION.
4. FROM AN IMPROVED CLIMATE, THANKS TO A REDUCTION IN THE OVEN EFFECT

IN HIS IMMEDIATE ENVIRONMENT; EXTREMES OF HOT AND COLD WILL BE MODERATED.
5. EVEN UNKIND VOICES CANNOT DESCRIBE BUTTERFLIES AS DESTRUCTIVE VERMIN.
6. ANTI-GREENING NEIGHBOURS CAN EASILY CLEAR THEIR OUTSIDE WALLS OF GREENERY - THAT IS THEIR WINDOW RIGHT.
7. JUST AS IT IS THEIR RIGHT TO PREVENT THE GREENING OF THEIR OUTSIDE WALLS, SO THEY MAY NOT STAND IN THE WAY OF A NEIGHBOUR WHO ENCOURAGES GREENERY ON HIS OUTSIDE WALL.

TREE TENANTS
IN THE EXAMPLE OF THE RUPERTINUM, SALZBURG

THE TREE TENANTS ARE LOCATED ON THREE SIDES OF THE RUPERTINUM, SO THAT AT LEAST ONE IS ALWAYS VISIBLE FROM WHEREVER YOU LOOK. TREE TENANTS ARE INTENDED TO SYMBOLIZE THE PROFOUND REORIENTATION OF THE COMING EPOCH, WHEN VEGETATION AND TREES WILL ONCE AGAIN BE ACCORDED IMPORTANT STATUS AS MAN'S PARTNERS.
THE RECOGNITION THAT ART IS THE BRIDGE BETWEEN MAN AND NATURE MUST BE MADE MANIFEST AT THE RUPERTINUM AND MUST NOT REMAIN THEORY. THE ADVANTAGES ARE OBVIOUS AND WILL INCREASE OVER TIME, ANALOGOUS TO THE GROWING SIZE OF THE TREE TENANTS:
THREE DIFFERENT SPECIES OF TREE TENANTS SHOULD BE GIVEN ACOMMODATION, NAMELY:
- THE ACER PSEUDOPLATANUS SYCAMORE
- THE AILANTHUS ALTISSIMA TREE OF HEAVEN
- THE FAGUS SYLVATICA BEECH
THE SYCAMORE HAS ALREADY PROVED SUCCESSFUL ON A BALCONY IN PRINZ-EUGEN-STRASSE IN VIENNA. THERE IS A TREE OF HEAVEN GROWING OUT OF A GROUND-FLOOR DOOR IN STIFTSGASSE IN VIENNA. THE BEECH WOULD BE A SLOW-GROWING BEAUTY. IT IS WELL REPRESENTED IN HAMBURG, E.G. IN MAGDA-LENENSTRASSE. TREE TENANTS CANNOT GROW VERY TALL SINCE THEIR GROWTH IS CHECKED BY THE ROOT SPACE AND SOIL VOLUME AVAILABLE.
PRACTICAL EXPERIENCE OF TREE TENANTS ALREADY EXISTING AND INSTALLED:
1. ALSERBACHSTRASSE/LIECHTENSTEINSTRASSE IN VIENNA
2. ROSENTHAL AG SELB FACTORY
BOTH INITIATED BY MYSELF.
THE TREE TENANT PAYS RENT IN A MORE VALUABLE CURRENCY THAN A HUMAN TENANT:
1. AS AN OXYGEN SUPPLIER
2. AS A CLIMATIC REGULATOR; EXTREMES OF HEAT AND COLD, HUMIDITY AND DRYNESS ARE MODERATED
3. AS A DUST HOOVER WHICH IS CONSTANTLY IN OPERATION
4. AS AN ECHO DAMPER
5. AS A BEAUTY DISPENSER VISIBLE FROM AFAR
6. AS A MOOD REGULATOR FOR URBAN-DAMAGED PEOPLE
7. AS A SYMBOL AND STIMULATOR OF THE REORIENTATION OF OUR SOCIETY AND AS AN EXAMPLE OF THE FORESTATION OF CITIES, EVEN - AND IN PARTICULAR - ON VERTICAL FAÇADES.
FURTHER ADVANTAGES: CLEANING OF WASTE WATER AND RAIN WATER; DEPOSIT FOR HUMUS FROM HUMUS PLANTS; PROTECTION FOR WALLS AGAINST ULTRAVIOLET RAYS.
THE PROPOSED LOCATIONS OF TREE TENANTS MAY BE ALTERED. TREE TENANTS HAVE THE ADVANTAGE OF TAKING UP ONLY A LITTLE INDOOR SPACE WHILE AT THE SAME TIME VITALIZING AND ENRICHING INTERIORS.
TREE TENANT LOCATIONS MUST BE STATICALLY CALCULATED AND CORRECTLY INSULATED. WINDOWS ARE TAKEN BACK TO BEHIND THE TREE TENANT, PRODUCING A SORT OF SMALL BAY WINDOW IN REVERSE OCCUPYING SOME 1-3 M OF FLOOR SPACE. WINDOWS SHOULD ALSO BE BUILT ON EACH SIDE OF THE TREE TENANT, PROVIDING LATERAL VIEWS THROUGH THE TREE TENANT'S TERRITORY. THE WINDOWS RETAIN THEIR USUAL APPEARANCE, WITH A WINDOW CROSS. ONLY THE WINDOW PANES ARE REMOVED.
FOR THE PURPOSES OF BETTER STATIC PLACING OVER THE OUTSIDE WALL, AND TO SAVE SPACE, THE ROOT AREA OF ONE OR TWO TREE TENANTS MAY BE BUILT AS A TRIANGLE, WITH ONE POINT FACING INTO THE ROOM AND TWO SIDES TOWARDS THE WINDOW, INSTEAD OF HAVING THREE WINDOW SIDES. IN THIS WAY, VOLUME AND WEIGHT LESSEN TOWARDS THE CENTRE OF THE ROOM AND INCREASE TOWARDS THE OUTSIDE WALL.

THE CLIMBER PARTENOCISSUS TRISCUSPIDATA AMPELOPSIS VEITSCHII MUST ALSO BE TRAINED UP SOME PARTS OF THE WALL BOTH AS PROTECTION AND FOR THE ADVANTAGES THEY BRING, NAMELY THE SAME AS THOSE OF TREE TENANTS.
FRIEDENSREICH HUNDERTWASSER
VIENNA, THE MORNING OF 16 OCTOBER 1981
WRITTEN IN BED

THE ARCHITECTURE DOCTOR

OUR HOUSES HAVE BEEN SICK FOR AS LONG AS THERE HAVE BEEN INDOCTRINATED URBAN PLANNERS AND STANDARDIZED ARCHITECTS. THEY DO NOT FALL SICK, BUT ARE CONCEIVED AND BROUGHT INTO THE WORLD AS SICK HOUSES.
THESE MANY HOUSES, WHICH WE ALL ENDURE IN THEIR THOUSANDS, ARE UNFEELING AND EMOTIONLESS, DICTATORIAL, HEARTLESS, AGGRESSIVE, GODLESS, SMOOTH, STERILE, UNADORNED, COLD AND UNROMANTIC, ANONYMOUS AND YAWNINGLY VOID.
THEY ARE AN ILLUSION OF FUNCTIONALITY. SUCH IS THEIR DEPRESSING NATURE THAT BOTH THEIR RESIDENTS AND PASSERS-BY FALL SICK.
CONSIDER THIS: WHILE 100 PEOPLE LIVE IN A HOUSE, 10,000 WALK AND DRIVE PAST IT EVERY DAY; THESE LATTER SUFFER JUST AS MUCH AS THE RESIDENTS, IF INDEED NOT MORE SO, FROM THE DEPRESSING IMPACT OF THE FAÇADE OF A HEARTLESS HOUSE. BUT THE HOSPITALS ARE THEMSELVES SICK.
LEVELLING, CONCENTRATION-CAMP AND BARRACK-STYLE BUILDINGS DESTROY AND STANDARDIZE THE MOST VALUABLE THING A YOUNG PERSON BRINGS TO SOCIETY: SPONTANEOUS, INDIVIDUAL CREATIVITY.
HAD ARCHITECTS BEEN ABLE TO CURE THESE SICK AND AND SICK-MAKING BUILDINGS, THEY WOULD NOT HAVE BUILT THEM AT ALL.
SO A NEW PROFESSION IS NEEDED: THE ARCHITECTURE DOCTOR.
THE SOLE TASK OF THE ARCHITECTURE DOCTOR IS TO RESTORE HUMAN DIGNITY AND HARMONY WITH NATURE AND HUMAN CREATION. WITHOUT FIRST TEARING EVERYTHING DOWN, BUT BY MAKING CHANGES ONLY AT STRATEGIC POINTS, AND WITHOUT GREAT EFFORT OR FINANCIAL RESOURCES. THIS INCLUDES DEREGULATING CORRECTED RIVER COURSES, BREAKING UP STERILE, FLAT SKYLINES, CONVERTING AREAS OF GROUND INTO UNEVEN, UNDULATING SURFACES, LETTING SPONTANEOUS VEGETATION GROW IN GAPS BETWEEN COBBLES AND CRACKS IN WALLS, WHERE IT DISTURBS NO ONE, VARYING WINDOWS AND IRREGULARLY ROUNDING OFF CORNERS AND EDGES.
THE ARCHITECTURE DOCTOR IS ALSO RESPONSIBLE FOR EVEN MORE DECISIVE SURGICAL OPERATIONS, SUCH AS CUTTING AWAY WALLS AND POSITIONING TOWERS AND PILLARS.
WE SIMPLY NEED TO ALLOW WINDOW RIGHTS, PLANT ROOFS WITH GRASS AND TREES, LET CLIMBERS GROW AND INSTALL TREE TENANTS.
IF YOU LET WINDOWS DANCE BY DESIGNING THEM IN DIFFERENT STYLES, AND IF YOU ALLOW AS MANY IRREGULARITIES AS POSSIBLE TO APPEAR OR HAPPEN IN FAÇADES AND INTERIORS, HOUSES WILL RECOVER. HOUSES WILL BEGIN TO LIVE.
EVERY HOUSE, HOWEVER UGLY AND SICK, CAN BE CURED.
HUNDERTWASSER   24 JANUARY 1990

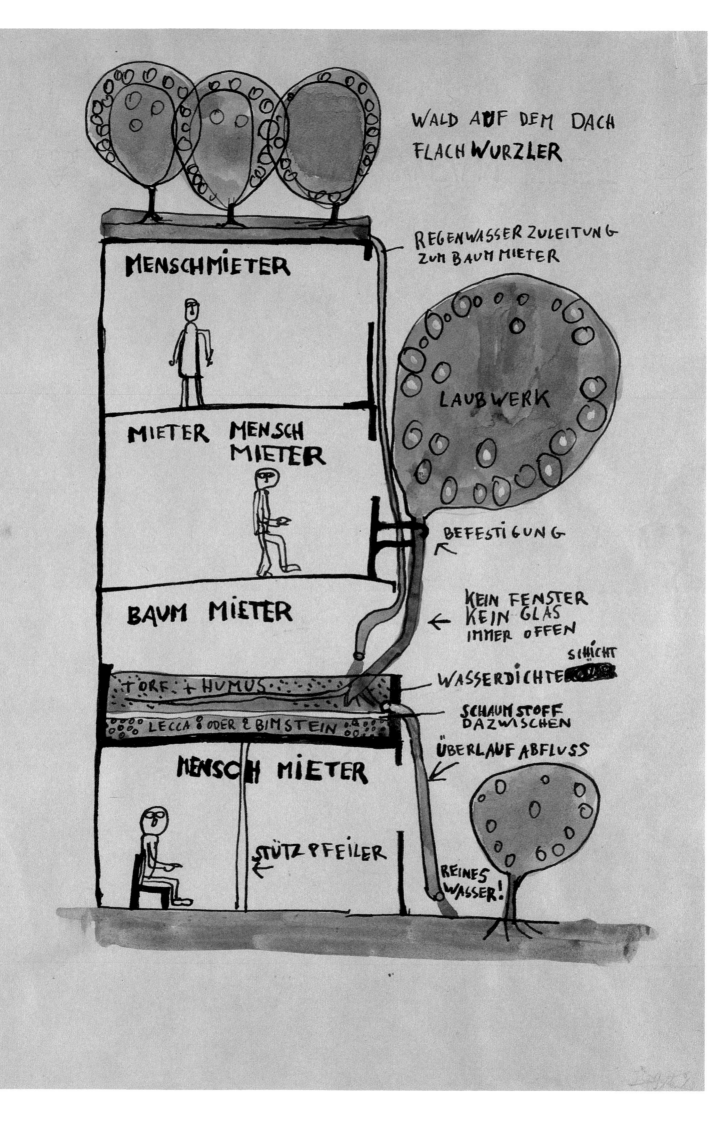

BAUMMIETER-BRIEF   Auckland, Neuseeland, 9. Juni 1973, Winter

Caro Giulio Macchi,

Endlich habe ich Zeit, mich um die Triennale von Mailand zu kümmern. Ich bin sehr geehrt, daß ich daran teilnehmen kann. Ich habe viele Ideen zu realisieren.

Erstes Projekt:

Ein Baum oder mehrere Bäume sollen aus den Fenstern wachsen. Große Bäume aus dem dritten oder vierten Stockwerk zum Beispiel. In einem Haus in der Ausstellung oder nicht in der Ausstellung. Dies soll etwas Bleibendes sein, also nicht nur für die Ausstellung.

Um ein Beispiel zu geben:

So viel Raum in der monotonen sterilen Stadt ist nicht bewohnt. Also warum soll nicht ein Baum anstatt eines Menschen in einer Wohnung wohnen, wenn der Sauerstoff rar wird? Man braucht nur ein Fenster einer Wohnung und etwas Raum dahinter.

Dies ist etwas sehr Wichtiges und kann die Stadt mehr revolutionieren als wenn man nur die Dächer mit Wäldern bedeckt. Denn die Baum-Mieter, die sich aus den Fenstern lehnen, die sieht man schon von weitem, an denen kann sich jeder freuen, die Dachgärten und Dachwälder sieht man meist von der Straße nicht.

Die dem Baum vermieteten Wohnräume müssen mit einer Lage Pirelli-Gummi oder Plastikfolie oder anderem Material isoliert werden bis zur Höhe des Fensterbretts. Dann eine Woche mit Wasser angefüllt lassen zur Probe, ob alles dicht ist.

Die Wohnungen werden dann mit Erde bis zum Fensterbrett angefüllt in zwei Schichten, erst Lecca oder Bimssteine, dann leichte Humus- oder Torferde, dazwischen eine wasserdurchlässige Schaumstoffschicht.

Die Baum-Mieter werden mit Kränen von außen durch die Fenster in die Wohnungen gehievt, so daß die Wurzeln im Erdreich fußen und die Baumkronen in den Luftraum der Straße ragen.
Die Wurzeln sind im dunklen Zimmer vergraben, das Laubwerk im hellen Tag.

Die Fenster müssen immer offenbleiben ohne Fensterscheiben, so daß also Luft, Regen, Hitze, Kälte, Wind, Schnee ungehindert eindringen können.

- 2 -

Dies ist der neue Lebensraum des Baum-Mieters, der eben etwas anderes braucht als ein Menschen-Mieter. Der Raum muß vom Rest des Hauses total isoliert werden durch Isolierungsspezialisten.

Das Regenwasser muß vom Dach mit einem Rohr eingeleitet werden und der Überschuß durch ein zweites Rohr wieder abgeleitet werden.

Die Autos haben die Bäume in die Stockwerke verdrängt. Die senkrechten sterilen Wände der Häuserschluchten, unter deren Aggressivität und Tyrannei wir täglich leiden, werden wie grüne Täler, wo der Mensch frei atmen kann.

Der Baum-Mieter zahlt seine Miete mit Sauerstoff, durch seine Staubschluckkapazität, als Anti-Lärmmaschine durch Erzeugung von Ruhe, durch Giftvertilgung, durch Reinigung des verseuchten Regenwassers, als Produzent des Glücks und der Gesundheit, als Schmetterlingsbringer und durch Schönheit und mit vielen anderen Valuten.

Dies läßt sich alles in Geld umwechseln und ist mehr als ein Mensch-Mieter mit einem Scheck bezahlen kann.

Cordiali saluti

tuo Federico

An der Via Manzoni wurden etwa 15 Bäume in Wohnungen eingepflanzt. Die Straße wurde eine Nacht lang vom Verkehr gesperrt, um die Kranhebearbeiten durchzuführen. Auch der Triumphbogen wurde mit Bäumen besetzt. Die Aktion kostete mehrere Millionen Lire.
Es gab eine Pressekonferenz und zwei Kataloge.

Tree tenant action, Via Manzoni, Milan, 1973

Tree tenant action, Milan, 1973

Left: *Baummieter – Tree Tenant,* June 1973
Drawing accompanying letter to Giulio Macchi (top)

171

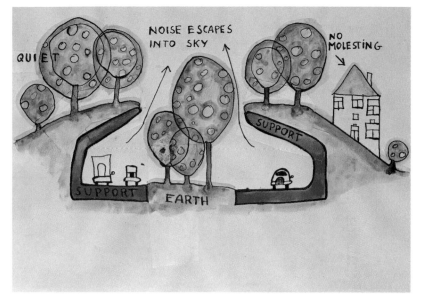

Drawing of the Green Motorway

Model of the Terraced House

Tree Tenant Model

Model of the Green Motorway

Model of the Service Station

Model of the Spiral House

ARCHITECTURE MODELS

The models were built from balsawood in the studio of modelmaker Peter Manhart, Vienna, during 1974 and 1975.

Model of the Underground House

Model of the "Slit Eye" House

Model of the Tunisian Underground House

Model of the Grass-Roofed House built in New Zealand by Ivan Tarulevic

Model of the Green Motorway

Pedestrian zone, Seilergasse, Vienna

GOOD PAINTING

Stowasser STOWASSEN

Fritz FRITZ

Friedrich FRIEDRICH

Friederich FRIEDERICH

Friedereich FRIEDEREICH

Friedenreich FRIEDENREICH

Hundertwasser HUNDERTWASSER

Friedensreich FRIEDENSREICH

Regentag REGENTAG

Dunkelbunt DUNKELBUNT

750 *Blind Venus Inside Babel – Blinde Venus in Babel,* Bay of Islands, New Zealand, Craig's Hut,
August 1975, Barge, September-November 1975
Mixed media: egg tempera, polyvinyl, oil and tinfoil glued to two horizontal chipboard panels
with UHU, 114 x 90 cm

793 *Unwohlsein – Schwarze Spirale – Malaise – Black Spiral,* Hahnsäge-
Venice, June-July 1978
Mixed media: egg tempera, oil and tinfoil glued with Pattex onto irregularly shaped fibreboard primed with chalk, zinc white and polyvinyl,
52 x 72 cm

H. R.: What makes a good painting?
F. H.: If the painting is full of magic. If you feel some happiness from it, if it makes you laugh, or cry, if it gets things moving. It should be like a flower, like a tree. It should be the same as nature. It should be that when it is not there you should miss it. It is a person. I have always compared paintings with trees. A painting is only good when it can stand comparison with a tree, or a living being.

H. R.: That is hard to explain to people who don't like painting. But it is the truth. You have to create something with its own vitality. Yet if you set out too purposefully you will certainly fail. It must be done nearly inadvertently, and the real successes are almost unanticipated – though the level of intention is complex and stealthy. How do people know they want to be painters?

F. H.: It is difficult, because painters want to be painters for many reasons, as a form of self-induced therapy, to depict something, on account of beauty or money, for politics or religion or to be "in" or to print visions of the future.

QUALITY AND PERMANENCE

F. H.: Today, all art which is openly beauti-

Humus Toilet, 1980

SHIT CULTURE - HOLY SHIT

VEGETATION HAS TAKEN MILLIONS OF YEARS TO COVER THE SLUDGE, THE TOXIC SUBSTANCES WITH A LAYER OF HUMUS, A LAYER OF VEGETATION AND A LAYER OF OXYGEN, SO THAT MAN CAN LIVE ON EARTH. BUT UNGRATEFUL MAN THEN FETCHES THE SLUDGE AND THE TOXINS, COVERED WITH PAINSTAKING COSMIC CARE, BACK UP TO THE EARTH'S SURFACE. THUS THE ATROCIOUS ACT OF IRRESPONSIBLE MAN MAKES THE END OF THE WORLD THE SAME AS THE BEGINNING OF TIME. WE ARE COMMITTING SUICIDE. OUR CITIES ARE CANCEROUS ULCERS. YOU CAN SEE THAT CLEARLY FROM THE AIR. WE DO NOT EAT WHAT GROWS IN OUR OWN COUNTRY, BUT IMPORT OUR FOOD FROM FAR AWAY, FROM AFRICA, AMERICA, CHINA AND NEW ZEALAND. NOR DO WE KEEP OUR SHIT. OUR EXCREMENT, OUR WASTE IS WASHED FAR, FAR AWAY, WHEREBY WE POLLUTE RIVERS, LAKES AND OCEANS, OR WE TRANSPORT IT TO HIGHLY-COMPLEX, COSTLY SEWAGE WORKS, AND ONLY RARELY TO CENTRALIZED DECOMPOSITION PLANTS, OR OUR WASTE IS DESTROYED. SHIT NEVER RETURNS TO OUR FIELDS. NOR TO THE PLACES WHERE OUR FOOD COMES FROM. THE CYCLE FROM FOOD TO SHIT IS WORKING. THE CYCLE FROM SHIT TO FOOD HAS BEEN BROKEN. WE HAVE A FALSE NOTION OF OUR WASTE. EVERY TIME WE FLUSH THE TOILET, THINKING IT A HYGENIC ACTION, WE VIOLATE COSMIC LAWS. FOR IN TRUTH IT IS A GODLESS DEED, A WANTON ACT OF DEATH. WHEN WE GO TO THE TOILET, LOCK OURSELVES IN AND FLUSH AWAY OUR SHIT, WE SIGN AND SEAL THE MATTER. WHY ARE WE ASHAMED? WHAT ARE WE AFRAID OF? WHAT ACTUALLY HAPPENS TO OUR SHIT AFTERWARDS IS SOMETHING WE IGNORE, LIKE DEATH. THE BOTTOM OF THE PAN IS LIKE A DOOR OPENING ONTO DEATH; WE SIMPLY WANT TO GET AWAY AS FAST AS WE CAN, FORGET THE DECAY AND PUTREFACTION. BUT WE ARE QUITE WRONG. IT IS WITH SHIT THAT LIFE FIRST BEGINS. SHIT IS MUCH MORE IMPORTANT THAN FOOD. FOOD NOURISHES ONLY MANKIND, WHICH REPRODUCES ON A MASSIVE SCALE, DIMINISHES IN QUALITY AND HAS BECOME A DEADLY THREAT TO THE EARTH, A DEADLY THREAT TO VEGETATION, THE ANIMAL WORLD, WATER, AIR, THE HUMUS LAYER. BUT SHIT IS THE FOUNDATION OF OUR RESURRECTION. EVER SINCE MAN COULD THINK, HE HAS SOUGHT IMMORTALITY. MAN WANTS TO HAVE A SOUL. SHIT IS OUR SOUL. SHIT WILL ENABLE US TO SURVIVE. SHIT WILL ENABLE US TO BE IMMORTAL. WHY ARE WE AFRAID OF DEATH? THE PERSON WHO USES A HUMUS TOILET HAS NO FEAR OF DEATH, FOR OUR SHIT MAKES FUTURE LIFE AND REBIRTH POSSIBLE. IF WE FAIL TO VALUE OUR SHIT AND TURN IT INTO HUMUS TO THE GLORY OF GOD AND THE WORLD, WE LOSE OUR ENTITLEMENT TO BE PRESENT ON THIS EARTH. IN THE NAME OF FALSE HYGENIC LAWS WE LOSE OUR COSMIC SUBSTANCE, WE LOSE OUR REBIRTH. DIRT IS LIFE. STERILE CLEANLINESS IS DEATH. THOU SHALT NOT KILL, AND YET WE STERILIZE ALL LIFE WITH POISON AND CONCRETE. THAT IS MURDER. MAN IS JUST A TUBE. HE PUTS THINGS IN AT ONE END AND PASSES THEM OUT, DIGESTED, AT THE OTHER. THE MOUTH IS AT THE FRONT, THE ANUS AT THE BACK. WHY? IT SHOULD BE THE OTHER WAY ROUND. WHY IS EATING POSITIVE? WHY IS SHIT NEGATIVE? WHAT COMES OUT OF US IS NOT WASTE, BUT THE MATERIAL OF WHICH THE WORLD IS MADE, OUR GOLD, OUR BLOOD. THE LUNATIC INTERRUPTION TO THE CYCLE OF LIFE MAKES US BLEED, OUR CIVILIZATION BLEED, OUR EARTH BLEED. THE PERSON WHO SIMPLY LETS BLOOD, ONLY LOSES BLOOD AND NEVER REPLACES IT, WILL BLEED TO DEATH. FREUD WAS RIGHT WHEN HE SAID IN HIS INTERPRETATION OF DREAMS THAT SHIT IS A SYNONYM FOR GOLD. WE MUST NOW REALIZE THAT IT IS NOT JUST A DREAM, BUT A REALITY. WHEN PASOLINI HAD ACTORS EAT SHIT IN A FILM, IT WAS A SYMBOL OF THE CONTINUATION OF THE CYCLE, A DESPERATE SHORT CUT. WE MUST DEVOTE THE SAME LOVE, THE SAME TIME AND ATTENTION TO WHAT COMES OUT FROM "BEHIND" AS TO WHAT GOES IN "IN FRONT". THE SAME CEREMONY AS FOR MEALS, WITH TABLE-LAYING, KNIVES, FORKS AND SPOONS, CHOPSTICKS, SILVER CUTLERY AND CANDLE-LIGHT. WE SAY GRACE BEFORE AND AFTER MEALS. NO ONE SAYS GRACE WHEN THEY SHIT. WE THANK GOD FOR OUR DAILY BREAD, WHICH COMES FROM THE EARTH. BUT WE DO NOT PRAY FOR OUR SHIT TO BE TRANSUBSTANTIATED. WASTE IS BEAUTIFUL. THE GRADING AND REINTEGRATION OF WASTE IS A JOYOUS ACTIVITY. AN ACTIVITY WHICH TAKES PLACE NOT IN CELLARS AND REAR COURTYARDS, DUNG HEAPS AND TOILETS, BUT WHERE THERE IS LIGHT AND SUNSHINE, IN OUR LIVING ROOMS, OUR BEST ROOMS. THERE IS NO SUCH THING AS WASTE. WASTE DOES NOT EXIST. THE HUMUS TOILET IS A STATUS SYMBOL. WE HAVE THE PRIVILEGE OF BEING WITNESSES, WITH THE HELP OF OUR OWN WISDOM, TO THE TRANSFORMATION OF OUR OWN WASTE, OUR OWN SHIT INTO HUMUS, JUST AS A TREE GROWS AND THE HARVEST RIPENS. AT HOME WITH US, AS IF IT WERE OUR OWN CHILD. HOMO - HUMUS - HUMANITAS, THREE FATEFUL WORDS WITH THE SAME ORIGIN. HUMUS IS TRUE BLACK GOLD. HUMUS HAS A GOOD SMELL. THE FRAGRANCE OF HUMUS IS HOLY AND CLOSER TO GOD THAN THAT OF FRANKINCENSE. ANYONE WHO WALKS IN THE WOODS AFTER THE RAIN KNOWS ITS SMELL. IT IS NATURALLY SOMETHING OF A PRODIGIOUS STEP TO PLACE THE RUBBISH BIN IN THE CENTRE OF OUR APARTMENTS AND TO SITE THE HUMUS TOILET ON THE MOST BEAUTIFUL SPOT AS THE SEAT OF HONOUR. BUT THIS IS PRECISELY THE ABOUT-TURN WHICH OUR SOCIETY, OUR CIVILIZATION MUST NOW MAKE IF IT IS TO SURVIVE. THE SMELL OF HUMUS IS THE SMELL OF GOD, THE SMELL OF RESURRECTION, THE SMELL OF IMMORTALITY.

FRIEDENSREICH HUNDERTWASSER
ALGAJOLA, VENICE, NEW ZEALAND, 1979-1980

THE HUMUS TOILET

WORKS INDOORS, INCLUDING IN THE LIVING ROOM. NO SMELL, NO FLIES (WHEN WASTE IS CAREFULLY COVERED WITH DAMP HUMUS). NO SEWAGE PIPES, NO FLUSHING. NO CHEMICALS, NO OUTLET PIPES. NO POWER SUPPLY (FOR HEAT AND VENTILATOR SUCH AS IN THE SMALL SCANDINAVIAN UNITS ON SALE; ONLY CLIVUS MULTRUM REQUIRES NO ELECTRICITY). ONLY DISADVANTAGE COMPARED TO PURCHASABLE HUMUS TOILETS REQUIRING ELECTRICITY: ONLY A LIMITED AMOUNT OF URINE CAN BE ABSORBED. WHEN FLUID DRIPS INTO THE SAUCER, STOP ADDING FLUID (POUR BACK ON TOP OR USE FOR PLANTS). COVERING WASTE WITH HUMUS MEANS THE HUMUS TOILET WILL BE FULL WITHIN A SHORTER TIME (IN 2 MONTHS INSTEAD OF 4 FOR 2 PEOPLE WITH KITCHEN WASTE). IN RETURN YOU ARE ENTIRELY INDEPENDENT OF THE POWER GRID. IF POSSIBLE, DRY ANY LEAVES OR FRUIT AND VEGETABLE PARINGS (E.G. IN THE SUN) BEFORE ADDING THEM TO THE HUMUS TOILET. THIS ACCELERATES THE HUMUS PROCESS, AND BULK IS REDUCED BY FASTER LOSS OF WATER CONTENT. WATER ACCOUNTS FOR 90-95% OF VOLUME AND WEIGHT. ONLY 5-10% REMAIN AS HUMUS. ENQUIRIES TO HUNDERTWASSER, C/O HAREL, POSTFACH 145, A-1013 VIENNA. TO CLEAN URINE AND DOMESTIC WASTE WATER, A BIOLOGICAL TREATMENT PLANT SHOULD BE EMPLOYED. IN LIGHT AND WARM INTERIORS, USE AQUATIC PLANTS: CALLA, CYPRESS GRASS, WATER HYACINTHS, CYPERUS TEXTILIS, PAPYRUS, SCOURING-RUSH, TRADESCANTIA ZEBRINA, ALOCASIA, BAUMEA ARTICULATA (NEW ZEALAND RUSH), FICUS PUMILA. OUTDOORS, USE RUSH, REED, CAT'S TAIL, WATER MINT, WATER FLAG. THE DIRTY WATER MUST FLOW THROUGH THE ROOT AREA OF THE AQUATIC PLANTS AND THROUGH THE COLONIES OF BIODEGRADING BACTERIA, AND IN THIS WAY IS NATURALLY PURIFIED. THE DIRT IS CONVERTED IN PART INTO PLANT MATERIAL AND IN PART INTO MINERALIZED SOIL.

ful and positive is discarded. It must be something terrible, negative, disgusting, perverse – then it has a chance of being re-marked on by museum directors and critics, then it has a chance of being bought by col-lectors. This is a kind of collective hysteria. I have another rule; it concerns the painter and his studio. I found out that the bigger the studio is, the bigger the windows, the worse is the painter and the paintings. The smaller the studio, the smaller the windows, the bet-ter the paintings. When you have big win-dows you tend to look outside and if you have small windows you tend to look inside – which is better.

H. R.: How concerned are you about the permanence of your paintings and prints? Does it matter to you that they survive for a long time?

F. H.: I would like them to survive, of course. My technique is quite good and I spend more time preparing the painting than in painting. It is an important part of the paint-ing, the preparation. For instance, I start with making the frame, glueing and then putting on the canvas, then putting on the paper – because I glue paper on the canvas. The glue is a mixture of wall-paper glue and polyvi-nyl; it stretches the canvas like a drum. Then I whitewash it and prime it. The primer is chalk and zinc white and polyvinyl. Before, I tried it with rabbit glue, which is very com-plicated and does not hold very well. Also, the mice ate it sometimes and it is not water-resistant and so it tends to mould.

1975 was busy; Hundertwasser published a second Japanese wood-block portfolio, *Midori No Namida.* His retrospective ex-hibition was shown at the Haus der Kunst, Munich. He published his "Humus Toilet

Manifesto", half invention, half exhorta-tion for a reasonable balance between con-sumption and investment in the ecosystem. During 1975–1976 a world travelling ex-hibition, "Austria Presents Hundertwasser to the Continents", was shown in thirty-five cities on five continents. The Albertina ex-hibited Hundertwasser's complete graphic works, which began a U.S. museum tour. Then, in contrast to all these social events, Hundertwasser sailed the "Regentag" in the Caribbean. His Paris exhibition at Galerie Paul Facchetti's elegant new premises yielded reviews that admired Hundertwasser's strong colours and his "baroque" designs. Reviewers appreciated the balance of orientalism and modernity in Hundertwasser's work. His variety of de-signs and inventive use of material were also praised.

Then he exhibited again in a New York gallery and, as in Paris, the critics were more understanding. The Americans ap-preciated that Hundertwasser's environ-mental actions took place in the "real" world; insults to the environment are not a major subject in his art. To that degree imagination and fantasy are far apart. He can imagine solutions to the world's prob-lems, but these are not to be enacted through fantastic or irrational means. Hun-dertwasser's outlook is quintessentially so-cial and all his efforts are on behalf of indi-viduals living in accord with nature.

THE SALZBURG FESTIVAL

At the 1977 Salzburg Festival, Léopold Sédar Senghor, President of the Republic of Senegal, paid Hundertwasser a supreme compliment in the Festival's Opening Ad-dress, "Austria as Expression of Universal Culture". Senghor's talk was devoted to Mozart, Rilke, and Hundertwasser: "The three artists whom I have chosen to illus-trate Austrian culture, as different as they are from each other, all witness the same truth which is essential, the universality in the Austrian spirit: they have made of

Ill. p. 178: 769 *Window out of the Pond – Window into the Pond,* Vienna, 1978
Aquatint colour etching from 4 copper plates in 3 versions: yellow-brown 1–75, yellow-blue 76–150, green-blue 151–280, 65 x 50 cm (39.7 x 32.6) Edition of 280 and XXXXVIII proofs, all signed and numbered. Printed by Robert Finger, Vienna. Published by Gruener Janura, Glarus

Ill. p. 179: 763 *Regenbogenhaus – Rainbow House,* Kaurinui, August 1976, Hahnsäge, January 1977
Mixed media: watercolour, egg tempera, polyvinyl, oil and lacquer on paper, glued to canvas with polyvinyl and wallpaper glue, primed with chalk. Wooden frame constructed by Hundertwasser, 117 x 88 cm

diverse cultural influences a harmonious symbiosis in order to express the being of Austria and by extension the universal being of man."

Senghor's vision of the rejuvenation of the West in a new synthesis was epitomized by Hundertwasser. Senghor hoped the world might attain a pan-cultural assimilation of every tradition's best features and analogized from Austria's past as microcosm of assimilation and exchange. From that past Hundertwasser's artistic ancestors arose.

H. R.: How do you explain that living in Vienna – the capital of a small country – you feel at home everywhere in the world rather than a stranger everywhere?

F. H.: Vienna is an international city in the centre of Europe. Maybe because I'm half Jewish (but this has nothing to do with Vienna). I would feel at home everywhere in the world if I were born in Madrid. That has something to do with me, not with Vienna.

H. R.: Do you know what that "something" is?

F. H.: Yes, that is a special gift from heaven that I feel like a world-citizen.

For Hundertwasser the present moment offers special possibilities, a diversity of choices among good and evil that coexist as complementaries, "light and shadow".

F. H.: All times are good and all times are bad at the same time. There is no good time without a bad time, no light without shadow. The stronger the light, the more you feel the shadow and the more you live in darkness, and the more happy you are with your bit of light. It is always equal. Of course there are tremendous dangers today. The biggest danger results from our brains not developing as fast as our machines. Now we have been seeing the strange situation that a man without much brains has great power.

H. R.: Is this also visible in architecture?

F. H.: Yes, very much in architecture, more than in our art; because you can escape art, you can escape a painting.

MORALITY

H. R.: Does being an artist involve a specific morality?

F. H.: I think so, but maybe not all artists conceive it that way. In some societies artists are dangerous to those in power because they don't fit into the system. The artist sets an example of how everybody should cope with life.

An artist is completely outside the hierarchy. An artist is neither rich nor poor; he is at home with all classes of people. An artist is at home with the poor, with the beggar, with the farmer, the worker, and the ruling classes – it's all the same. He can go just as he is, dressed as he is, with his mentality just as it is; he can go and sit with beggars, or "clochards", and an hour later he is invited to the Rothschilds and eats at their table, and later he goes back to the "clochards" – he is just outside the system, neither of the rich nor the poor. A real artist does not even have to paint. I know many artists who don't paint.

H. R.: Are they really artists?

F. H.: Yes, they are artists, they are artists of life.

H. R.: Do artists do good?

F. H.: They can do good only if they show a way. If they show a feasible way of creation. For example, the arts have at least the duty to give people hope and show them beautiful paths alone which they can go. Art has to do good. I want – and I do it instinctively – to demonstrate to people, to paint for them, a paradise that can belong to everyone, if only they will reach out for it. Paradise is always there, but we destroy it. I want to show how simple it is, basically, to find paradise on earth.

You have to live as if there were a war on, when everything is rationed. Man has to be cautious, has to think for himself, be economical, not wildly extravagant.

H. R.: If you could own a work of art, what would you want to look at?

F. H.: Maybe a painting by Egon Schiele, *Die tote Stadt,* though I am quite happy without it and would be quite happy with a reproduction.

H. R.: Why do you suppose that other people want art on their walls?

F. H.: Nobody can answer that question satisfactorily because there are so many reasons.

H. R.: Why do people want art?

F. H.: Generally collectors are abnormal. I said this is an interview and it was published and one of my collectors got completely mad and he telephoned me and wrote a letter that he is not abnormal, and he was insulted. But the fact is that collectors are abnormal because if they are true collectors (who don't collect for money or prestige) then they need the painting because they are not creative. If a collector were creative he would not need art; he would somehow be happy with his own creativity [. . .]

Our society has two strong activities which are compensations: art and sport. Sport is seeing others run and jump and play football, and reading about it in the newspapers and television makes you a sports fan, but you yourself don't participate. This is one of the big symptoms of our sickness

as a society, the fact that we have art and sport.

In 1978 Hundertwasser produced a remarkable colour etching and aquatint, *Window out of the Pond – Window into the*

768 *Abendländer – The Occidental*, Vienna, May 1978
Aquatint colour etching from 2 copper plates in 2 colour versions on Arches Büttenpaper, 76 x 56.5 cm (59.5 x 34.5)
Edition of 220 and XVIII proofs, all signed and numbered, green 1–110, blue 111–220. Printed by Robert Finger, Vienna. Published by Gruener Janura, Glarus

Left: 781 *Grüne Stadt – Green Town,* Venice, 1973/78
Mixed media: watercolour, oil, lacquer and china ink on printed paper,
glued to canvas with polyvinyl and wallpaper glue, 97.1 x 145 cm

Bottom: 761 *Gib Acht wenn Du über die Prairie gehst – Take Care When
You Walk Over the Prairie,* Vienna, 1976
Aquatint colour etching from 2 copper plates in 2 colour versions: green
and blue, 50.6 x 66 cm (30 x 39.6)
Edition of 214 and XIII proofs, all signed and numbered. Printed by Robert
Finger, Vienna. Published by Grueuel Janura, Glarus

Pond (p. 178), done to appear as if one were looking up from the murky water of a pond and another version – inked from the same plates – to create the sensation of looking down through the water. Looking up through the pond becomes an experience akin to fathoming the great space under a cathedral's dome. Hundertwasser's work explores the water-world and captures its refractive light.

When Senghor met Hundertwasser at Salzburg he invited the artist to visit Senegal as his guest, and in 1978 Hundertwasser accepted the invitation; during the following year he completed a set of three postage stamps for Senegal. Anxiety about the condition of the world prompted Hundertwasser to paint through the summer of 1978 – first at Hahnsäge, then in Venice: *Malaise – Black Spiral, Malaise – Spiral Noire, Unwohlsein – Schwarze Spirale* (p. 176). The spiral throbs with suffering, a suffering that transforms the world, and all is tinged with misery. The charming landscape is now steeped in omens and brooding. Such paintings usher in Hundertwasser's later style. Increasingly, he has treated social questions directly in architecture, and his painting has become more and more the place for personal statements.

Hundertwasser's belief in modern architecture's failure is unwavering, and academic architects are the focus of his displeasure – although what "academicism" represents at this moment is problematic.

F. H.: Architects believe that they have to study and they have to show that they are able to fulfil these rules based on a Bauhaus philosophy, worldwide. This Bauhaus philosophy was only philosophy, never practical, even at the beginning. Its philosophy was that you should abandon the lies of façades and decorations and get to the point.

GARDEN DWARFS

Stowasser STOWASSER

Fritz FRITZ

Friedrich FRIEDRICH

Friederich FRIEDERICH

Friedereich FRIEDEREICH

Friedenreich FRIEDENREICH

Hundertwasser HUNDERTWASSER

Friedensreich FRIEDENSREICH

Regentag REGENTAG

Dunkelbunt DUNKELBUNT

830 *Les doges – Die Dogen – The Doges,* Kaurinui, February-June 1982, Vienna, July 1982
Mixed media: watercolour, egg tempera, polyvinyl, oil and lacquer on chipboard primed with chalk and polyvinyl, 51 x 73 cm

803 *Pardonnez-moi, Mustafa – Excuse Me, Mustafa*, Senegal, 1978, Bacca-lu-Algajola, July 1979
Mixed media: watercolour, egg tempera, acrylic, oil and paper on the back of a drawing by Mustafa Wade, glued to canvas with polyvinyl, 45 x 54.5 cm

F. H.: Dwarfs – unfortunately Disney has conformed them into stupid things – but you must think about the garden dwarfs before Disney came. I find garden dwarfs every-where now. You can buy them anywhere. That is very strange, where you buy these dwarfs. You cannot buy them in a shop, you cannot buy them in a gallery. If you go to a modern sculptor and say: "Please, I want to buy a garden dwarf, can you make me one", he will throw you out. You buy a garden dwarf in a nursery. That is amazing. Where you buy plants and seeds, potted plants, books about plants, they have a department where they have garden dwarfs. There is something mysterious about that. Why do they sell garden dwarfs together with plants? It must have something to do with ecology, or it is the God of Ecology.

People like to put garden dwarfs inside their gardens under plants and small trees, under flowers in a kind of little hill, and they put something else next to them, sometimes a small animal or a rabbit or other statues of figures in sagas, old fairy tales. It looks like an altar. It is very similar to the corner where they have the crucifix, Jesus hanging there, or in the Orient they have Buddha some-

where. The only thing is, it is in the garden. But not all people have it, just some people. When you ask them why they have it they can never answer the question. They only say, "Oh, because I like it, because my father had it, or it belongs to him". My the-ory is that the garden dwarf is a mind of god, the god of very ancient times which was de-stroyed – maybe even destroyed by our monotheism. He personifies the bad con-science of man towards nature. When people feel that they wrong nature they place this garden dwarf as an excuse. He is small because grass and flowers are small, so he is smaller and can talk better to the snails and the rabbits and the animals who are generally small – as we can no longer do. He is always there, in the sun, in the rain.

A fertility god, Priapus, was the god of gar-dens, their protector. It takes little imagi-nation to understand the suppression of this phallic deity by the Christian world, his replacement by a usurping dwarf lacking a huge (fertilizing) penis and the final neutralizing of this figure as a harmless ninny – where once a wise and powerful

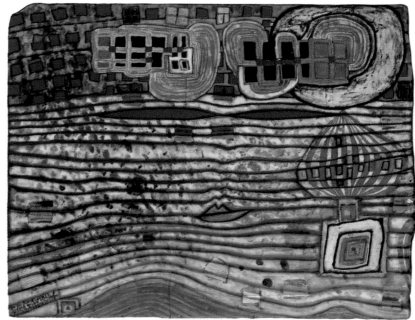

807 *Wavelength – Wellenlänge*, Algajola, 1979
Mixed media: watercolour, egg tempera, acrylic, oil and tinfoil on paper primed with chalk and polyvinyl, 53 x 63 cm

figure presided. Art explores its own implications; it carries us forward. Simultaneously, it acts to remind us of what we forget, much as do garden dwarfs.

F. H.: Yes, he is the symbol of fairy tales. People cannot live without dreams. He symbolizes that dream. He is dreaming the dream which people sometimes have not the time to dream.

The architects hate it. For a rational architect the worst enemy is the garden dwarf. When you see an architect – in the style of Le Corbusier, or a Bauhaus-style architect like Mies van der Rohe – the worst thing you can do for him, the worst offence, is when you invite him to dinner and you put a garden dwarf on the table.

In the summer of 1978 Hundertwasser began a painting that was to occupy his attention for three years as he struggled with its disturbing subject. Unusually rich in the mixed media employed, in addition to the usual watercolour and egg tempers – often supplemented with acrylic and oil paints – *Der Führer* (pp. 190–191) uses lacquers and numerous metal leafs and foils of tin, gold, silver, and copper. All was painted on a fibreboard surface extended with glue and sawdust mounds on a polyvinyl white ground.

Early in his career, Hundertwasser had used irregularly shaped supports (torn paper, a tailor's pattern, etc.), but increasingly he painted fictive spaces behind the picture plane. Transparent space is compromised when a picture's edges call attention to themselves; but "Der Führer" required something different. The subject occasioned a rupture with the past.

A Nazi salute erupts from the countryside, but looms above everything and pro-

jects outside space. That hand is the Führer's, and is also his public saluting him. That hand was omnipresent during the Hitler era. The hand raised in adoration was one of an ocean of hands so raised. The hand waved frantically with joy. Hands saluted the Führer and his image. Throngs rushed forward in giddy delight, their hands raised in recognition, their hands raised to do the work of *Der Führer,* but today we cannot find these crowds of happy saluters. That hand was everywhere, and today, like the unicorn, no one claims to have seen it.

Beginning in 1975, Hundertwasser worked on an idea for a painting that became *Song of the Whales* (HW 777) (p. 187), a mixed media triptych that he finished in February 1978 at Hahnsäge,

777A *Gesang der Wale – Song of the Whales,* Tokyo-Vienna, 1978/79
Japanese woodcut in 34 colours and 2 versions: blue 1–150,
green 151–250, 57 x 42.5 cm (51.8 x 37)
Edition of 250, all signed and numbered. Cut by Hideo Maruyama, Kyoto.
Published by Gruener Janura, Glarus

Bottom: 791 *Hundertwasser Wavy Face – Tête Hundertwasser dans le cadre ondulé – Hundertwasserkopf im welligen Quadrat*, Coin design V, New Zealand, July-August 1978
Pencil on drawing paper, 29.5 x 20.6 cm

Ill. p. 189 left: 787 *Onion Rain – La tour d'onion sous la pluie d'or – Zwiebelturm im Goldregen*, Coin design I, New Zealand, July-August 1978
Pencil on drawing paper, 29.5 x 20.6 cm

where he was meeting René Brô – just before Hundertwasser left to visit President Senghor in Dakar. The picture radiates the calm the artist felt after settling in New Zealand.

RECYCLING THE DEAD

F. H.: With the entry into an ecological age we can see that there is no waste, nothing dies, everything is alive constantly, only transformed into other forms – and this is not a religious philosophy, only facts. Because of a wrong conception, the Last Judgement, resurrection, people still believe like the old Egyptians – if you can conserve a man in his corporeal appearance, then at the Last Judgement he will continue to live. But this is complete nonsense. A person should be buried only half a metre, or two feet, below the surface. Then a tree should be planted there. He should be buried in a coffin that decays so that when you plant a tree on top the tree will take something out of his substance, and change it into tree-substance. When you visit the grave you don't visit a dead man, you visit a living being who was just transformed into a tree. He continues to live in the tree. You say, "This is my grandfather, the tree is growing well, fantastic". You can develop a beautiful forest which will be more beautiful than a normal forest because the trees have their roots in the graves. That forest can spread over the landscape and, as we don't have enough forest, the forest will be conserved at the same time. It will be a park, a place for pleasure, a place to live, even a place to hunt. A fantastic place where you can live in constant contact with life and death. I don't think that any authority should be against that. Dead people should be everywhere – in one's own garden. The cities of death will also be forests of life. The trees will mark the graves. People will choose different trees so it will not be a mono-culture but a most incredible forest. This place will turn into a paradise, a Garden of Eden.

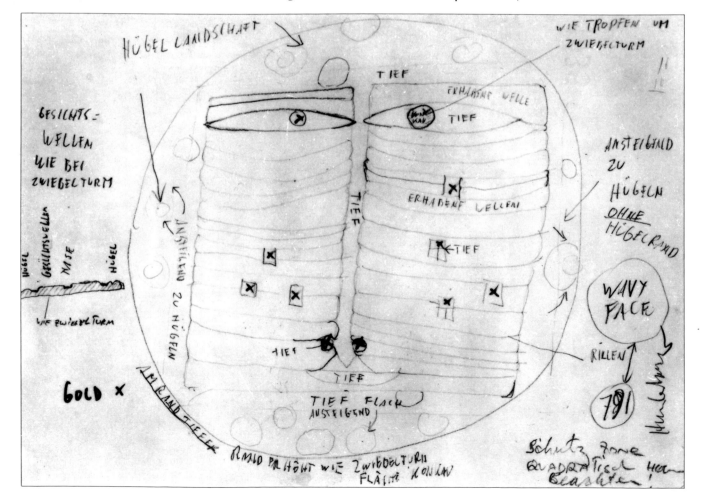

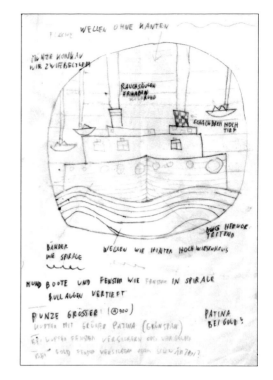

This idea first appeared in his *Garden of the Happy Dead* (p. 59), and Hundertwasser practises what he preaches. He applied for, and received, permission to be buried on his own land, amid the trees he had planted in New Zealand. On 14 June 1985, the Minister of Health, A. G. Malcolm, wrote to Hundertwasser that it is most unusual for a Minister to give authority for the burial of a person except in a burial ground. On those few occasions, the authority has always been given after the person's death and it is therefore even less common for a Minister to give authority before a person has died or indeed at a time when there is no prospect for that person's death.

What has been worrying me, however, is my certainty that you should be buried in the Bay of Islands if that is your wish; my certainty [is] that if you were to die tomorrow I would approve your burial there. Why should I not approve your burial there today even though you may not die for another 25 years? I can find no answer to that question except bureaucratic answers, and I see no reason to deny you of satisfaction while you are alive so as to give you satisfaction when you are dead.

I have, in view of all these thoughts, signed an authority for you to be buried in a special place.

MEDALS

In 1979 the Austrian Mint coined five medallions according to Hundertwasser's designs (on which he had been working during the previous year). In one drawing Hundertwasser pictured the front view of a steamship underway, with smaller ships in the background supporting the larger vessel as angels in Byzantine art fill the spaces around the Christ Child and His Mother. The design's strict frontality and symmetry suggests something hieratic and noble. Hundertwasser intended a note of theocratic heraldry for this project.

Never trained as a sculptor, Hundertwasser was initially reluctant to venture into coinage. But one idea proved compelling, of carrying "coins with me in my pocket as small works of art which I show everybody". He designed the coins in plaster on a scale "the size of a soup plate" and continued shaping and refining details until the design satisfied him. Then a technician

Top centre: 788 *Window Spiral – La spirale aux fenêtres – Fensterspirale,* Coin design II, New Zealand, July-August 1978
Pencil on drawing paper, 29.5 x 20.6 cm

Top right: 794 *Steamer from Front with Ships – Vapeur de front avec bateaux – Dampfer von vorne mit Schiffen,* Coin design VI, New Zealand, July-August 1978
Pencil on drawing paper, 29.5 x 20.6 cm

189

Ill. pp. 190/191: 820 *Der Führer – The Leader,* Kaurinui, August 1978, Paris, December 1978, Porquerolles, August 1980, Giudecca, January 1981
Mixed media: watercolour, egg tempera, acrylic, oil lacquer, tinfoil, gold, silver and copperleaf on fibreboard primed with polyvinyl, wooden fingers glued on, 47 x 62 cm (53 x 62)

Bottom: 810 *Die Fenster gehen nach Hause – The Windows Are Going Home,* Venice-Vienna, 1978/79
Mixed media: watercolour, acrylic, egg tempera, oil and tinfoil glued onto canvas with polyvinyl, 64 x 91 cm

reduced them in size. "From time to time you touch it with your fingers, you take it out of your pocket and look at it all wet in the pouring rain or in the bath under water or in a glass of water or in the sun, or it shines in candlelight when you turn it about".

THE FIRST FLAG

For *Friedensfahne 1978 für das Gelobte Land,* Hundertwasser combined the colour symbolism of Moslem green with the blue of the sky and water. "The green Arab crescent moon is infinite like the horizon, like a cup of open hands holding the blue Jewish star like a precious jewel; the Arab moon is protecting the Jewish star . . . It is the flag of union. It is the flag of the Promised Land." (Statement of 3 September 1978.) In a world where idealism rarely amounts to very much, Austria's Chancellor Bruno Kreisky sent the peace flag to the heads of state of the Middle Eastern countries. Whether or not it fostered understanding is anybody's guess, although the emblem saluted the underlying similarity of the cultures dwelling together in that region. "I received very nice letters from the Arabic side as well. I got a letter from Bourguiba, from King Hussein of Jordan, from Shimon Peres, who came to Vienna especially to meet me for this flag."

DIRT

There are different kinds of dirt. Common sense yields the distinction between litter and dirt (soil, humus). To misplace dirt makes it visible. Littering (decontextualization) demarcates ecology just as the propriety of art (the borders of *kitsch*) is cen-

834 *La prochaine dimension – (le mal et le bien) – Die nächste Dimension – (Böse und Gut) – The Next Dimension – (Good and Evil)*, Kaurinui, April-June 1982, Vienna, July 1982
Mixed media: watercolour, egg tempera, polyvinyl, oil, lacquer, silver leaf and china ink on paper, glued to canvas with cellulose, primed with chalk, zinc white and polyvinyl, frame made in New Zealand, 90 x 90 cm

tral to Hundertwasser's aesthetic concerns. The risks are high in distinguishing between dirt (soil) and litter, between human beings as exploitative parasites or a benign part of the world.

Hundertwasser says, "To be conscientious in our society is not to be afraid of dirt anymore." In the last two hundred years we have learned to think differently about dirt and cleanliness. Class was hardly an indicator. Kings, queens and emperors rarely washed, and were unimaginably polluted by today's standards. Excrement was a commonplace even in royal households, and castles stank offensively. In the last three centuries, science has increasingly taught the relationships between health and hygiene. As a result the infant mortality rate has dropped. Life expectancy has risen. Plagues have vanished. Smallpox has been eradicated and polio has all but disappeared; the potential to control syphilis and tuberculosis is at hand.

F. H.: But at the same time as these deadly sicknesses disappeared others arrived as humans went too far in one direction. Now we have a completely clean and sterile environment, especially in America, Sweden,

Germany, Switzerland – in Europe anyhow. We now have sicknesses which are just as bad as the plague and those epidemics of the Middle Ages. Now we have cancer and poisoning – all kinds of poison through radiation, through the food chain, and especially through the medicines which are used to make us clean, like the antibiotics and DDT. Now we know that cancer is an environmental sickness.

The longer I live the more I have the feeling that I must contribute to restore the dirt, just by being a little bit more dirty than others. Of course, I wash myself like others, but I don't see why the windows should be constantly clean, why the walls should be blank and sterile, why the toilet should be sprayed with poison? This is dangerous not only for us but for the environment. Extreme cleanliness is one big part of the reason why our environment is poisoned, why our forests are dying.

Like Chagall and Matisse, Hundertwasser is one of those exceedingly rare modern ar-

818 *Let Us Pray Manitou Wins*, Venice-Spinea, 1979/80
Serigraph: 10 versions in 14 colours with metal embossing in 2 colours, 56 x 76 cm
Edition of 428 and XC proofs. Coordinator Alberto della Vecchia. Printed by Studio D'Arte Serigrafica di Claudio Barbato, Spinea, Venice 1981

tists who can maintain colour harmony in a single painting that contains the entire spectrum. Creating a sympathetic agreement of colours that normally conflict when adjacent is no easy thing, and there is no set formula to accomplish it. Like Chagall, Hundertwasser, in *Wavelength, Wellenlänge* (p. 186), brings the most diverse colours into proximity without disharmony. When recent Modernists have delighted us – like Morris Louis – they have relied on restricted means: a limited palette, for example. *Wavelength* is a joyous riot of colour, somehow all subdued and glowing. These lush tones coexist contiguously, adding strength to their neighbours. Nor is the colour intensity uniform. Saturated reds, blacks and blues can be found near lower-intensity but less saturated colours. Value shifts are encountered when the underlying white of the primed support shows through (a technique akin to watercolour). Glazing animates the whole and produces a translucence through which we look to gather the painting's bounty of colour.

In *The Windows Are Going Home, Die Fenster Gehen Nach Hause* (p. 192) Hundertwasser reconsidered a motif he had used previously: windows returning to their home in the sky (cf. p. 116). The recapitulated theme is handled with a suavity that, if lacking the initial urgency, has gained grace and eloquence. Not every artist can return to material and reinvigorate it. Indeed, Hundertwasser is not always successful in recapturing the vitality of an earlier image, no more than we regain love's aura when we meet former lovers – but only a cynic spurns such reacquaintance. It is not to be scorned. Moments of artistic infatuation can, and should, be savoured again. Art history overly stresses the recitation of careers that roar through styles and periods without a backward glance. A certain gentleness is thereby lost, to say nothing of thoroughness. Art can grant that a moment be reentered.

The latter version of *The Windows Are Going Home, Die Fenster Gehen Nach Hause* is not inferior to the first, but differ-

ent. The new version is sweeter. Mystery has given way to knowledge. Hundertwasser created a rapturous levitation where houses rise through the middle of the picture into the lavender concave sky that enfolds the background. In the foreground, great blue concentric rings pulse with golden centres. The whole is surrounded by a green border.

In 1980 Hundertwasser travelled to Qatar, Sri Lanka, and the Maldive Islands before returning to New Zealand. He was awarded the Austrian State Prize for Visual Art, which automatically made Hundertwasser a member of the Kunstsenat.

THINKING ABOUT BUILDING

F. H.: I was asked to make a speech about colour in architecture for human planning. It was at a symposium somewhere in Austria, in Zell am See. I thought a long time. I wrote an essay, but I did not go there because I had a girl and did not want to miss her, so instead of making that speech I wrote it and sent it to them. They were very angry, but the speech is interesting because what is wrong with the colour in architecture is that it is always one colour. There is monoculture in our architecture, and monoculture is always bad. (Monoculture is chain-production, is forests where you plant only one species, and monoculture is in our pre-fabricated objects.) There might be a man, maybe the assistant mayor of the town, to whom the paint manufacturers bring a catalogue of colours, and he can choose all kinds of pink. Whole blocks of flats will be painted pink, on the decision of a man who doesn't understand anything. That pink will turn grey, will get dirty ten years later, and rain will wash over it. The sunny side of the building will fade while on the shady side it will remain, and on the rainy side it will get dirty. Strangely, that building will get better with time – though people will not admit it, they will think it is dirty.

831 *Tender Dinghy* – Kaurinui, February-June 1982, Vienna, July 1982
Mixed media: watercolour, egg tempera, polyvinyl, oil, lacquer and gold leaf on chipboard primed with chalk, zinc white and polyvinyl, 64 x 43 cm

When you have a building in one colour which is damaged somewhere on the outside, then they repair it, but they don't repair the hole, they repaint the whole building. For one tiny defect they must repaint the whole building. They are unhappy if there is some divergence from the monoculture, from the evenness of the building, that destroys the sterile unity, the unity of death. I would be very happy; I would mark it and repair it in another colour, for instance, red, just like if we have a shirt and there is a hole in it. I don't waste a lot of time and energy running around trying to find exactly the same colour to repair it, or to give it to a specialist who can repair it so that afterwards you cannot see where the damage was. That is silly. On the contrary, you should be happy about the damage because this is a gift given by nature. It makes you richer, not poorer; you just put a patch on it, and when you have a blue shirt use a yellow patch. That is normal.

Hundertwasser was given charge of a master class in the Vienna Fine Arts Academy; more remarkably, the Municipality of Vienna agreed to erect an apartment building in the heart of the city following a Hundertwasser plan. During the summer of 1980 a professional model maker worked with Hundertwasser to prepare a model for the

proposed building. When presented at a press conference by Vienna's mayor, Leopold Gratz, the success of the model ignited the usual controversies that greeted Hundertwasser's efforts on his native soil. His usual critics were predictable in their vitriol. But the house project moved on to glorious success.

H. R.: How do you schedule your time, when to do architecture, when to paint?
F. H.: I think architecture was the aim all the time. I painted because I was not allowed to do architecture. So I dreamt on a small scale what I was not allowed to do on a big scale. I was dreaming that the paintings were nothing but sketches and models for bigger things.

***Let Us Pray Manitou Wins*, 1981 (p. 193), extended the range of his graphics. The de-**

Top left: Kohlenwäsche in Hamm before renovation

Top right: Hundertwasser's model of the Kohlenwäsche in Hamm

Right: Hundertwasser's second model of the Kohlenwäsche in Hamm

196

sign of the central section of *Let Us Pray Manitou Wins* derives from *Downtown-plane* (HW 698), a painting Hundertwasser began in 1970 and finished in 1971. The title refers to an Amerindian prophecy that the hunting grounds would be destroyed by white people and that vengeance would follow. The work is a terrestrial equivalent for *Song of the Whales* (p. 187), a dire warning against rampant and thoughtless human growth. The print carries all manner of quotes, including a miniature of Leonardo's version of the Vitruvian Man, a late example of Kampmann's glass trees, various Hundertwasser houses and windows, and a rising column of smoke from the foreground house.

1982 was an extraordinarily busy year, even for a man as energetic as Hundertwasser. From winter until late May, Hundertwasser worked in New Zealand on sixteen paintings. He travelled to Chieng Mai (Thailand) in June, then, via Vienna, to Venice, where in August he finished the pictures started in New Zealand – before he went on to Sardinia in September. One of these 1982 works, *The Doges* (p. 184), is an interesting composition. Three large magicians occupy the right side. Each wears a different coloured tall hat (recalling the Doges' mitres and also stovepipe hats). Their feet invisible, each stands before a green band bordered with buildings – the islands of Venice. Their gorgeously patterned robes of office are all different.

Their mouths are the shape of boats, and the central wedge is golden-hued water with kiss-boats. After thirty years this motif – which first appeared in *Yellow Kisses – Yellow Boats* (p. 34), 1951, whose punning title elided boat and mouth – reappeared to good effect. In contrast to its lavish colour, *The Doges's* lower left presents a dark figure in grisaille, with a red-speckled face and lank blond hair. This figure, perhaps a perforated woman, seems to be moving left, out of the picture, toward a corner bordered by a speckled red stream. (In an unfinished state – preserved in an archival photograph – this reddish border-stream was grey with a series of bands over which was glazed the final, much stronger, colour. In the finished work these subtle colours contribute bountifully textured complexity, orchestral in its tonal variety.)

Another of the paintings that originated during this productive period was *Tender Dinghy* (p. 195), whose title, like *The Doges,* concerns the connection of people to land and water. *Tender Dinghy* returns to Hundertwasser's favourite vantage, the bird's-eye view. Below us water shimmers, reflecting rainbow stripes as water breaks

Hundertwasser at a preliminary meeting at the Kohlenwäsche in Hamm, 1982

sunlight. A sky-blue boat is moving gently on the water.

Recalling an earlier emotional state and to examine his motives and growth, Hundertwasser undertook one of his rare self-portraits. In *The Next Dimension (Good and Evil)* (p. 193), Hundertwasser divided his face left and right. The left eye and nostril were covered with metallic silver leaf. The right eye and nostril were treated with black china ink, which absorbs all light. Opacity and reflectivity contrast the inner and outer worlds.

ARCHITECTURE DOCTOR

During this period, Hundertwasser worked as an "architecture doctor" – a profession of his own invention whose calling is to modify and beautify existing structures, structures sterile and soulless in character. In that capacity Hundertwasser embellished the façade of the Rosenthal factory at Selb. He met with the Federal Governor to propose the application of ceramic "beard-tongues" to the façade of the Rupertinum Museum in Salzburg. Hundertwasser also presented a large model for the transformation of an old coal mine in Hamm.

He began to lecture on architecture and the environment, speaking in Manila in June, then Seattle and Washington, D.C. In San Francisco, "Hundertwasser Week" was declared for 5–12 December 1982, and he unveiled two posters for Greenpeace and the Jacques Cousteau Society. The most memorable of his architectural addresses took place in the San Francisco office of the architecture group of Skidmore, Owings & Merrill. "When I have to read a speech I cut pieces out of books and already printed

Photo of the American Institute of Architecture in Washington D.C., painted over for a television teaching film, December 1982

speeches and glue them together with my new writings to make a roll, sometimes ten metres long. Then I hold the roll and start reading and the roll unfolds; as I talk I unroll it, and at the end of the speech you have a long roll running into the audience." On this occasion his talk resulted in some serious and protracted difficulties. He read a manifesto.

F. H.: I talked about inhuman architecture and especially the inhuman architecture done in that office, for which the architects there were all responsible. I said that humans should have the right to transform the insides and outsides of the places in which they live. This "third skin" of human beings has to develop, to change and undergo mutations, and if you impede this process, it is as criminal as if you prevent a child from growing. And that is what is done constantly in architecture, and that is why I got angry.

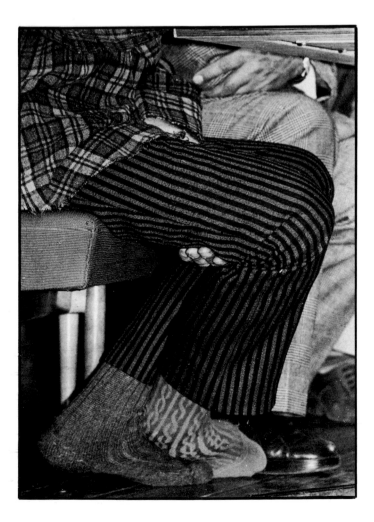

But then Hundertwasser departed from his speech – offensive enough to his audience in the very bosom of corporate Modernist architecture. He wanted to demonstrate his ideas with an action. He drew on a wall.

F. H.: Just to manifest my right to be present in this room. The building was built by humans, but the people who enter it are not allowed to leave a trace on the wall or floor or anything. When this human being is gone nothing is left in that room. (When I make a speech on architecture I always take out my knife and leave a mark on the lectern, and then generally the organizers get very angry and they send a bill for the whole lectern. I have to change the whole lectern because I gave life to the lectern by making a tiny mark. The friendly faces suddenly get very cool; then we have long discussions by letter.) On that occasion I did a beautiful drawing; it was made quickly on the wall but it was still a Hundertwasser drawing and it was worth some money.

They billed Hundertwasser for damages and he wrote back that there was no damage because a drawing of that size was worth thousands more than the cost of the panel. He asked for the panel back, promising to pay for a replacement. But, by then, the drawing having been destroyed, he refused to pay. This legal quagmire continued to exhaust all parties until, finally, Hundertwasser paid through his agent in San Francisco. "I did the same thing in Washington and they were very pleased with the drawing on the wall." In fact, Hundertwasser's Washington representative, Manfred Baumgartner, had arranged for Hundertwasser to paint a mural on a school building collaboratively with children.

Hundertwasser always wears "mismatched" socks

MODEL

HÜGELWIESENLAND

ROSENTHAL FACTORY, SELB

Before renovation

Hundertwasser and factory owner, Philip Rosenthal

View of the façade after Hundertwasser's "intervention"

Below: Letter dated 12. November 1982 from Hundertwasser to Mierka, the owner of the grain silo in Krems, Austria, in which he confirms their plans to transform the building over a period of several years.

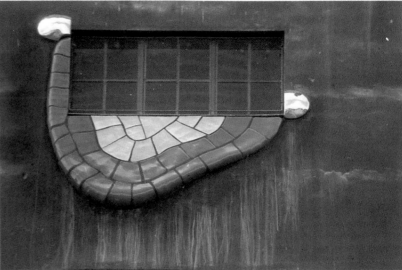

12. NOV. 82 WIEN

LIEBER FREUND MIRKA

ICH FREUE MICH SEHR ÜBER
UNSERE LANGJÄHRIGE ZUSAMMEN ARBEIT
DIE IN DEM AUGEN BLICK BEGANN UND
BESIEGELT WURDE ALS WIR ZUSAMMEN TRAFFEN.
IHR SILO WIRD LANGSAM ÜBER DIE
JAHRE ENTSTEHEN UND ICH FÜHLE ES
WIRD EIN WERK WERDEN DAS VIELE
BAUWERKE ÖSTERREICHS ÜBER LEUCHTEN
WIRD. EIN BAUWERK AN DER DONAU

GRAIN SILO, KREMS

WÜRDIG DER BURGEN DER WACHAU DER KIRCHEN UND TÜRME IN KREMS UND DEN BAUTEN WIENS. ES WIRD LANGSAM ENTSTEHEN UND SEINE AUSSTRAHLUNG VON JAHR ZU JAHR MEHREN WIE EIN RIESENBAUM DER PLÖTZICH SICH ENTSCHLOSSEN HAT WIEDER ZU WACHSEN UND JEDES JAHR NEUE UND NOCH WUNDERBARERE BLÜTEN BRINGT DIE KEIN MENSCHEN= AUGE JE GESEHEN HAT. SO EIN LANGSAM ZUR VOLLENDUNG REIFENDES

BAUWERK DASS SEINE WANDLUNG VON ALLEN AUGEN VOLLZIEHT HAT ES SEIT DER ZEIT DER GROSSEN KATHE= DRALEN NICHT GEGEBEN VON VIELEN HUNDERTEN VON JAHREN, GERADE IN UNSERER ZEIT DES SCHNELL SCHNELL KONZIPIERTEN, SCHNELL GEMACHTEN UND SCHNELL VERGANGENEN SO WIE IN DER MODE IST IHR SILO WIRD IHR SILO ZU EINEM WENDEPUNKT ZU EINEM NEUEN DENKEN ZU EINEM NEUEN MENSCHEN UND NATURGERECHTEN

ZEITALTER DASS BEGINNT.
MAN WIRD SICH FREUEN DIESES IHR WAHRZEICHEN ZU ERBLICKEN AUF DEM WEG VON WIEN NACH KREMS UND MAN WIRD DAS TEMPO VERLANGSAMEN UM BESSER UND LÄNGER DIE FUNKELNDEN EINZELHEITEN ZU BETRACHTEN.

INZWISCHEN HERZLICH IHR

RUPERTINUM, SALZBURG

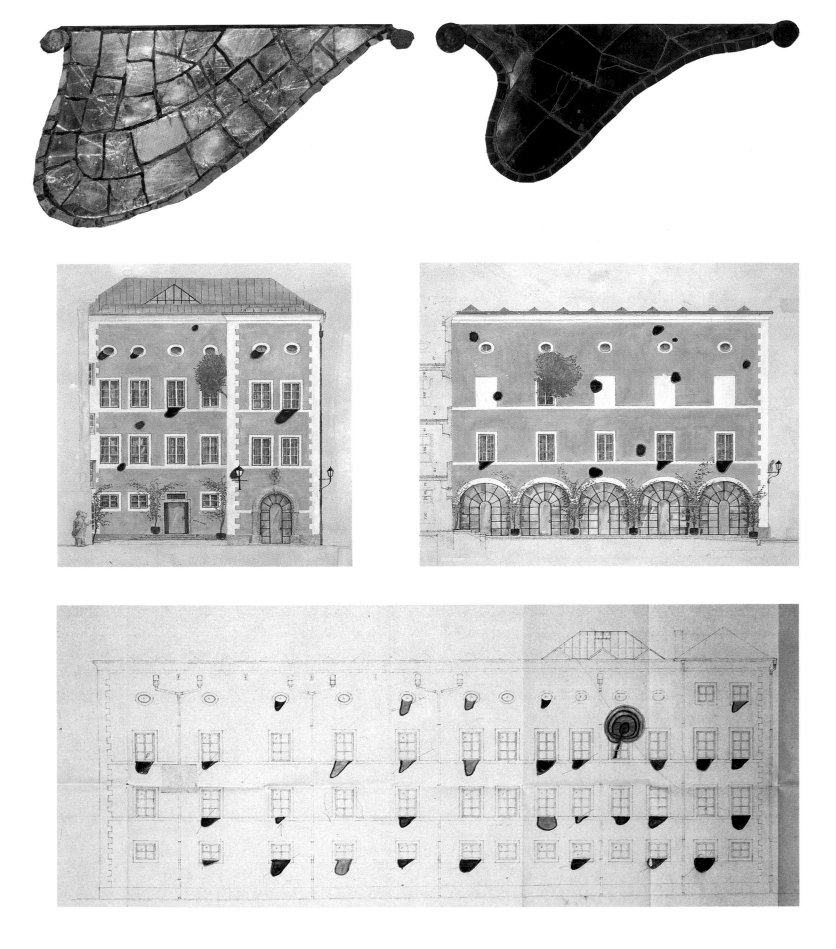

THE HUNDERTWASSER HOUSE

	Stowasser	STOWASSEN
	Fritz	FRITZ
	Friedrich	FRIEDRICH
	Friederich	FRIEDERICH
	Friedereich	FRIEDEREICH
	Friedenreich	FRIEDENREICH
	Hundertwasser	HUNDERTWASSER
	Friedensreich	FRIEDENSREICH
	Regentag	REGENTAG
	Dunkelbunt	DUNKELBUNT

839 Löwengasse – La Troisième Peau – The Third Skin, Porquerolles, 1980,
Wolfgangsee, 1981, finished in Venice, August 1982
Mixed media: watercolour, egg tempera, polyvinyl, oil and lacquer on cardboard with aluminium,
primed with chalk and polyvinyl, 57 x 63 cm

Miraculously, the city of Vienna requested Hundertwasser to build one of his utopian structures. The officials, haunted by the images Hundertwasser painted, wanted something special to exemplify his ideals. At first things did not go very well. The architect assigned to assist Hundertwasser tried to pervert his notions. No other architect could be hired "because of problems with the architectural lobby, the architect organizations, and the architect unions." Instead, the state offered to collaborate, to assign a staff architect (Herr Pelikan) who worked on salary to transcribe Hundertwasser's thoughts and to assure structural and mechanical tolerances.

Hundertwasser frequently refers to the three skins we possess: skin, clothing, and architecture. Accordingly, he shows bleeding architecture, buildings suffering from boils and eruptions – maladies his buildings would not possess. The Löwengasse structure is actually a vertical village; each coloured flat reads as a solid mass within the building – a discrete unit. One can stand in the street and, pointing up to one's apartment, say, "I live in that red apartment. That's my home."

The renewable plaster on the walls (to shoulder height) can be drawn on by children and adults. A doctor's office is on the premises. Dignity returns to the dweller, who becomes more than the furniture, which is replaced with each lease. The tenant is much more of a factor in the history of the place than a fly who meanders in only to circle the room and sail out again into the sunlight.

The vaulting joyous roofline evokes Gaudí's *Casa Mila* which (though Antonio Gaudí designed parks) did not contain a roof garden, or an indoor winter garden, or numerous terraces – reachable by stairs from apartments below. As in Gaudí, opulent stairs lead to the street, a virtual extension of the street, and angled supports recall Gaudí's *Park Güell* project. The great curving parabolic entry arch recalls Gaudí, although Hundertwasser surpassed Gaudí by using the internal space – of what is in reality a hyperbolic saddle arch – for a playroom. In comparison to Hundertwasser's "usefulness" of every part, Gaudí can seem overdone, and forced. Gaudí magnified small details into huge unnatural features; and scale did not justify this enlargement, except in terms of the explosion of love and life Gaudí meant to communicate: "Yes, of course. [My building] will have something of Gaudí". Hundertwasser could envision that someday he might have Gaudí's same lavish means at his disposal.

"Yes, then I could do better, I could do more. In a sense, mine is painted architecture. The plaster has various colours throughout, each flat being a different colour. It has hollows and bumps, and at the edges it has been rubbed by hand into rainbow patterns, using other colours.

H. R.: Will you get a hand-made building or a sculpture?
F. H.: It is a kind of sculpture, of course. It can be considered as a sculpture, but one can't live happily inside a sculpture.

Surface delight had been lacking in modern building since Gaudí's death. Hundertwasser's concrete is tinted in the material so that weathering will not eliminate the colour. A patchwork of ornamental tiles (metallic silver in some places) refreshes the façade with the luxury formerly associated with a princely mode of decoration. Expensive materials for palatial buildings appear on a downtown corner, an architectural phoenix amid otherwise drab and uniformly grey buildings. Before the Löwengasse building was finished – when it was all models and drawings, scaffolding and clambering workmen confused at the rising mass of the structure – even Hundertwasser could not conceive the sensation of walking through those corridors, so unlike anything else in the history of recent architecture. It is one thing to theorize, quite another to live with the results of speculation. Before the building was occupied I asked Hundertwasser what surprises the house held for him when it was finished.

F. H.: It is much more evident and living – human, part of nature and the universe – than I ever dared to believe that it could be. It is a kind of living sculpture. The house is

Matchbox model, 1979

like a dream. Until now, houses were the extreme opposite of dreams, indoctrinating, dictatorial, oppressive. In the old days the church and kings showed their power to the common people. When somebody built a house, he showed his importance to the others by big portals, by steps going up. And this state of affairs continues in much stronger evidence than at the time of kings because, for instance, the banks and insurance companies oppress people to a much bigger extent than ever any king or emperor would have dared. Even these flat apartment buildings show the power of the state. Bauhaus architecture showed power, the power of the machine, and the powerlessness of the individual to revolt. People stand in front of my house with open mouths, and they cannot believe that a dream can be re-

KINGS

It is clear how Hundertwasser feels about the modern corporation. This faceless, anonymous, stateless entity is bound by no authority, and is ultimately irresponsible, since the employees, like soldiers, can claim that "I was innocent, I was only following orders". Hundertwasser admires the responsibility and visibility of royalty and he believes there is a place for kings in the modern world.

F. H.: When the people see the king walking in fantastic clothes with a white ermine cape and a sceptre, with a long coat to the floor, with white horses, a castle with golden onion domes, then the people are content. It is strange but true. If you take a king or an emperor away from the people they feel bad. Austrians and Germans – everybody has everything, cars, money, television – they have a high standard of living, but something is missing. It is the king, Emperor Franz Josef.

H. R.: The Habsburgs furnished sovereigns to Austria from 1278–1918, and to Spain from 1516–1700; are there many Habsburgs around?

F. H.: Yes, there is a Habsburg, Otto Habsburg, and I am in touch with him. The next step would be to convince Austrians to reinstate the Habsburgs. I like difficult tasks.

H. R.: Which type of government would you prefer to see rule?

F. H.: I would like a constitutional monarchy.

H. R.: What you seem to have in mind is that your house should provide a people's Neuschwanstein, a fantastic, regal palace for all. This is the service of builders for kings, emperors and popes. Who is your favourite architect?

ality. They have to look twice, because this is exactly what they dream; this house is out of the world of dreams. This house satisfies the deep, real longing people have.

The building unfacetiously expresses people's desires stripped of any pretentious need to make an "appearance". The imperiousness of fashion – of changing styles which are dictated by a few professional tastemakers – has been nullified, and natural desires blossom unrepressed. Hundertwasser's audience is considerably greater than that of the avant-gardists, who work for themselves against the longings of ordinary people, but, then again, that is the supposed position of post-modernism.

F. H.: Gaudí, of course, and Cheval, the French postman and Simon Rodia in Los Angeles who built the Watts Towers. Of course, there are many nameless and countless American young architects who make self-made houses who have that dream and fulfil it every day for their own housing. America, especially California, is now very advanced; there is a huge movement of thousands and thousands of people who are moving in that direction.

Hundertwasser's house proves that mass production can yield cost-effective variety. None of the locks or doorknobs are the same on any of the apartments; though ordered from hardware catalogues, they are not uniform throughout building, nor are the doors, or the windows – everyone has a uniquely individual living situation that they can further change at will.

H. R.: Suppose someone had no feeling at all for the building and you wanted to explain why the walls are uneven, dappled and irregular.
F. H.: They have the feeling already, I mean that I've found that it's deep inside every human being. Humans today get lost because of the straight line and because of the levelling effect of mass production.

Rather than insisting on manufacturing handmade elements which would drive the cost of the buildings up astronomically, Hundertwasser specified "off-the-shelf technology" (pre-existing mass-produced elements – doorknobs, windows, doors, plumbing fixtures, etc.) and combined them in novel ways. Rather than specifying one style of architectural element for a whole building, by mixing different manufactured parts already available in the marketplace, Hundertwasser harmonized the best of both worlds. The industrial capacity for efficient and low-cost mass production based on uniformity of manufacture is maintained while the luxury of variety is present in every element of the house.

Just as he had long imagined he could, Hundertwasser planted trees arranged to grow atop his building in the heart of the city. These trees provide shade, ornament (as no carved foliage could), add colour, clean the air, and suggest a kind of aristocratic opulence formerly available only to large landholders. Significantly, stairs lead from lower floors so that dwellers below the top floor can have an apartment with a roof garden even if the roof is not the ceiling of their apartment.

Although bureaucrats opposed every

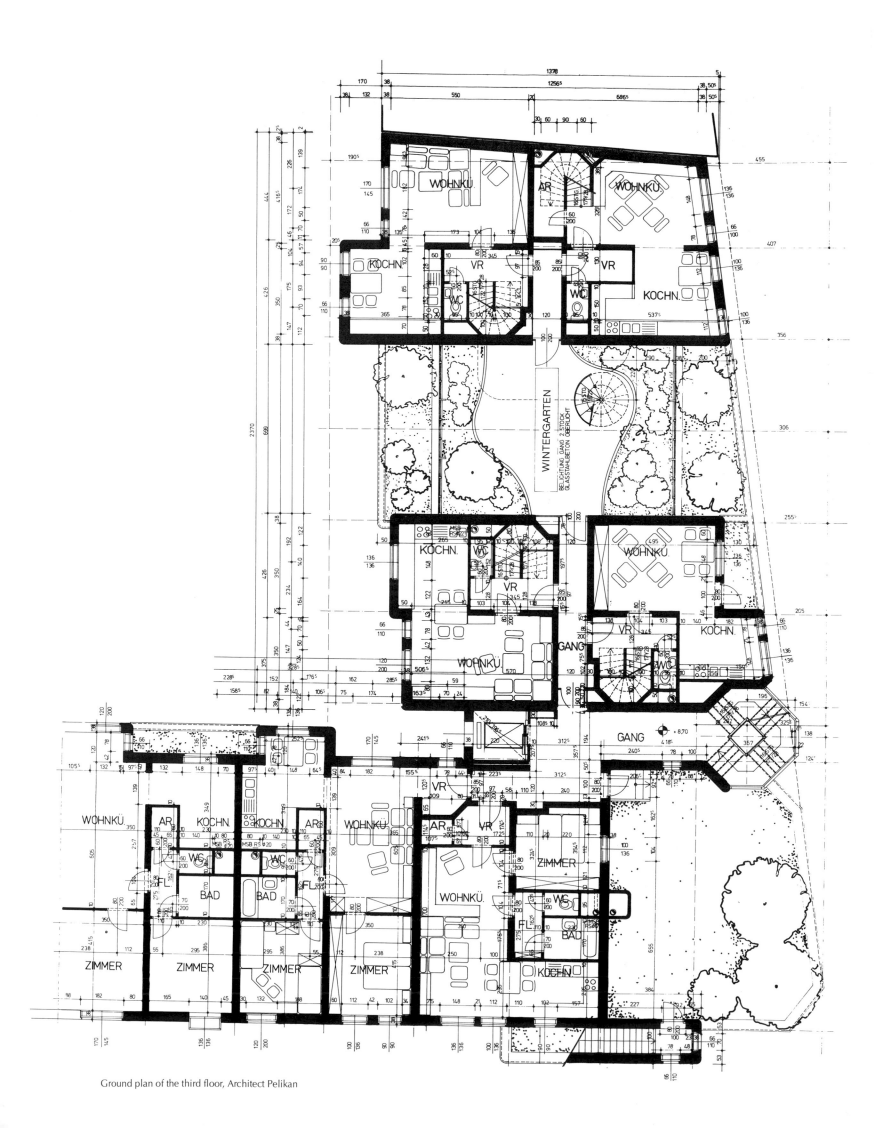

Ground plan of the third floor, Architect Pelikan

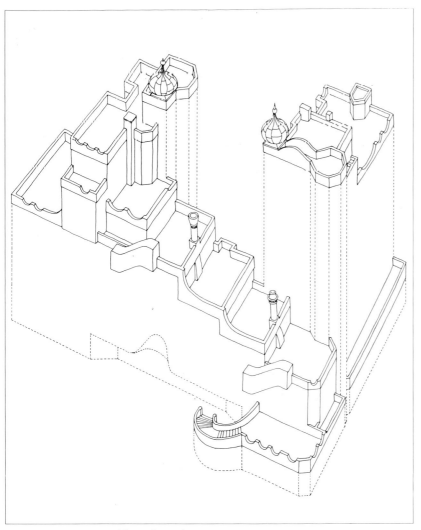

Axonometric projection of the roof, Kegelgasse

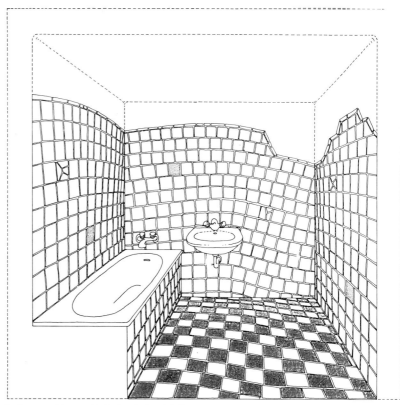

Bathroom with organic design, industrial tiles

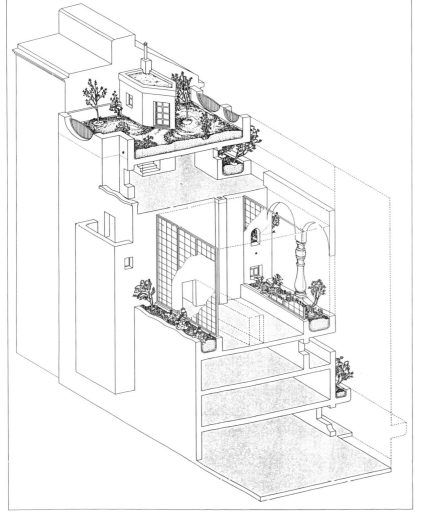

Axonometric projection, winter garden and roof terrace

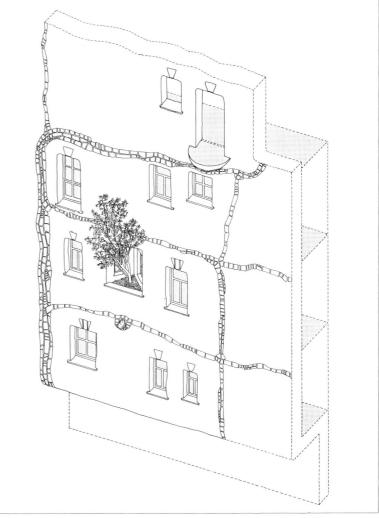

Façade detail, coloured lines and room outlines

deviation from municipal codes, the apartment block proved an astounding success. Demand for flats in the building is 600 % above subscription possibilities. This is a model for the rest of the world to follow. The health of the individual can be markedly improved by living in the settings Hundertwasser advises. (Like any other medicine, not all prescriptions will be correct for all people; there are undoubtedly personalities who require the ordering grid.) For the most part creative faculties will be improved by Hundertwasser's architecture, which uses the conveniences of modern technology without insisting that the house itself is a machine.

Children living in Hundertwasser's house undergo the same sort of awakening he experienced as a child. One of the tenants remarked: "It's very good for kids", because in contrast to her former residence – when the child lived in a modern apartment and painted houses with straight triangular roofs – now the little girl draws flowers and undulating rooflines; her mother remarks that "Since she has lived here, her drawing has been colourful and imaginative again." ("New York Times", 8 January 1987). The interesting point is that the mother – perhaps unconsciously – sees the new apartment as remedying a condi-

tion imposed by soulless modern architecture, for she speaks of her child's drawings as being lively "again", as if vitality had been draining from the girl as she was formed into a model, dull, citizen.

This massive building project had, inadvertently, no freelance architects. The architectural profession's own stubbornness excluded them from the enterprise.

F. H.: Nowadays it is the job of the artist because the architects have failed as a profession. They did not live up to their "Hippocratic oath", so to speak. That is, they build houses which make people sick, mentally and otherwise, and that is why the revolution must come from outside, and I think it comes from the artist.

Because I am not an architect, the city gave me an architect to fulfil my wishes, to transcribe them into plans and make them feasible, but the architect made everything square – he squared everything out. The irregular windows he made regular, the onion-domed towers he transformed into cubes – and he gave nasty interviews in the newspapers about how good he is and how bad I am and that what I do is completely impossible. He is the serious architect and he cannot allow this insanity, which is detrimental to the public. What he said was not true, but he said it and the newspapers printed it. He gave something like twenty interviews. All the newspapers sided with

Plan of plaster colouring for façade. Plan by Arch. Pelikan, coloured by Hundertwasser

216

the architect and they all attacked me and the politicians who commissioned the work.

Yet you have talked to Herr Bruckner, the overseeing construction engineer – it has gone as fast as a normal flat building. The reason is very strange, but it is a normal and human reason. The workers who work on the building like working there. They like to work in variations. They like to mix different colours, like to make curved forms, like to work on windows which are not all the same; that makes them involved in the building. They do not have the feeling that they are just machines who assemble pre-fabricated items. Because they are interested and because they work joyfully, they identify themselves with the work and work quicker. When you force workers to assemble things just like on the assembly-line they are not interested and find it disgusting and work without pleasure – and their

rhythm slows down. Then the workers say to the employer, "When you force me to do this uninteresting work, you will have to raise my wages or let me work less." Then they strike and ask for higher wages.

Everybody would say – every architect, every socialist would say, "We must make the houses all the same, then we can build

is disappearing, when franchised foods and mass-produced goods of every sort force an insistently alien rhythm into our lives, our houses can be made with industrially fabricated elements but assembled in a way that gives variety to the cityscape and joyful employment to skilled workers who might otherwise be underemployed. In the modern welfare state (which means most developed countries) the cost of unemployment far exceeds the cost of creating jobs that add visual and cultural interest. In fact, such workers should be construed as part of the new service industries; the element they contribute, not simply fabrication of the building, is the "service" of quality workmanship, for which we are willing to pay in all other aspects of our lives as consumers.

There are ten different sizes of windows in the building, and Hundertwasser worked out their arrangement, first on paper, then on a model.

quicker, faster." But this is not true. The contrary is true. Rationalization goes to a certain point, but then all of a sudden it turns into the contrary.

For a post-industrial age, Hundertwasser's building technique should be preferred, as it employs a great number of people in skilled crafts. In an age when work's dignity

F. H.: Together with the model-maker we decided there would be ten different kinds of windows displayed in different ways, in different places. I thought I must make this compromise with the builders, otherwise

they would go crazy if every window were really different. It would be terribly expensive because that would mean every window was handmade – on a building with 300 windows.

H. R.: Are the windows grouped in functional units?

F. H.: I tried to make the windows for the living rooms bigger than for the kitchens, and to make the windows where they don't have much light anyhow (on the courtyards) bigger than up near the top of the building. I tried only to make windows that look good from the outside. I thought that if they look good from the outside they will look good from the inside, too.

H. R.: In a regular building people on the ground floor get the same size windows as the people on the top floor.

F. H.: The interesting thing is that until one hundred – or even as recently as fifty – years ago windows were not the same size on all the storeys. Even the storeys were different heights; the ground floor was higher, the next lower, the one above it still lower, and the last the lowest. At first the rich people were on the ground floor and they had big windows and high ceilings while on the top floors were the servants. The higher up you went in one of these buildings the poorer the people. Today we have another reason, which is a very human reason.

On the ground floor in cities you have less light so you must have bigger windows; on the top floors there is a lot of light, you are much nearer the sky, and you don't have the shadow from the neighbouring houses – so you have smaller windows. In fact, with the smaller windows you get just as much, maybe even more, light than down on the ground floor, or the first with a huge window. I don't understand why buildings have the storeys all the same height. You have

one grid and you repeat it up 20, 30, 100 storeys – this is madness. Another thing: as windows get smaller and smaller as you go up the façade of the building you get a feeling of perspective as the building gets higher. You get a good feeling that the building is standing solidly like a pyramid with a broad base.

Black lines surround the chosen colours to accentuate the outlines, which shade out to grey, which is rubbed into the concrete to

ated into the building, and this is a dream that Modernist architects have long harboured. Le Corbusier's Marseilles Block, which was ultimately a failure, represented an attempt to unite the elements of a free-standing building and a town.

KEYSTONES

H. R.: Your drawings for the building feature keystones of red and blue.

F. H.: I put keystones in red ceramics; they should not be done in stucco. The keystones are a kind of crown. It is like a tie for a man; something is missing if there is not a keystone on top of the windows.

PLANTS AND ARCHITECTURE

F. H.: You can bring plants inside the house and raise them just by using the electric light for a good purpose; that means making plants live where plants generally don't live. You can very well have plants in caves if you have electric light, tube lights of ultraviolet. You can make plants work for you too, for instance, cleaning your garbage, transforming your garbage into humus and your waste and even your washing water. They can do all that, but even if it were only partly successful – if you could say, "okay, only 10 % or 20 % or 50 % of my dirty water is cleaned by my own houseplants" – it would still be a big achievement.

H. R.: Is any plant water purification system built into the house?

F. H.: No, not yet. Rainwater runs down the terraces and waters the trees and plants there.

soften the edges of the forms. In effect, each colour is framed by a darker grey, then black, which finally becomes an irregular black ceramic ribbon. These shiny ribbons outline the apartments and public spaces – staircases, elevators, public grounds or children's playgrounds, etc. The parts for individual use are colourful on the outer walls, the public parts grey.

Such houses are more like cottages that have been stacked to make a self-contained village. All the elements – a café, bookstore, laundry facility, playroom (which could be a nursery school), garage, private gardens – of a village are incorpor-

The house is a stylistic, not an ecological advance. It is a social, not a scientific/technological statement. In Hundertwasser's words, "The house is a step in human progress in the direction of harmony with nature and creativity."

As if 1983 were not a sufficiently exciting year for Hundertwasser, he also produced a set of stamps for the United Nations, in honour of the 35th anniversary of the Charter of Human Rights, at the invitation of the Secretary General.

LIVING IN THE WORLD

H. R.: Was there one time which you think of as the happiest time of your life?
F. H.: No, I think now is.

H. R.: What is the best thing that ever happened to you?
F. H.: That is hard to say. I could answer that I am alive, or that I got to be a painter and to live independently. I don't know to what I should give preference. I could say that I live in Venice or in New Zealand.
H. R.: Why did you decide to go to Venice?
F. H.: I never decided to go. Things just happen in my life. The same with the boat, it happened.

Hundertwasser believes that "Venice is a town for chosen people. To live there is different from being a tourist there." Now Hundertwasser tries to spend about three months a year in Venice, and while he might like to divide his time differently,

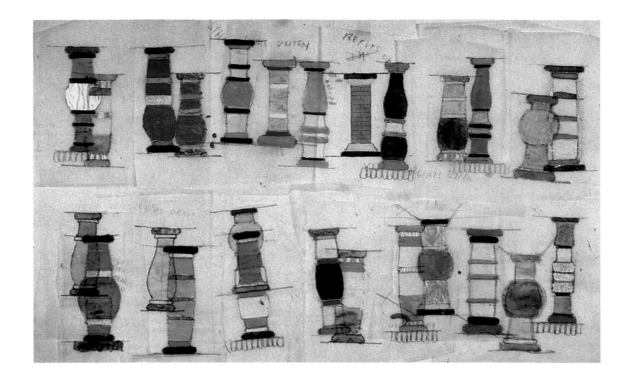

spending more time in New Zealand or in Vienna, Venice is captivating, a place whose spell is hard to break. "When I am there, yes, it is hard to leave; when I am anywhere else, it isn't. When I am there I want to stay."

H. R.: How much of the year do you spend in New Zealand?
F. H.: About three months a year, maybe six months.

On another occasion, Hundertwasser spelled out his thinking on dual, or multiple, identity and citizenship.

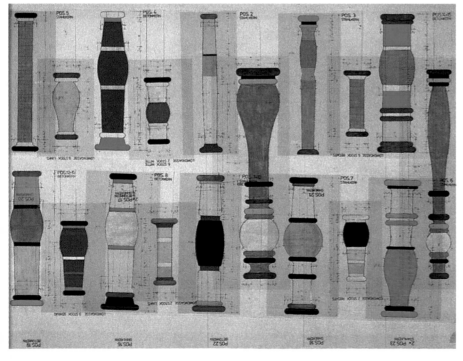

F. H.: I can't stop being a citizen of Vienna. It's very difficult to live in Vienna, and living there permanently would be a kind of torture . . . Vienna is a city closed in upon itself, it has few connections with the outside world, defending itself in this way from unhealthy modern influences. All the mistakes of present-day culture arrive in Vienna late, when they have already lost their cutting edge. As a result Vienna is not obliged to follow the same development as New York, Paris, Stockholm, Amsterdam and Tokyo. But because Vienna is such a difficult city an atmosphere is gradually created. The cultural level of people in Vienna is much higher than in other cities in the world. The Viennese are very proud, they think they know everything, and at the same time they are also great individualists. ("Domus", October 1983)

NEW ZEALAND

Known to the native Maori as Aotearoa, or "Long White Cloud", and discovered by a Dutchman, hence called Nieuw Zeeland – this island nation was a distant part of the British Empire. New Zealand today is still a

Drafts of pillars by Hundertwasser
Finished artwork by Architect Pelikan

country in search of its identity, and Hundertwasser designed a flag for it (p. 234).

No one seeing his design would be surprised at the appearance of a spiral as the artist's central motif. What was astonishing was how well that design harmonized with the heritage, spirit and mythology of his adopted country. Hundertwasser's whole career seemed pre-ordained to create this emblem. Perhaps the latent emblem had been growing in his unconscious and only needed New Zealand's air and soil to blossom. The indigenous curling fern exemplified humanity's harmonious peace with nature. The flag (for so Hundertwasser envisioned the emblem's use, not so much as a graphic design on paper, but as a standard) would be a symbol of New Zealand's leadership in a new age. With great visual economy, the white spiral within the fern's green recalls the central myth of the Maori (a story that may very well have solid historical foundation): that their ancestors came to the great island by sailing toward a long streaming white cloud which arose in the highlands and drifted continually out to sea. Recapitulating some of his ideas about the New Zealand flag, Hundertwasser turned his attentions to designing a flag for Australia (p. 235).

THE FUTURE

H. R.: What do you prefer about your current work compared to your past?

F. H.: I have the feeling that I have now come to a decisive point. It is like an onion dome. You start the dome from different points and now I come to the conclusion where the ends meet. I started as a sailor, I started as an architect, I started as an ecologist, I started as a painter, stamp designer, and so forth, and all these activities now

come closer and closer and meet at one point that makes me happy and that justifies my activities. I know that all the things I have done came to the same conclusion, that I do on a small scale what humanity is arriving at anyhow.

In times of extreme danger, humanity comes together and diversities start to lessen because then we have a common danger. For instance, only fifty years ago it would have been impossible to have Communists, priests, artists, bankers, factory owners at the same table – even nuclear energy producers meeting with ecologists, politicians, farmers, doctors and gardeners. Now it happens that they sit together at one table, in the last ten or five years, and ever more frequently, they come and sit. You see the artist with a long beard, a hippie-type, and next to him sits the banker with a tie and next to

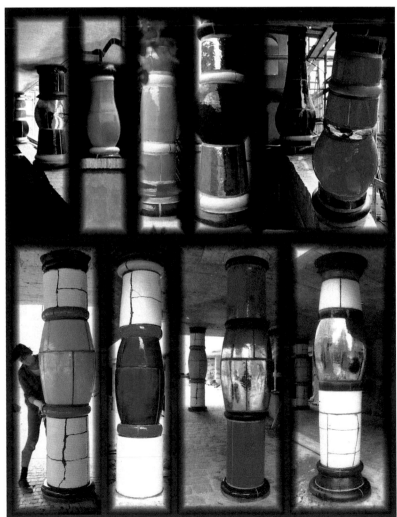

The pillars

Ill. p. 224: The mosaics

Ill. p. 225: The collaborators

Window-washers

Gardeners

Masons

Asphalters

Plasterer

Plumbers

Tilers

Carpenters (Doors)

Electricians

Painters

Carpenters (Windows)

Tiler

him the bishop, then the farmer – completely different kinds of people. They have nothing in common, yet they not only sit together and talk, but they come to similar conclusions about what has to be done to save humanity. This is amazing and it fills me with a kind of hope that something can be done, because never before have such diverse people come to the same conclusions.

H. R.: Would you like to have disciples?

F. H.: No. Disciples are the end of everything.

H. R.: Who will carry on what you do, besides the trees?

F. H.: The trees carry on, that is enough.

Trees and human beings are at the height of their respective evolution. Trees are higher than grasses, shrubs, mosses and so on. Humans are higher than the other four-legged beings, birds, snakes, worms and microbes, etc.

Trees and humans have got much in common. They are both vertical, a link between the sky and the earth. The tree develops its manifold foliage towards the sky, but man has got his innumerable brain cells related towards the sky, the spirit. Only his feet touch the soil. The sky/earth polarity of the tree is even stronger because its feet not only touch the soil but its feet are roots anchored deep within the soil; the tree has ramifications towards the sky and into the soil.

That is why trees and men are brothers in the evolution of the universe.

Though, perhaps, it could have been expected in some dialectial sense, as a swing of fashion's pendulum away from abstraction, at the end of the twentieth century figurative art has reappeared. Yet this neo-figuration has not revived Romanticism. Even in Germany, the home of sentimentality, the figure is never shown to exalt the human being. Instead the figure always expresses something of the depressing moral and physical circumstances with which the future, the past, and current prospects are

viewed. The individual and society are

equally indicted. Unremittingly, thoughtlessly, this new art expresses an exhaustion which may have been genuine at one time. Today such cynicism has long since ceased to indicate anything but mannerism. Moreover, when practised by artists who have not mastered the basic draughtsmanship to render the figure convincingly, or even gesture (as had the masters of abstraction who preceded them), the debasement of the figure is a sham.

Ignorance masquerades as stylish disgust, for disenchantment is a legitimate inheritance of the avant-garde's judgement of deranged society. Sadly, the new figurative art did not derive from the avant-garde, but is the offspring of journalism, and has triumphed momentarily, thanks largely to marketing. Compared to such well-fed cynical pandering, Hundertwasser's semi-figuration could have served as a guiding spirit. His work should be a touchstone for the young artist, for he has been treating art's current agenda for decades.

After a highly successful period of abstraction, Hundertwasser's representationalism suggests how a career of serious experimentation with imagery can be conducted. When pseudo-expressive art (distortion for the sake of commercial advantage) gained prevalence, Hundertwasser did not budge, did not add scenes of torture, dogs with triangular teeth, or sexual exploitation. To some, this made him seem oblivious (and hence inconsequential). Nevertheless, it was clear throughout the 1970s and 1980s that such hyped imagery was a pervert's confection offered for general consumption and accepted out of uncomfortable lack of self-assurance. Hundertwasser's genuinely emotional painting merits consideration over the current darlings of publicity.

The invention of all-over design (a legitimate and important discovery in the wake of Surrealism) exempted artists from responsibility. Their work was no longer

Onion dome

Ill. pp. 228–231: Hundertwasser House, Vienna

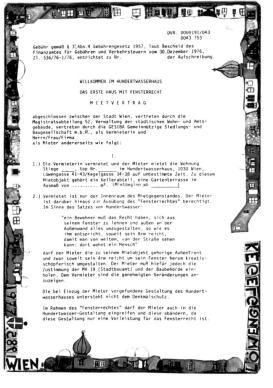

WILLKOMMEN IM HUNDERTWASSERHAUS

DAS ERSTE HAUS MIT FENSTERRECHT

M I E T V E R T R A G

abgeschlossen zwischen der Stadt Wien, vertreten durch die
Magistratsabteilung 52, Verwaltung der städtischen Wohn- und Amts-
gebäude, vertreten durch die GESIBA Gemeinnützige Siedlungs- und
Baugesellschaft m.b.H., als Vermieterin und
Herrn/Frau/Firma
als Mieter andererseits wie folgt:

I.

1.) Die Vermieterin vermietet und der Mieter mietet die Wohnung
Stiege   top Nr.   im Hundertwasserhaus, 1030 Wien,
Löwengasse 41-43/Kegelgasse 34-38 auf unbestimmte Zeit. Zu diesem
Mietobjekt gehört ein Kellerabteil, eine Gartenterrasse im
Ausmaß von .... m². (Mietbeginn ab _____)

2.) Vermietet ist nur der Innenraum des Mietgegenstandes. Der Mieter
ist darüber hinaus zur Ausübung des "Fensterrechtes" berechtigt.
Im Sinne des Satzes von Hundertwasser:

    "ein Bewohner muß das Recht haben, sich aus
    seinem Fenster zu lehnen und außen an der
    Außenwand alles umzugestalten, so wie es
    ihm entspricht, soweit sein Arm reicht,
    damit man von weitem, von der Straße sehen
    kann: dort wohnt ein Mensch"

darf der Mieter die zu seinem Mietobjekt gehörige Außenfront
und zwar soweit sein Arm reicht um sein Fenster herum kreativ-
schöpferisch umgestalten. Der Mieter muß hiefür jedoch die
Zustimmung der MA 19 (Stadtbauamt) und der Baubehörde ein-
holen. Dem Vermieter sind die genehmigten Veränderungen an-
zuzeigen.

Die bei Einzug der Mieter vorgefundene Gestaltung des Hundert-
wasserhauses untersteht nicht dem Denkmalschutz.

Im Rahmen des "Fensterrechtes" darf der Mieter auch in die
Hundertwasser-Gestaltung eingreifen und diese abändern, da
diese Gestaltung nur eine Vorleistung für das Fensterrecht ist.

7

NATIONS UNIES

FS 0.40

DROITS DE L'HOMME 1948·83

TROISIEME PEAU

their own, but that of someone else: their unconscious. Stain painting further emphasized the "stuff", the materials of the painter, as the theme of painting, at the expense of expression. Stain painting, too, offered the chance for irresponsibility. This was not true of its first practitioners, but subsequent field painters abjured responsibility for their paintings' compositions. In contrast, Hundertwasser's unceasing care for the appearance of his designs should attract young painters. His vision of control, rational if not logical, stands in vivid contrast to the juvenile shrieks that pass for despair.

Hundertwasser's paintings never were very large. They have not grown appreciably larger with time. He has taken his large-scale concerns to architecture. Neither reductions of grand pictorial urges nor the enlargement of miniatures, Hundertwasser's paintings are not pretentiously sized. This sense of premeditated scale and mastery has been absent from recent art for some time.

For numerous reasons Hundertwasser should be a pre-eminent artist at the end of the twentieth century. So much of what he has doggedly, but not condescendingly, preached has proven correct. So much of what he has advocated has weathered

mere fashion. In contrast to "throw-away" culture, his works are as richly worked as precious objects. And yet, until recently, the idea that an art object could be anything but a precious object did not even need to be questioned because of the labour-intensive investment it represented (to the artist and the community who supported him). Then artists gradually became aesthetic engineers, "liberated" by Duchamp from making anything at all. Hundertwasser's is a reasonable response to our times.

His painting is based on a well-understood tradition. He does not parody tradition, and that sense of a living heritage and an artistic pedigree is rare in the modern world. Understandably, earlier in his career he had almost no effect on the history of art, being an outsider, a loner, and the extreme example of an individualist. More surprisingly, Hundertwasser's art – which effectively responds to the rhetorical position of so much that has constituted itself "post-modern" – has not found its champions in the critics who have become the entrepreneurs of post-modernism. (By which we learn that in the short run art politics and money are stronger than rhetoric or history.) One has only to consider this artist's sincerity to learn from him

Ill. pp. 232/233: Stamp designs for the United Nations on the occasion of the 35th anniversary of the Charter of Human Rights; created in Kaurinui, New Zealand on 16 March 1983.
Watercolour on white primed paper, 30 x 23 cm

Left: Hundertwasser's flag design for New Zealand, Bay of Islands, March 1983

 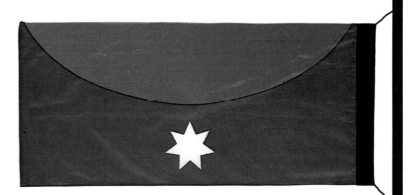

the appropriate responses to those who wish to leave modernism behind. Hundertwasser is an artist **in** whose work we can begin to see the resolution of current predicaments that lack resolution in mainstream art.

H. R.: What do you think the art that comes after yours should be?
F. H.: The arts should be positive, free, romantic, beautiful, something like a jewel, something which you cannot do without.

Right: Hundertwasser's flag design for Australia, Sydney, 1986

THE DICTATES OF FASHION

MAN HAS THREE SKINS: HE IS BORN IN THE FIRST, THE SECOND IS HIS CLOTHING AND THE THIRD IS THE FAÇADE OF HIS HOUSE.

I AM AGAINST CONFORMISM, AGAINST THE FASHIONS WHICH CHANGE EVERY YEAR. IN THE PAST THINGS WERE DIFFERENT. FASHION HAS ONLY EXISTED FOR ABOUT A HUNDRED YEARS; BEFORE THAT THERE WERE SIMPLY CLOTHES.

WHEN OUR SECOND SKIN FALLS SICK OR IS MADE INTO A UNIFORM OR DOES NOT SUIT ITS WEARER, THE PERSON, IN OTHER WORDS THE ORGANISM BENEATH IT, WILL SIMILARLY FALL SICK.

THE URGE TO IMITATE THE WORTHLESS IS PARTICULARLY PRONOUNCED IN CONTEMPORARIES OF THE PRESENT CIVILIZATION.

READY-MADE GOODS AND OFF-THE-PEG FASHIONS INCREASINGLY DISCOURAGE US FROM CREATIVELY DESIGNING OUR OWN CLOTHING, WHICH IS MORE THAN JUST SOMETHING WE WEAR ROUND ABOUT US.

WHICH BRINGS ME AGAIN TO THE DICTATES OF THE KINGS OF FASHION, THE DICTATES OF THE FASHION MAFIA. THE FASHION MAFIA IS JUST AS EVIL AS THE MODERN ART MAFIA, IF INDEED NOT MORE SO. THE FASHION MAFIOSI ARE BASED IN PARIS, NEW YORK, THE BIG CITIES, GERMANY. THEY ARE TRUE EXPLOITERS, RECKONING AND CALCULATING WITH THE STUPIDITY OF PEOPLE IN GENERAL AND THE FEMALE SEX IN PARTICULAR.

MEN WEAR EMPHATICALLY IDENTICAL, LEVELLING CLOTHING. ALWAYS THE SAME GREY TROUSERS. THEY ARE NEITHER BLACK NOR WHITE NOR GREEN NOR YELLOW, NOR ARE THEIR TROUSERS PINK OR BROWN; MEN'S TROUSERS ARE GREY.

THERE ARE THUS TWO FORMS OF DEPENDENCY: WOMEN ARE DEPENDENT ON THE FASHION MAFIA, MEN ON A HORRIFYING LEVELLING OF INDIVIDUALITY WHICH HAS BEEN GOING ON FOR THE PAST 100 TO 150 YEARS.

BOTH WOMEN'S AND MEN'S FASHIONS ARE TOTALLY ENSLAVED. A SLAVERY IMPOSED BY A FALSELY-UNDERSTOOD TRADITION ON THE ONE HAND AND THE FASHION MEDIA ON THE OTHER. THE FASHION DICTATES OF THE FASHION MEDIA MUST BE BROKEN, WHICH MEANS THAT PEOPLE MUST BE SHOWN HOW STUPID THEY ARE WHEN THEY BLINDLY OBEY THE LATEST DICTATE OF FASHION. MORE STUPID THAN A FLOCK OF HYPNOTIZED HENS, THEY ALLOW THEMSELVES TO BE DICTATED A NEW FASHION EVERY FEW MONTHS, EACH MORE ABSURD THAN THE LAST.

IT IS A PHENOMENON WHICH IS QUITE UNBELIEVABLE. CLOTHING IS SOMETHING ETERNAL, JUST LIKE ART. CLOTHING MUST ONCE AGAIN BECOME ART AND MUST CEASE MERELY TO BE FASHION.

HUNDERTWASSER   15 DECEMBER 1989

OUR TUBE DEPENDENCY

SOME OF US HAVE, FORTUNATELY, ONLY HEARD OF INTENSIVE CARE UNITS; MANY OF US HAVE EXPERIENCED THEM AT FIRST HAND OR THROUGH VISITING FRIENDS AND RELATIVES IN HOSPITAL.

TUBES GO INTO PEOPLE TO SET UP BLOOD TRANSFUSIONS INTO ARMS AND VEINS; OXYGEN TUBES GO THROUGH THE NOSE, WITH OR WITHOUT FACE MASKS, DILUTED FOOD IS ADMINSTERED THROUGH TUBES, AND "WASTE DISPOSAL" ALSO TAKES PLACE VIA TUBES IN THE ANUS AND CATHETERS FOR URINE.

A HORRIBLE PICTURE, BUT NECESSARY TO KEEP PEOPLE ALIVE. YOU NEED ONLY CUT OR PULL OUT ONE OR SEVERAL OF THE VARIOUS TUBES, AND THE PERSON WILL DIE.

HE IS DEPENDENT UPON THOSE TUBES.

BUT WE HAVE GIVEN NO THOUGHT TO THE FACT THAT WE ARE ALL DEPENDENT UPON TUBES, I.E. THAT WE ARE ALL OF US, AND ESPECIALLY CITY DWELLERS, KEPT ALIVE BY ARTIFICIAL, UNNATURAL MEANS.

PIPES BRING WATER TO OUR APARTMENTS, PIPES BRING INDUSTRIAL HEAT, ELECTRIC CABLES SUPPLY THE POWER WITHOUT WHICH WE WOULD HAVE NO LIGHT, NO ELECTRICAL EQUIPMENT SUCH AS TELEVISION, RADIO, LIFTS ETC. TELEPHONE WIRES CONNECT US WITH THE REST OF THE WORLD, AS DO ANTENNAE AND THE CABLES OF CABLE TELEVISION. GAS PIPES BRING US GAS ALL THE WAY FROM SIBERIA, ALONG WITH ANY NUMBER OF OTHER TUBES TO WHICH WE ARE "CONNECTED", E.G. LIFTS, BECAUSE WE CANNOT CLIMB STAIRS ANY MORE. THEN THERE ARE THE "WASTE DISPOSAL TUBES" FOR REFUSE, DRAINAGE SYSTEMS, FLUSH TOILETS. EVERY TUBE, EVERY PIPE TO WHICH WE ARE CONNECTED INCREASES OUR DEPENDENCY UPON A DISTRIBUTOR TYRANT.

AND TELEVISION, RADIO AND ADVERTISING SPRAY US WITH PYSCHOLOGICAL POISON AND BRAIN-WASHING, WHICH ONLY INCREASE OUR TUBE DEPENDENCY.

IT IS A GIGANTIC NETWORK OF SLAVERY AND TUBE DEPENDENCY.

ARE WE AWARE OF THIS?

IF WE ARE BAD, THE DISTRIBUTOR TYRANT MAY DESTROY US AT ANY TIME BY CUTTING OFF THE SUPPLY AND WASTE PIPES UPON WHICH WE ARE DEPENDENT. WE ARE THUS ALL FED ARTIFICIALLY, KEPT ALIVE ARTIFICIALLY, AS IN AN INTENSIVE CARE UNIT.

IN ORDER TO REGAIN OUR FREEDOM, OUR HUMAN DIGNITY, OUR INDEPENDENCE, WE MUST SLOWLY PART FROM THESE TUBES. HOW? WITH GREAT DIFFICULTY. BUT THERE IS NO OTHER SOLUTION IF WE WANT TO SURVIVE.

HUNDERTWASSER   24 JANUARY 1990

THE CULTURAL EXPERTS AND THE ARTISTIC ADVISERS

IN A WORLD OF RATIONALISM, FEELINGS ARE UNWANTED AND ARE PRESENTED AS WEAKNESS OR KITSCH. BUT ART SHOULD APPEAL TO THE SENSES AND FEELINGS AND ACT AS A COUNTERBALANCE TO THE COLD CALCULATEDNESS, THE FUNCTIONALITY AND RATIONALISM OF OUR AGE. ADVISERS AND EXPERTS ARE THE PUPPETS OF THE TASTE MAFIA AND OTHER INTEREST GROUPS. WHO OBSTRUCT AND IGNORE PEOPLE'S DESIRES. THE HEADS OF INDUSTRY AND THE ECONOMY ARE PROUD, INDEPENDENTLY-MINDED DECISION-MAKERS WHO DO NOT SHIRK RESPONSIBILITY FOR THEIR ACTIONS. IN MATTERS OF ART, HOWEVER, THEY SHIT IN THEIR PANTS AND ARE AFRAID OF MAKING THEMSELVES LOOK RIDICULOUS BY FOLLOWING THEIR FEELINGS. SO THEY ACT UPON THE ADVICE OF ART EXPERTS AND ADVISERS, DESPITE A SENSE OF LATENT UNEASINESS AND A BAD CONSCIENCE, ONLY TO BE THROWN INTO CONFUSION BY THE SPONTANEOUS REACTION OF THE CLEANING LADY, WITH WHOM THEY SECRETLY AGREE.

IN THE CASE OF PUBLIC COMMISSIONS, IT IS CLEAR THAT SO-CALLED EXPERT ADVICE RESULTS IN A YAWNING VOID WHICH FAILS TO FIND POPULAR APPROVAL.

EVERYTHING USED TO BE BEAUTIFUL AND GOOD. THE BEAUTIFUL WAS BEAUTIFUL. THE UGLY WAS UGLY. DISSONANCE WAS DISSONANCE. HARMONY WAS HARMONY AND WAS EXPERIENCED AS SUCH WITHOUT PROBLEM BY EVERYONE. THEN THE SO-CALLED CULTURAL EXPERTS CAME ALONG AND SOWED CONFUSION. FOR EXAMPLE, WITH ESOTERIC OVER-INTERPRETATIONS SEEN THROUGH FIXED, IDEOLOGICAL-SOCIAL EYES. BEAUTY BECAME BAD. UGLINESS BECAME GOOD. DISSONANCE WAS DECLARED TO BE HARMONY. THE SO-CALLED ADVISERS AND EXPERTS AGREE ON EVERYTHING AMONGST THEMSELVES, FEEL THEMSELVES TO BE THE GUARDIANS OF MODERN CULTURE, TO BE TREND-SETTERS, EVEN TEACHERS, SEEKING TO FORCE UPON PEOPLE STYLES OF THEIR OWN CHOOSING.

IT IS LIKE EXPERTS TRYING TO TALK SOMEONE OUT OF A PAIR OF SHOES WHICH ARE ATTRACTIVE AND WHICH FIT HIM WELL, AND INTO A PAIR HE DISLIKES WHICH HURT. THEY WILL ARGUE, THESE EXPERTS, THUS: MY DEAR SIR, BY NOT WEARING THESE SHOES YOU WILL MAKE YOURSELF A LAUGHING STOCK. ALL THE LEADING FIGURES ARE WEARING THESE SHOES. THE FELT PAIN IS AN INTEGRAL ELEMENT OF THE NEW, WORLDWIDE SHOE-WEARING EXPERIENCE. IT HAS TO BE LIKE THAT!

HUNDERTWASSER   7 FEBRUARY 1990

REFLECTIONS

IN 1952 I SPOKE OF THE SHAM CIVILIZATION FROM WHICH WE NEED TO FREE OURSELVES, MY OWN SELF FIRST OF ALL. I SPOKE OF THE GREY COLUMNS OF MARCHING MEN HEADING UNCREATIVELY TOWARDS SELF-DESTRUCTION. IN 1953 I REALIZED THAT THE STRAIGHT LINE LEADS TO THE DOWNFALL OF MANKIND. THE STRAIGHT LINE IS TRUMPS. THE STRAIGHT LINE IS THE LINE DRAWN LAZILY WITH A RULER, NOT EXISTING IN NATURE, UPON WHICH OUR WHOLE CIVILIZATION IS BASED. IN BUILDING, THINKING, EDUCATION, ADMINISTRATION - EVERYWHERE. WE NEED BEAUTY BARRIERS.

BEAUTY BARRIERS ARE NON-REGULARIZED, NON-CONTROLLED IRREGULARITIES. THE STRAIGHT LINE IS GODLESS AND IMMORAL. THE STRAIGHT LINE IS A FICTION. THE STRAIGHT LINE IS THE ONLY UNCREATIVE LINE, AND ONE WHICH DOES NOT CORRESPOND TO MAN AS THE IMAGE OF GOD. THE STRAIGHT LINE IS THE CURSE OF OUR CIVILIZATION. EVERYTHING BUILT WITH ITS AID IS BORN DEAD. EVEN CREATIVITY IS PREFABRICATED. PREFABRICATED CREATIVITY IS STERILITY AND SIGNIFIES THE END OF HUMANITY. ONLY THOSE WHO THINK AND ACT CREATIVELY ARE ALIVE. WE ARE ACTUALLY DEAD, BECAUSE WE ARE NOT CREATIVE. WE ARE CREATIVELY IMPOTENT.

THAT IS OUR TRUE ILLITERACY.

I AM AN INTROSPECTIVE PERSON. I DO NOT LIKE TO PREACH; I PREFER TO LIE UNDER A TREE AND THINK THINGS OVER AND GRADUALLY TURN INTO HUMUS MYSELF.

I AM A KING. I CROWNED MYSELF. I AM RICH. WEALTH STREAMS AFTER ME. IT IS SAD THAT NOT EVERYONE IS A RICH KING. YOU NEED ONLY TO PLACE A CROWN ON YOUR HEAD AND RECOGNIZE YOUR WEALTH. BUT WE ARE TOO COWARDLY. I WOULD PREFER TO LIVE IN A VALLEY OF RICH KINGS THAN IN A VALE OF TEARS. THEN I COULD MEET OTHER RICH KINGS. WE MUST ALL START LIVING AS IF IT WAS WARTIME. MAN MUST BE CAUTIOUS, MUST THINK FOR HIMSELF, MUST BE ECONOMICAL, MUST NOT SQUANDER BLINDLY. MAN MUST ENSURE THAT THE CYCLE OF LIFE IS WORKING. YOU CAN CUT DOWN A TREE IN FIVE MINUTES. BUT IT TAKES 50 YEARS TO GROW. WHICH IS APPROXIMATELY THE RATIO BETWEEN TECHNOCRATIC DESTRUCTION AND ECOLOGICAL RESTRUCTURE.

HUNDERTWASSER   15 FEBRUARY 1990

THE MADNESS OF EXTREMES

MAN IS ONLY SUCH WHEN HE CONFESSES HIMSELF AN INDIVIDUAL WHO THINKS AND ACTS INDEPENDENTLY AND CREATIVELY. IN MASSES, IN HUMAN MARCHING COLUMNS HE BECOMES A HERD ANIMAL HEADING BLINDLY TOWARDS HIS DOWN-

FALL, EVEN WHERE THE ORIGINAL IDEA INSPIRING THOSE MASSES WAS A GOOD ONE.
FOR IDEAS, TOO, GROW OLD AND DIE. FURTHERMORE, AS IN A GAME OF CHINESE WHISPERS, THE ORIGINAL IDEA IS SOON SO DISTORTED THAT IT BECOMES THE EXACT OPPOSITE OF ITSELF.
WHERE THE MULTITUDE RECOGNIZES A MISTAKE, IT SEEKS TO CORRECT IT BY DOING THE OPPOSITE. ONLY THIS EXACT OPPOSITE INEVITABLY REVEALS ITSELF TO HAVE BEEN AN EVEN GREATER MISTAKE. BUT THIS WE ONLY DISCOVER LATER, THROUGH EXPERIENCE. THE FACT THAT MAN IS PROUD AND WILL NOT ADMIT TO MISTAKES LEADS TO TERRIBLE CONFLICTS. EMOTIONAL CONFLICTS WITHIN HIM-SELF, THEN CONFLICTS WITH OTHERS, WHO HAVE NOT YET THOUGHT SO FAR, AND FINALLY CIVIL WAR AND WAR. AFTER THE CATASTROPHE, PEOPLE SAY: "IF ONLY I HAD KNOWN...", OR "NOBODY TOLD US...", "WE HAD TO DO IT" ETC.
ENEMIES ARE PRONOUNCED FRIENDS AND FRIENDS ENEMIES. BEAUTY IS MADE A CRIME AND UGLINESS AND DISHARMONY ARE MADE WORTHWHILE GOALS. CON-FUSION IS COMPLETE. THIS CAN ONLY HAPPEN TO MAN.
THE SITUATION REACHES SUCH EXTREMES THAT WHEN AN "ENEMY" PLANTS A TREE WE UPROOT IT, JUST IN CASE ANYONE SHOULD SAY THAT THE PERSON WHO PLANTED THE TREE DID A GOOD DEED, AND WAS THUS GOOD AND NOT BAD. SO THE TREE HAS TO GO. IN OUR SHORT-SIGHTEDNESS, PECULIAR ONLY TO MAN, WE ARE QUITE UNABLE TO SEE THAT FUTURE GENERATIONS WILL RELAX IN THE SHADE OF THIS TREE, GENERATIONS WHOSE VERY DIFFERENT PROBLEMS WILL NOT IN-CLUDE THE QUESTION OF WHETHER THE TREE WAS PLANTED BY A CHRIST OR AN ANTI-CHRIST, A FASCIST, A GREEN, A MADMAN, A MURDERER OR A COMMUNIST. THEY WILL SIMPLY BE HAPPY IT IS THERE!
HUNDERTWASSER   17 FEBRUARY 1990

THE PREJUDICE TRAP

I RECENTLY DESCRIBED HOW A - FUNDAMENTALLY INTELLIGENT - PERSON WOULD RATHER UPROOT A TREE AND THEREBY DAMAGE HIMSELF THAN ADMIT THAT, EVEN THOUGH IT WAS PLANTED BY AN "ENEMY", IT IS IN FACT A GOOD THING.
PREJUDICE ADDICTION IS A SICKNESS SUFFERED BY INTELLECTUALS WORLDWIDE, BUT ONE WHICH IS NEVERTHELESS PARTICULARLY AUSTRIAN.
ONCE YOU HAVE STYLIZED AND BRANDED AN ENEMY, WHETHER SOCIALLY OR POLITICALLY, EVERYTHING HE DOES IS BAD AND LOATHSOME, INCLUDING HIS FAMILY, HIS CIRCLE, THE WATER HE DRINKS, THE PLACE WHERE HE LIVES, THE CLOTHES HE WEARS - IN SHORT, EVERYTHING CONNECTED WITH THIS MON-STROUS PERSON.
BY THE SAME TOKEN, WHERE SOMEONE IS REGARDED AS GOOD AND EXEMPLARY BY THESE SAME INTELLECTUALS, EVERYTHING HE DOES IS OUTSTANDING, FOR THE BENEFIT OF MANKIND, PIONEERING, EXTREMELY GOOD, ACCEPTABLE WITHOUT CRITICISM, AS IN THE CASES OF, E.G., HITLER, STALIN, MAO, ETC.
AS SOCIALLY-ORIENTED INTELLECTUALS GOVERNED BY THE SPIRIT OF THE AGE, WE FALL INTO THE TRAP OF PREJUDICE IN OUR HORDES. AND THE WORST PART IS THAT, ALTHOUGH WE TRY TO SUPPRESS IT, WE GET THE VAGUE FEELING OF BEING JOINTLY RESPONSIBLE FOR TERRIBLE THINGS.
TODAY WE ARE STILL TRAPPED IN THE SAME SITUATION. WE CAN ESCAPE FROM IT BY INDEPENDENT, UNPREJUDICED THINKING AND CAN THEN WARN OTHERS HEADING INTO THE DEAD-END ABYSS.
TYPICAL SYMPTOMS OF OUR PREJUDICE-POISONED SOCIETY INCLUDE, E.G., THE FACT THAT A SCIENTIST, A DOCTOR, AN ARTIST, A MUSICIAN, A POLITICIAN, A RELIGIOUS GURU ETC. WILL JOIN FORCES WITH THE DEVIL IN ORDER TO DESTROY ANOTHER DOING THE SAME JOB, ONLY BETTER.
HUNDERTWASSER   19 FEBRUARY 1990

THE GARDEN DWARF

THE ABSENCE OF KITSCH MAKE OUR LIVES UNBEARABLE.
WE CAN'T MANAGE WITHOUT ROMANTICISM.
THE GARDEN GNOME SYMBOLIZES OUR RIGHT TO DREAMS AND OUR YEARNING FOR A FAIRER, BETTER WORLD.
THE GARDEN GNOME IS A BULWARK AGAINST THE SOULLESS, NIHILISTIC DICTATES OF OUR TIMES. JUST AS WE HUNT DRACULA WITH GARLIC AND CRUCIFIXES, SO WE USE THE GARDEN GNOME TO DRIVE OUT STERILE, TYRANNICAL DOGMA.
AGGRESSIVE RATIONALISTS AND PASSIVE DREAMERS OF A BETTER, MORE BEAUTI-FUL EXISTENCE PART COMPANY AT THE GARDEN GNOME.
LONG BEFORE THE CHRISTIAN WORLD PICTURE, LONG BEFORE THE GODS OF THE ANCIENT ROMANS AND EGYPTIANS, LONG BEFORE HISTORY WAS EVER RECORDED, WE WERE ABLE TO TALK TO THE BIRDS, THE ANIMALS, THE PLANTS AND THE TREES, INDEED EVEN TO WATER, ROCKS AND CLOUDS, AND COMMUNICATION BROUGHT HARMONY.
THUS IT IS WRITTEN IN FAIRY TALES.
THE GARDEN GNOME, TOGETHER WITH THE ELVES, PIXIES, GNOMES, GIANTS AND THE WHOLE HOST OF MAGICAL BEINGS, IS A LAST SURVIVOR FROM THAT DISTANT PAST.
MAN LIVES BY VIRTUE OF HIS IDENTITY, BY VIRTUE OF HIS MEMORY OF THE ROOTS

OF HIS BEING. WE MAY NOW BE VERY "INTELLIGENT", BUT WE HAVE FORGOTTEN THE LANGUAGE OF NATURE.
HENCE THE SMALL GNOME IN THE GARDEN.
YOU TALK TO THE GRASS AND THE BIRDS FOR ME,
I NO LONGER KNOW HOW.
AND ASK NATURE FOR FORGIVENESS FOR THE EVIL WE DO HER,
AND HELP ME AGAINST THE COLD, ALL-POWERFUL ENEMY.
I NO LONGER KNOW HOW.
HUNDERTWASSER   APRIL 1990

BIOGRAPHY

1928   Born 15 December in Vienna as Friedrich Stowasser.

1929   Death of his father, technical civil servant and officer in World War 1.

1934   First juvenile drawings.

1936   Attends the Montessori school in Vienna for one year. His report refers to his "unusual sense of colour and form".

1938   Following Austria's annexation, forced removal to his aunt's and grandmother's home on Obere Donaustraße.

1943   First deliberate crayon drawings after nature. During this year 69 Jewish relations on his mother's side are deported and killed, including his aunt and grandmother.

1948   School-leaving certificate. Spends three months at the Academy of Fine Arts in Vienna under Prof. Robin Christian Andersen. Lastingly influenced by a Walter Kampmann exhibition in the Albertina and by Schiele exhibitions.

1949   Start of extensive travelling: Leopoldskron, Styria, Naples, North Italy, Tuscany, Sicily, where he meets René Brô and follows him to Paris. Develops his own style and adopts the name Hundertwasser.

1950   Stays in Paris with Brô and the Dumage family. Paints two murals with Brô in St. Mandé. Leaves the Ecole des Beaux-Arts on the very first day.

1951   Spends winter and spring in Morocco and Tunisia. Becomes a member of the Art Club of Vienna.

1952   First exhibition in Art Club of Vienna: *European Holding His Moustache*. Brief decorative-abstract period.

1953   Paints the first spiral. Second stay in Paris. Works in Brô's studio in St. Maurice. Second exhibition in Art Club of Vienna: *99 Heads*.

1954   First exhibition in Paris at Paul Facchetti's: *Garden of the Happy Dead*. Spends September and October in Santo Spirito hospital in Rome with jaundice and paints a large number of watercolours. Develops the theory of "transautomatism" and begins to number his works.

1955   Exhibition at Carlo Cardazzo's Galleria del Naviglio, Milan.

1956   Second exhibition at Facchetti's in Paris: *The Great Way*. In summer he sails from Söderhamm to Hull on the SS Bauta together with Hans Neuffer. Publishes the text "The Visibility of Transautomatic Creation" in "Cimaises" and "Phases" in Paris. Friendship with Siegfried Poppe, Hamburg.

1957   Buys "La Picaudière", a farmhouse in Normandy. Publishes *The Grammar of Seeing*.

1957-1960   Contract and exhibition in Galerie H. Kramer, Paris.

1958   Marries in Gibraltar (divorced 1960). Reads his "Mould Manifesto against Rationalism in Architecture" on the occasion of a congress in Seckau monastery on 4 July.

1959   Receives the Sanbra Prize at the 5th São Paulo Biennale. Together with Ernst Fuchs and Arnulf Rainer, founds the "Pintorarium", a universal academy of all creative fields. As guest lecturer at the Academy of Fine Art in Hamburg, he draws the Endless Line with Bazon Brock and Herbert Schult. Resigns lectureship following scandal.

1960   Nettle campaign in Paris in conjunction with Alain Jouffroy's Antiprocès – "how one can live independently". Exhibition in Galerie Raymond Cordier, Paris.

1961   Visits Japan. Receives the Mainichi prize at the 6th International Art Exhibition, Tokyo. Successful exhibition in Tokyo. Visits Hokkaido and Siberia.

1962   Marries Yuko Ikewada (divorced 1966). Paints in a studio on the Guidecca, Venice. Very successful retrospective at the Venice Biennale, organized by Vinzenz Ludwig Oberhammer.

1963   Travels to Greece. Accompanied by Siegfried Adler.

1964   Climbing trip in the Tyrolean Alps. Large retrospective in the Kestner-Gesellschaft, Hanover, organized by Wieland Schmid. The exhibition also travels to Amsterdam, Bern, Hagen, Stockholm and Vienna. The Kestner-Gesellschaft publishes the first oeuvre catalogue.

1965   Essay: 35 Days in Sweden. Touring exhibition very successful in the Moderna Museet, Stockholm.

1966   Unhappy in love. Ferry Radax films the first documentary on Hundertwasser in La Picaudière and the woods. Exhibition at Hammerlund's, Oslo.

1967   Visits Uganda and the Sudan. Touring exhibition in galleries in Paris, Geneva, London, Berlin. Nude speech in Munich.

1968   Nude speech and reading of Los von Loos [Loose from Loos] in Vienna. Visits northern California. At the University of California, Berkeley, prepares a large catalogue for his museum exhibition (organized by Herschel Chipp). Sails from Sicily to Venice in the "San Guiseppe T", an old wooden sailing ship.

1968-1972   The ship is converted into the "Regentag" in the dockyards in the Venice lagoon.

1969   Museum exhibition in Berkeley, Santa Barbara, Houston, Chicago, New York, Washington.

1969-1971   *Good Morning City - Bleeding Town* print in 120 colour variations, followed by a court case in Munich lasting 5 years. Represented by Hans Brockstedt. Lives and works on board the "Regentag" in the Venice lagoon.

1970-1972   Collaboration with Peter Schamoni on the film "Hundertwassers Regentag". Works on the Regentag print portfolio in Dietz Offizin in Lengmoos, Bavaria.

1971   Works on the Olympia Poster for Munich in Lengmoos. Sails down the Dalmatian coast in the "Regentag" with Peter Schamoni and Manfred Bockelmann; balloon flight with the two of them from Bavaria into Austria.

1972   Friendship with Joram Harel. In the TV series "Wünsch Dir was", demonstrates roof forestation and individual façade design. Publishes manifesto: Dein Fensterrecht - deine Baumpflicht [Your window right - Your tree duty]. The Regentag film is shown in Cannes. Sails to Elba in the "Regentag". Death of his mother.

1973   First portfolio with Japanese woodcuts: *Nana Hiaku Mizu*. Hundertwasser is the first European painter to have his works cut by Japanese masters. Trip to the Cape Verde Islands and to New Zealand to his touring exhibition (organized by Hertha Dabbert) in Auckland, Wellington, Christchurch, Dunedin, Stommonta, New Plymouth, Palmerston North. Takes part in the Triennale di Milano, where 12 Baummieter [tree tenants] are planted in windows in the Via Manzoni. Publishes *Inquilino Albero*. Exhibition at Aberbach Fine Art, New York.

1974   Touring exhibition through museums in Australia: Melbourne, Canberra, Sydney, Mornington. "Stowasser 1943 - Hundertwasser 1974" exhibition in the Albertina printroom, Vienna, as well as "Friedrich Stowasser 1943 - 1949", featuring his entire juvenile oeuvre. Paints a Conservation Week poster for New Zealand and receives the Conservation Award. Presents his proposals for a pedestrian precinct in Vienna's Seilergasse. Sails to Tunisia, Cyprus and Israel in the "Regentag". Exhibition at Facchetti's, Paris.

1975   Second Japanese woodcut portfolio: *Midori No Namida*. Retrospective in Haus der Kunst, Munich. Publishes his *Humustoilette* manifesto in Munich. Designs a stamp for Austria: the Spiral Tree, engraved by Wolfgang Seidel. Hereby launches the series *Moderne Kunst* in Austria. The world touring exhibition "Austria presents Hundertwasser to the Continents" (with catalogue) begins in Paris and goes to Luxemburg, Marseilles, Cairo. The Albertina exhibition of his entire graphic oeuvre begins a tour through the USA: New York, Boston. Sails from Tahiti via Rorotonga to New Zealand in the "Regentag".

1976   Sails the "Regentag" across the Atlantic, through the Panama canal to the Pacific. World touring exhibition: Tel Aviv, Warsaw, Reykjavik, Copenhagen, Dakar and the USA.

1977   Following two accidents, spends two months in Kawakawa hospital in New Zealand. Travels from Asia to South America. From Manaus, sails in an open boat down the Rio Negro and Rio Branco. Speech to the "Premières Rencontres Européennes du Cadre de Vie" at UNESCO in Paris in December. World touring exhibition: Tokyo, Hong Kong, Cape Town, Pretoria, Rio de Janeiro, Brasilia, São Paulo, Caracas.

1978   Spends two months in the woods in snow with his friend Brô and paints seven pictures. Completes a 3-D object, *Fall in cloud fall in fog fall out*, with Alberto della Vecchia. In Venice, designs a peace flag for the Middle East with a green Arab sickle moon and blue Star of David against a white background. Publishes peace manifesto. Travels to Senegal as guest of President Léopold Sédar Sen ghor. World touring exhibition: Mexico City, Montreal, Toronto, Brussels, Budapest. Albertina exhibition of graphic works in Canada, FRG, Morocco.

1979 Travels to New York, San Francisco, Tahiti, New Zealand. Peace flag and manifesto are sent by Federal Chancellor Bruno Kreisky to Middle-Eastern heads of state. Three stamps printed for the Republic of Senegal and one for the Republic of the Cape Verde Islands. Creates five coin objects in Vienna. Reads Die heilige Scheiße [Holy Shit] manifesto in Pfäffikon on the Lake of Zurich. Designs the book *Ao Tea Roa* together with Hans Brockstedt. Spends the summer painting in Algajola on Corsica. World touring exhibition: Madrid, Pfäffikon. Albertina exhibition of graphic works in Portugal, Spain, FRG, Italy and Great Britain. The "Hundertwasser Is Painting" touring exhibition with 40 new works starts in Aberbach Fine Art, New York.

1980 At the start of the year, travels to Qatar, Sri Lanka, the Maldives and New Zealand. On Open House Day presents 5 model designs for the house at Löwengasse/Kegelgasse commissioned by the Municipality of Vienna. Hundertwasser Day in Washington, D.C., on 18 November, proclaimed by Mayor Marion Barry, Jr. The first 12 of 100 trees are planted in Judiciary Square, Washington, D.C., and the anti-nuclear poster *Plant Trees - Avert Nuclear Peril* is handed over to Ralph Nader along with the environmental poster *Arche Noah 2000* for the FRG. Speaks on ecology, against nuclear power and for an architecture befitting man and nature in the US Senate, the Corcoran Museum, the Philipps Collection in Washington, in Berlin on the occasion of the 2nd European Ecology Symposium, in Vienna and Oslo Technical Universities. Spends the summer painting on the island of Porquerolles. World touring exhibition: Rome, Milan, Oslo, Cologne. Albertina exhibition of graphic works in France, FRG, USA. "Hundertwasser Is Painting" touring exhibition: Tokyo, Hamburg, Paris, Oslo.

1981 At the start of the year, travels with Brô to India, Nepal, New Zealand. Receives the Grand Austrian State Prize on 14 February (awarded 1980) and speaks on "The Wrong Art". Austrian Nature Preservation Prize. Paints by the Wolfgangsee in summer. Lectures on the environment, architecture and art in Cologne, Munich, Frankfurt, Graz, Vienna, East Berlin, Hamburg. World touring exhibition: Vienna, Graz, East Berlin, Helsinki, Bucharest. Albertina exhibition of graphic works in France, South America, FRG and USA. "Hundertwasser Is Painting" touring exhibition: Vienna. 1 November: appointed head of the master class for painting at the Academy of Fine Arts, Vienna.

1982 Finishes 16 works in New Zealand (until May) and Venice (until August). Travels to Chieng Mai and Sardinia. As "architecture doctor", redesigns the façade of the Rosenthal factory in Selb. Produces models of redesigned coal-washing plant in Hamm, Westphalia, and ceramic tongue-beards for the Rupertinum, Salzburg. *Artists for Peace* poster. Talks on environmental protection in Sydney, Manila, Seattle, San Francisco, Washington, D.C., in November and December. Hundertwasser Week in San Francisco from 5 to 12 December to mark the presentation of the two posters *Save the Whales* and *Save the Seas* to Greenpeace and the Jacques Cousteau Society, proclaimed by Dianne Feinstein, Mayor of San Francisco. Presentation of the poster *You Are a Guest of Nature* to the Centre of Environ-

mental Education, Washington, D.C. Travels to Tahiti and New Zealand. World touring exhibition in Sofia. Albertina exhibition of graphic works in France, FRG, South America, USA and Australia. Exhibition at Artcurial in Paris with 20 new and 20 old works. Catalogue with texts by Hundertwasser, Pieyre de Mandiargues, Alain Jouffroy.

1983 Designs six stamps for the United Nations (2 each for New York, Geneva and Vienna), printed in Austria, engraved by Wolfgang Seidel. Founds a committee for the preservation of the façade of the old post office in Kawakawa, New Zealand. Foundation stone of the Hundertwasser House is laid in Vienna. Works in Spinea on *10002 nights Homo Humus come va how do you do* in 10, 002 different versions. Mosaics on the outside walls of a silo in Krems harbour. Creates the open-air model of the Hochwiesenhaus [Highrise Meadow House] at the IGA garden exhibition in Munich in summer. Works on the book "Schöne Wege". Designs a flag for New Zealand, the Koru, an unfurled fern. Travels to Kenya, the Seychelles and New Zealand. World touring exhibition in England and Scotland. Lecture at the Royal College of Art, London.

1984 Lives in New Zealand, Tahiti, Venice and Normandy. TV broadcast "The Fall of the Avant-Garde" in Munich with Brauer, Fuchs and Hrdlicka. Signs 10,002 copies of *10 002 nights ... in Spinea*. Receives the City of Goslar's Environmental Protection Prize. Topping-out ceremony at the Hundertwasser House in Löwengasse/Kegelgasse, Vienna. Works on the building site. Receives the prize for the most attractive stamp and the gold medal from President Pertini for the 1.2 SFr stamp for the UN, Geneva. Exhibitions in Switzerland. Takes an active part in campaigns to save the Hainburg leas. Camps in the leas for a week. Designs the poster "Hainburg - Die freie Natur ist unsere Freiheit" (Free Nature Is Our Freedom).

1985 Works all year on the building site and at the same time on his book "Das Haus". 11 June: nominated "Officier dans l'ordre des arts et des lettres" by French arts minister Jack Lang. Returns to New Zealand at the end of the year. Exhibition of graphic works in the Musée Gauguin, Tahiti, in December.

1986 On 17 February the Hundertwasser House is presented to its tenants; 70,000 visitors attend the "Open House". 1000 green flags with fern design flown in New Zealand; great interest shown by the population, press and in parliament. Designs *Uluru - Down Under Flag* for Australia. Returns from New Zealand via Australia, India and Nepal. World touring exhibition: Czechoslovakia. Exhibitions in: Sweden, Austria, FRG, Switzerland, Liechtenstein. Works on the design of the Brockhaus encyclopaedia.

1987 *Cept Europalia 1987*, a Hundertwasser 6-Schilling special-issue stamp, appears in March. On 3 March receives the order of "Officier dans l'ordre des arts et des lettres" from His Exc. the French ambassador in Austria. Designs the poster for "Luna-Luna" by André Heller and the poster for the Europalia. Designs the Palais des Beaux-Arts in Brussels for the Europalia. Redesigns St. Barbara's church in Bärnbach, Styria, and plans a children's day centre in Heddernheim, Frankfurt. World touring exhibition: Czechoslovakia. Further work on the design of the Brockhaus encyclopaedia.

1988 More painting in the woods. Upon the invitation of mayor and head of provincial government Dr. Helmut Zilk, he assumes the planning and design of Vienna's Spittelau heating station, in collaboration with architect Peter Pelikan and the architectural firm of Prof. Möbius, Vienna. Travels to New Zealand; after his return, resumes work on the building of St. Barbara's in Bärnbach. Produces the colour etching *Bärnbacher Andacht* in two versions as a contribution towards the renovation of the church. Writes manifesto, *Das kulturelle Österreich gegen die Deportation und Zerstörung von Dörfern in Siebenbürgen, Rumänien (Cultural Austria against the Deportation and Destruction of Villages in Siebenbürgen, Rumania)*. Architecture exhibition in the Hilger gallery, Frankfurt. In July/August he teaches at the International Summer Academy in Salzburg. The newly-designed St. Barbara's church in Bärnbach is consecrated in September. Foundation stone of the children's day centre in Heddernheim is laid on 20 December. Joins the campaign to retain the existing form of Austrian number plate. Works on the design of the Brockhaus encyclopaedia. Awarded the Golden Medal of Honour of the City of Vienna and the Golden Medal of Honour of the Province of Styria.

1989 Further involvement in the campaign to preserve Austrian identity and individuality in the matter of number plates. The Brockhaus encyclopaedia appears in November. Creates *Semi-Dako (Flying Dragon)* for Japan. Builds *Hügelwiesenland [Hilly Meadow Landscape]* model. Architecture lecture on the "Green City" in Baden, Switzerland. Departs for New Zealand in December. Exhibitions in the USA, France, FRG, Switzerland and Austria. Museum exhibitions in Japan.

1990 Spends the spring in New Zealand. Lectures at Wellington, Christchurch, Dunedin, Auckland and Blenheim for the LIVING TREASURE PROGRAMMES and 30 min. TV film production.

1991 Completion of KunstHausWien. Opening on 9 April.

The works reproduced are in the possession of the artist or unknown collectors, unless otherwise indicated below: Anne Abels, Cologne: 56, 113 above; J.J. and J.J. Aberbach, New York: 37, 114, 135 below, 151; Collection Siegfried Adler, Montagnola, Switzerland: 34 above, 122; Micheline Brault, Paris: 20; Mme Dumage, Paris: 19 below, 25 below, 28, 30; André Feher, Brussels: 113 below; Colonel L. Franck, London/Switzerland: 96/97; Historisches Museum, Vienna: 22 above; Collection Tsutomu Inada, Tokyo: 110 above; Iynedjian, Lausanne: 52; Hélène Kamer, Paris: 79; Kunsthalle Hamburg: 116 above; Mme Marteau, Paris: 69 below; Galerie Moos, Geneva: 110 below; Siegfried Poppe, Hamburg: 82; Collection M. Puch, Paris: 87; Dieter and Edith Rosenkranz, Wuppertal: 116 below; Jerome Stern, New York: 34 below; Mr. Teraoka, Tokyo: 83 below; Mr. Kohichi Tsutiya, Japan: 78.

The photographs for this book were kindly provided by the Joram Harel Archive, Vienna. Photographic acknowledgements go to: Baar, Vienna: 41; Stephan Bröcher, Frankfurt: 48 (building); Aldo Cantarella, Milan: 171; Augustin Dumage, Paris: 53 above; Harald Hauswald, Berlin: 199; Foto Jucho, Hamm: 196 below; Karl Heinz Koller, Vienna: 228/9, back cover; Gerd Ludwig, Essen: 135 below, 158, 159; Ulrich Mack, Hamburg: 94; Stefan Moses, Munich: 138 below, 146; Pásztory: 166 above; Herbert Prasch, Vienna: 152; François René Roland: 212; Rosenthal-Bilderdienst: 202 below right; Seifert, Vienna: 59 above; Petra Spiola: 228/9; Peter Strobl, Vienna: 72 (model), 100 (model); Wolfgang Wiebold: 196 above left; Hans Wiesenhofer, Vienna: 72 right, 100, 101, 106-9, 227, 230/1; Renate Zimmermann, Munich: 135 above. The following models were constructed by Alfred Schmid: Service station, p. 29; Children's Day Care Centre, p. 48; school, p. 49; incinerator, p. 72; Wigast Service Station, p. 99; KunstHausWien, p. 160; Hügelwiesenland, pp. 200-1; Hundertwasser House, p. 213. The author and publishers wish to thank Mr. Hundertwasser and Mr. Harel for their generous co-operation and assistance.